Dedication

We dedicate this book to all the Ladies in Waiting, especially our daughters Jessica, Christen, and Lauren, who are seeking to become women of God.

Lady *in* Waiting

EXPANDED EDITION

Becoming God's Best While Waiting For Mr. Right

JACKIE KENDALL & DEBBY JONES

Destiny Image® Publishers, Inc.
P.O. Box 310
Shippensburg, PA 17257-0310

"Speaking to the Purposes of God for This Generation
and for the Generations to Come"

ISBN 0-7684-2310-4

Formerly published as
Lady In Waiting Second Edition © 1995 ISBN 1-56043-848-7
Lady in Waiting Meditations For the Heart © 2002 ISBN 0-7684-3034-8
Lady In Waiting Study Guide © 2002 ISBN 1-56043-298-5

For Worldwide Distribution
Printed in the U.S.A.

1 2 3 4 5 6 7 8 9 10 / 10 09 08 07 06 05

This book and all other Destiny Image, Revival Press, MercyPlace, Fresh Bread, Destiny Image Fiction, and Treasure House books are available at Christian bookstores and distributors worldwide.

For a U.S. bookstore nearest you, call
1-800-722-6774.
For more information on foreign distributors, call
717-532-3040.
Or reach us on the Internet:
www.destinyimage.com

Lady *in* Waiting

DEVELOPING YOUR LOVE RELATIONSHIPS

What Others Are Saying...

I have already ordered a number of books and sent them to pastors, youth leaders, single women, single moms, married women, high school girls, college women, career women, missionaries, and missionary kids in many parts of the world....

Rebecca Whisnant
Bible Study Leader for Single Women

Lady in Waiting is one of the most effective tools I have ever used in discipling single, young women. It has also been a great blessing in my own life as a single woman. I plan to use *Lady in Waiting* for many years to come in my ministry.

Brenda Rich
Dean of Women
Columbia International University

Too often in today's literature we emphasize reliance on self rather than on our Savior. *Lady in Waiting* goes beyond pop psychology and clings to the steadfast foundation of God's Word. Creatively integrating biblical truth with an honest evaluation of the struggles facing today's single woman, this book will add value to any woman's library!

Tara D. McClary
Former Career Women's Coordinator
Singles Ministry
Briarwood Presbyterian Church (PCA)
Birmingham, Alabama

After 22 years of marriage, *Lady in Waiting* has given me a sense of security in Christ that I never experienced before. This book helped me realize that my earthly father, my husband, or anyone else could not provide security—only God can. What a freeing principle—not only for me, but also for my husband! Now my marriage is better than ever because I no longer have unrealistic expectations of him!

Jimmie Davis
Coordinator of Deaf Ministry
First Baptist Church in Atlanta

Having been sent to teach missionary children in Kiev, Ukraine, *Lady in Waiting* was one of the few books I was able to pack. It will be a treasure "map" for me and will help me recognize a Boaz if he ever comes into my life.

Becky DeWitt
Foreign Missionary/SBC

In my job in the Education Department at the university, I have the opportunity at least weekly to talk to ladies about their relationships and have recommended *Lady in Waiting* many times.

Dottie Myatt
Education Department
Union University

Contents

Preface

Is this just another book for singles? No! We believe this book is unique because its emphasis is not on a woman's status (single, married, divorced, or widowed), but on the state of her heart. We want to direct a woman's attention toward the One who really understands the longing of her heart. Too many women grow up believing that the inconsolable ache in her heart is for "a man." To love a man, get married, and then have children is thought to be the only script that will satisfy her heart's deepest longing. But no man, woman, or child can appease this longing; it can only be satisfied by the ultimate Bridegroom, Christ Jesus. This book nudges a woman closer to God, while acknowledging any longing she may have to be loved and cherished by a man.

Lady in Waiting is not about finding the right man, but being the right woman. Thus it focuses on ten qualities of a godly woman that are found in the Book of Ruth. These qualities will not only enhance your love relationship with your heavenly Bridegroom, but also guide you as a single woman, guard you while you date, support you in marriage, and comfort you if you are ever widowed or divorced. As you read you will see these characteristics beautifully displayed in the life of Ruth. She recklessly abandons herself to the Lordship of Christ, diligently uses her single days, trusts God with unwavering faith, demonstrates virtue in daily life, loves God with undistracted devotion, stands for physical and emotional purity, lives in security, responds to life with contentment, makes choices based on her convictions, and waits patiently for God to meet her needs.

What are *you* waiting for? Is it for that perfect job, the ideal relationship, a home, a career, a child? What if you get what you are waiting for? Will it truly bring the fullness of joy you long for? Anything other than a love relationship with the Lord Jesus Christ, regardless of how good that thing may be, will bring you discouragement and disillusionment. So come and explore the life of Ruth and learn what it really means to be a godly woman, "a lady in waiting."

Lady of Reckless Abandonment

The big day is over. Your roommate married a wonderful guy and you were the maid of honor. You shared your roommate's joy, but now you wrestle with envy's painful grip. As the happy couple drives to the perfect honeymoon, you sit alone in an empty apartment, drowning your envy and self-pity with a half gallon of Heavenly Hash ice cream.

Does this scenario sound familiar?

Have you assumed that your ultimate fulfillment would be found in marriage? Have you privately entertained the notion that the only satisfied women are married women? Have you been expecting your career to satisfy you until you are married? If you have answered "yes" to any of these questions, then you have a prospect of disillusionment looming in the future. On the back cover of the book *Learning to Be a Woman* is a key quote about fulfillment as a woman: "A woman is not born a woman. Nor does she become one when she marries a man, bears a child and does their dirty linen, not even when she joins a women's liberation movement. A woman becomes a woman when she becomes what God wants her to be."[1] This priceless truth can help keep your perspective clear in relation to true fulfillment in life. Too many Christian women think that the inner longings of their heart relate only to love, marriage, and motherhood. Look a little closer and see if that longing isn't ultimately for Jesus. Gary Chapman once remarked, "I feel very strongly that marriage is not a higher calling than the single state. Happy indeed are those people, married or single, who have discovered that happiness is not found in marriage but in a right relationship with God." Fulfillment for a Christian woman begins with the Lordship of Christ in every area of her life.

A college professor (wife, mother of seven children, singer, and author) told a group of young women that when she was eight years old, her mother told her a secret that has guided her perspective on life. The most important thing her mother would ever tell her was, "No one, not even the man you will marry one day, can make you happy—only Jesus can." What a profound statement for such a little girl. This secret allowed her to grow up following Jesus with reckless abandonment.

Are you still convinced that having Mr. Right will chase away the blues? That's not surprising. On the front of a national magazine the lead story said, "Hollywood's hottest newcomer is selling more records than Madonna and filling her dance card with movie offers. All that is missing is MR. RIGHT!" Such a mind-set bombards singles daily. How can you renew your mind and rise above this stereotype? You can be an exception through understanding "the secret of the alabaster box."

The Secret of the Alabaster Box

In the days Jesus was on earth, when a young woman reached the age of availability for marriage, her family would purchase an alabaster box for her and fill it with precious ointment. The size of the box and the value of the ointment would parallel her family's wealth. This alabaster box would be part of her dowry. When a young man came to ask for her in marriage, she would respond by taking the alabaster box and breaking it at his feet. This gesture of anointing his feet showed him honor.

One day, when Jesus was eating in the house of Simon the leper, a woman came in and broke an alabaster box and poured the valuable ointment on Jesus' head (see Mk. 14:3-9). The passage in Luke 7 that refers to this event harshly describes the woman as "a woman in the city who was a sinner" (Lk. 7:37). This woman found Jesus worthy of such sacrifice and honor. In fact, Jesus memorialized her gesture in Matthew 26:13 (see also Mk. 14:9). This gesture had such meaning, for not only did she anoint Jesus for burial, she also gave her all to a heavenly Bridegroom. Yes, she was a sinner (who isn't according to Romans 3:23?), but this sinner had dreams and wisely broke her alabaster box in the presence of the only One who can make a woman's dreams come true.

What is in your alabaster box? Is your box full of fantasies that began as a little girl while you listened to and watched fairy tales about an enchanting couple living happily ever after? Have you been holding on tightly to your alabaster box of dreams, frantically searching for a man worthy of breaking your box? Take your alabaster box to Jesus and break it in His presence, for He is worthy of such honor. Having responded to your heavenly Bridegroom in such a manner, you can wait with confident assurance that, if it be God's will, He will provide you with an earthly bridegroom.

How do you know if you have broken your alabaster box at the feet of Jesus? Such a decision will be reflected in reckless abandonment to the Lordship of Jesus Christ. When the Lord gives you a difficult assignment, such as another dateless month, you receive His terms without resentment. Your attitude will reflect Mary's response to the angel when she, as a single woman, was given a most difficult assignment. Mary said, "I belong to the Lord, body and soul...let it happen as you say..." (Lk. 1:38 Phillips). Take your alabaster box, with your body, soul, and dreams, and entrust them to Jesus. When He is your Lord, you can joyfully walk in the path of life that He has for you.

Ruth's Reckless Abandonment

In the Book of Ruth, a young widow made a critical decision to turn her back on her people, her country, and her gods because her thirsty soul had tasted of the God of Israel. With just a "taste," she recklessly abandoned herself to the only true God. She willingly broke her alabaster box and followed the Lord wherever He would lead her.

*But Ruth said, "Do not urge me to leave you or turn back from fol-
lowing you; for where you go, I will go, and where you lodge, I will
lodge. Your people shall be my people, and your God, my God"*
(Ruth 1:16).

As you look at the following three areas of Ruth's life that were affected
by her reckless abandonment to God, consider the parallels to your own
price tag of commitment to God. Have you broken the valuable alabaster
box yet?

New Friends

When Ruth told Naomi, "your people shall be my people," she under-
stood that she would not be able to grow closer to the God of Israel if she
remained among the Moabites (her own people). Ironically, God called
Moab His washbasin (see Ps. 60:8; 108:9). One rinses dirt off in a washbasin. Ruth chose to leave the washbasin and head for Bethlehem, which
means the "house of bread."[2]

Even today there exist "Moabites" who will undermine your growth if
you spend too much time with them. Sometimes mediocre Christians resist
the zeal and commitment of a dedicated single woman. Realizing that one's
friends drive you either toward or away from God, you may need to find a
"new people" who will encourage your growth and not hinder it. "He who
walks with the wise grows wise, but a companion of fools suffers harm"
(Prov. 13:20 NIV).

Often the choice for deeper commitment produces resentment from
people who were once "such good friends." Do not be alarmed; you are in
good company. When the woman broke the alabaster box and poured it on
Jesus, the disciples did not applaud her act of worship. Instead, with indignation they responded, "Why this waste?" (Mt. 26:8 NIV) The disciples of
Jesus were filled with indignation because the woman obviously wasted the
ointment. But from a heavenly perspective, the great cloud of witnesses
rejoiced as they beheld the woman giving such honor to Jesus. The broken
alabaster box publicly evidenced the woman's reckless abandonment to
Jesus. Is there such evidence in your daily life?

This is not to advocate that you distance yourself from all who have not broken their alabaster box at the feet of Jesus. Just consider the ultimate influence your friends have on your commitment to the Lordship of Jesus Christ. Be careful if you spend most of your free time with a girlfriend who does not share your commitment to Jesus. It can affect your relationship with the Lord. If a non-Christian or a lukewarm Christian influences you rather than you influencing them, you may be headed for serious trouble. You mirror those who influence you. When a woman stops growing spiritually, the lack of progress can often be traced back to a friendship that undermined her commitment to Jesus.

Take a moment to think about the spiritual depth of the girlfriend who influences you the most. Is she daily becoming all that Jesus desires? If so, her growth will challenge you to grow. On the other hand, her apathy may ultimately be contagious. "Do not be deceived: 'Bad company corrupts good morals' " (1 Cor. 15:33). Have any of your friendships caused your spiritual life to go into a deep freeze?

Maybe you, like Ruth, need to distance yourself from those who, spiritually speaking, are more like a washbasin than a house of bread. The friends who influence you the most should be women who live by Hebrews 10:24 (NIV): "And let us consider how we may spur one another on toward love and good deeds." Your best friends should be cheering you on in your commitment to Jesus.

New Surroundings

Ruth had to relocate in order to be fed spiritually. Likewise, some single women may have to "relocate" because some of their former relationships keep them in a constant state of spiritual "hunger." They have to change jobs or even their church in order to continue to grow. In the same way, be open to a change that may benefit your spiritual growth. Like Ruth, look for something that will stimulate your growth in the Lord.

One young woman had to make a choice between playing on a championship volleyball team or being a part of a discipleship group. She knew that she was free to play volleyball if she wanted. But when she compared volleyball and the discipleship opportunity, the Lord showed her that the good often becomes the enemy of the best in life. Because of her reckless abandonment in following the Lord's leadership, she valued her growing commitment to the Lord more than playing volleyball, and it paid off. The discipleship training prepared her heart to respond to an invitation to serve as a short-term missionary in the Philippines. Another young woman may be called to spend her summer ministering to a volleyball team instead of being in a discipleship group, but the commitment to do as the Lord directs is the key.

Ruth moved from a hedonistic society into a culture that attempted to please the God of the universe rather than the sensuous gods of the flesh. Within our advanced society of the 21st century, we often encounter women engaged in becoming a part of self-serving singles' clubs, singles' dating services, singles' cruises, singles' meet markets…all created to keep singles busy in the waiting time of life. A committed single woman must be sensitive to the inevitable challenges she will meet in her attempt to live unselfishly in such a self-serving society.

One single was persecuted, not by non-Christians but by Christians, because she chose to spend her summer studying at a Bible Institute rather than playing in the sunshine with her friends. They actually accused her of thinking she was better than them because she planned to study the Bible intensively for eight weeks. Unfortunately, our self-centered culture in America has penetrated the Church so much that a young woman not only has to choose against the American culture, but sometimes against the more subtle, worldly Christian subculture tainting the Body of Christ.

Part of reckless abandonment is realizing how much our culture has affected our behavior patterns. You want to be Christlike, but your lifestyle is a reflection of *Vogue* magazine or *Cosmopolitan* rather than a new creation in Christ. A.W. Tozer said, "A whole new generation of Christians has come up believing that it is possible to 'accept' Christ without forsaking the world."[3] Ruth had to forsake the familiar and comfortable in order to receive God's best for her life.

Lady of Reckless Abandonment

New Faith

Ruth moved from a false religion into the only true and eternal relationship. Too many women have been involved in a form of religious worship, but have never had a vital, growing relationship with Jesus. Has your religious experience been like Isaiah 29:13b (NIV)? "…Their worship of Me is made up only of rules taught by men." Has your faith been a lifeless ritual rather than a vital love relationship with Jesus? Why not spend some of your free hours as a single woman beginning a journey away from rituals into a deep relationship with Jesus Christ?

One single woman expressed this vital relationship with Jesus in the following way: "I desired that my relationship with the Lord be an adventure. One where I would find out what pleased Him and then do it, devoting as much energy to Jesus as I would in a relationship with a boyfriend. I am falling more in love with Jesus every day." Do you know more about pleasing a boyfriend than you do about pleasing the Lord Jesus?

Dividends From a High Price

Ruth's choice was costly, but the return on this high price far outweighed her investment. Matthew 19:29 (NIV) says, "And everyone who has left houses or brothers or sisters or father or mother or children or fields for My sake will receive a hundred times as much and will inherit eternal life." Ruth made the choice to turn her back on all that was familiar and begin a whole new life. Her "hundred times as much" was a godly husband, a son who would be the grandfather of King David, and inclusion in the lineage of Jesus Christ. She turned her back on all that was familiar and God rewarded Ruth's critical choice.

Another costly aspect of Ruth's choice was the time frame in Israel's history. It was the age of the judges, a period of time described as "do your own thing"; "Everyone did what was right in his own eyes" (Judg. 21:25b). Ruth chose not only to break her family cycle, but also to challenge the lifestyle that many in Israel embraced. She wanted God's will, not hers; His blueprints, not her elementary scribbling; God's assignment, not her foolish plans.

Whenever a single woman decides to abandon herself completely to Jesus, as Ruth did, she will find herself out of step with society and, sometimes, even with her friends. A single woman today needs the boldness to challenge and break the cycle of the "American way" that exalts a relationship with a man as the answer to life. This "American way" blurs the reality of the ultimate answer to life found in a deep relationship with Jesus Christ. A modern-day Ruth wrote: "My deep satisfaction from my commitment to Jesus is constantly challenged by other believers. They treat me like some kind of Neanderthal, definitely out of step with the today's woman."

The Missing Puzzle Piece

Often a woman will attempt to find delight in a career if Mr. Right has not arrived. In time, even her "great career" will prove to be less than satisfying. A career, a marriage, or even motherhood is not enough to totally satisfy you by itself. God knows that you will never be complete until you really understand that you are complete in Jesus. Colossians 2:9-10 says, "For in Him all the fullness of Deity dwells in bodily form, and in Him you have been made complete, and He is the head over all rule and authority." When a single woman enters a career or even marriage without understanding that she is complete in Christ, she will be disillusioned and dissatisfied.

Incompleteness is not the result of being single, but of not being full of Jesus. Only the process of reckless abandonment to Jesus does any woman ever finally understand that, in Him, she is complete. When two "incomplete" singles get married, their union will not make them complete. Their marriage will be simply two "incomplete" people trying to find completeness in one another. Only when they understand that their fullness is found in a relationship with Jesus will they ever begin to *complement* one another. They can never *complete* one another. You were not created to complete another, but to *complement*. Completion is Jesus' responsibility and complementing is a woman's privilege. A woman not complete in Jesus will be a drain on her husband. Such a woman will expect her husband to fill the gap that only Jesus can fill. Only the single woman who understands this means of being complete in Jesus is mature enough to be a helpmeet (complement). "For in Christ all the fullness of the Deity lives in bodily form, and you have been given fullness in Christ..." (Col. 2:9-10 NIV). Are you feeling full yet? Ask the Lord right now to begin this process of revealing to your heart the reality of your fullness in Him. "But it is good for me to draw near to God..." (Ps. 73:28a KJV).

In her book, *Loneliness*, Elisabeth Elliot states, "Marriage teaches us that even the most intimate human companionship cannot satisfy the deepest places of the heart. Our hearts are lonely 'til they rest in Him."[4] Elisabeth Elliot has been married three times (twice widowed) and she knows from experience that marriage does not make one complete; only Jesus does.

Satisfied By a Heavenly Fiancé

Does your relationship with Jesus reflect reckless abandonment to Him, or does it reflect only tokenism, a superficial effort toward following Jesus? Are you content to offer to Jesus that which cost you nothing? Are you influencing those around you to consider a life-changing commitment to Jesus Christ? In the Song of Solomon, the Shulammite was so committed to the one she loved that other women wanted to meet him. They were anxious to go with her to seek for him. "Where has your lover gone, most beautiful of women? Which way did your lover turn, that we may look for him with you?" (Song 6:1 NIV) Who was this one so worthy of such reckless abandonment? Does your commitment to Jesus cause those around you to seriously consider whether Jesus is Lord of their lives? Or does your "token" relationship leave you and others still thirsty?

One of Jackie's single friends stopped by her home one day, glowing and grinning from ear to ear. When questioned about her grin, she replied, "I am on a honeymoon with Jesus." This woman had been through a brutal divorce (including losing custody of her children) and in her hopeless condition she met the One who gives everlasting hope. When she began to recklessly abandon herself to knowing Jesus as Lord, He began to fill the gaps in her heart left by the removal of her husband and children. In Christ she found comfort, healing, direction, and purpose for her life. Do you understand such a relationship with Christ? It doesn't come cheaply, but the high price is worth the results of such a commitment, especially today. The depth of your relationship with God is up to you. God has no favorites; the choice to surrender is yours. A.W. Tozer so brilliantly stated in his book *The Pursuit of God*: "It will require a determined heart and more than a little courage to wrench ourselves loose from the grip of our times and return to Biblical ways."[5]

Ruth had just such a determined heart, and the Lord honored her faith to move away from all that was familiar and take a journey toward the completely unknown. Ruth did not allow her friends, her old surroundings, nor her culture's dead faith to keep her from running hard after God. She did not use the excuse of a dark past to keep her from a bright future that began with her first critical choice: reckless abandonment to Jesus Christ.

Have you made this critical choice or you have settled for a mediocre relationship with Jesus? Amy Carmichael, one of the greatest single woman missionaries who ever lived, once remarked, "The saddest thing one meets is the nominal Christian."[6]

Choose right now to put mediocrity behind you; courageously determine to pursue Jesus with your whole heart, soul, and mind. As a single woman, this is the perfect moment to establish a radical relationship with Jesus and remove any tokenism from your Christian walk.

Becoming a Lady in Waiting begins with reckless abandonment to Jesus. The strength and discipline necessary to be a Lady of Diligence, Faith, Virtue, Devotion, Purity, Security, Contentment, Conviction, and Patience is discovered in this radical way of relating to your heavenly Bridegroom. If you find yourself struggling with any of the qualities discussed in the following chapters, you may want to reexamine your own commitment to Jesus. Is it real and all-encompassing, or merely ornamental? Do you remember a time when you broke your "alabaster box" in the presence of the Lord Jesus? The Lady in Waiting understands the pleasing aroma of the perfume that flows from one's "broken alabaster box." It is the irresistible aroma of reckless abandonment to Jesus Christ.

Becoming a Lady of Reckless Abandonment

From your perspective, what is the difference between "token commitment" and "reckless abandonment" to Jesus? Is your relationship with Jesus one of sacrifice or convenience? (2 Sam. 24:24)

The difference is that the immature "token commitment" is doing the "bare minimum" to try to get by, but the mature "reckless abandonment" is going out of the way to grow closer to Jesus

Have you broken your "alabaster box" at the feet of Jesus? (See Mark 14:3-9 and Luke 7:36-39.) Are you afraid to break your box at His feet? Why?

I think right now I'm learning to completely break my "alabaster box" and surrender every last drop of oil to Him.

Like Ruth, how has your relationship with Jesus affected your friends, your surroundings, and your faith? (Mt. 19:29)

I prefer being with my friends from youth group over my friends at school, and I always prefer youth group/church activities over any other activity.

Does your life have public and private evidences of your reckless abandonment to Jesus Christ? Explain.

People can see that I'm different by the way I talk, act, and make choices. Privately, I'm learning to get into my Bible daily, and surrendering every area of my life to Him.

Read Colossians 2:10. What does being complete in Jesus mean to you?
In what ways do you feel incomplete? How can that be changed?

To me, it is being entirely content in who I am in through
Christ, and not feeling any lack of anything by — prayer and
— Bible study
constantly growing in spiritual maturity. Right now I'm (lookadoo)
feeling incomplete in spiritual maturity, but that can be changed

Have you experienced the completeness that comes from the courtship
available with your heavenly Fiancé? Consider this dating prerequisite: You
must understand you are complete in Jesus before you ever date or marry.

Yes, I do feel complete in who I am in Jesus. It
would be fantastic to have someone to "complement," but
I don't see it as a need, nor do I feel lacking without it.

What does the following statement mean to you: "Any woman who does
not understand that she is complete in Jesus is susceptible to idolatry"?
(This idolatry is dependence on a guy to make her complete—thus putting
him in God's place.) Consider this verse: "How happy are those who know
their need for God..." (Mt. 5:3 Phillips).

Well, the statement in the parenthesis pretty much
sums up my thoughts.

Lady of Diligence

While getting ready for a speaking engagement, she managed to get the kids up, dressed, and fed; fill the lunch boxes; load everyone in the car; and take them to school. Then she hurried home to set her hair and do her makeup. Finally dressed and ready to go speak, she made one last dash for the bathroom. While washing her hands, she noticed that the toilet was overflowing—not a slow drip, but pouring out all over the floor and into her open-toed shoes and nylons. She scrambled for towels and used them to build a dike then rubbed her feet dry and squirted her shoes with perfume. She ran out the door and jumped into the car. Halfway to the church she realized that she had left her Bible and outlines on the kitchen counter.

Such is the drama of Jackie Kendall's daily life. This kind of insanity is not unique to her. Every wife and mother daily deals with the legitimate needs of her husband and children. These needs take precedence over anything she might want to do, regardless of how "noble" her desires are! To be involved in the simplest form of ministry may require the married woman three times as much time to accomplish, in comparison to the single woman. Although a single woman may long for the "chaos" of a family, she must not waste her time wishing for it. She must be diligent to use her single time wisely now. She has more control over her time and choices now than she will probably ever have again. (The single parent is not included in this comparison because her responsibilities are double that of a married woman. She must "solo" in raising children, increasing the burden of her daily priorities even more.)

The perfect time to make the most of every opportunity is while you are single. Every believer should use time wisely, as Ephesians 5:15-17 (NIV) says: "Be very careful, then, how you live—not as unwise but as wise, making the most of every opportunity, because the days are evil. Therefore do not be foolish, but understand what the Lord's will is."

John Fischer wrote this:

"God has called me to live now. He wants me to realize my full potential as a man right now, to be thankful about where I am, and to enjoy it to the fullest. I have a strange feeling that the single person who is always wishing he were married will probably get married, discover all that is involved, and wish he were single again! He will ask himself, 'Why didn't I use that time for the Lord when I didn't have so many other obligations? Why didn't I give myself totally to Him when I was single?' "[1]

The single woman can be involved in the Lord's work on a level that a married woman cannot because of the distractions and responsibilities of being a wife and mother. Ironically, some single women can be so distressed by their single state that they become emotionally more distracted than a wife and mother of four children.

Rather than staying home worrying about another "dateless" Saturday night, realize how much valuable time has been entrusted to you at this point in your life. Rather than resent your many single hours, embrace them as a gift from God—a package that contains opportunities to serve Him that are limited only by your own self-pity and lack of obedience.

No Time to Waste

Understanding God's promised provision for widows, Naomi sent Ruth to gather grain in the field of a kinsman. Ruth was willing to use her life working diligently at whatever her Lord called her to do. She would not be paralyzed by her lack of a husband. "And Ruth the Moabitess said to Naomi, 'Please let me go to the field and glean among the ears of grain after one in whose sight I may find favor.' And she said to her, 'Go, my daughter' " (Ruth 2:2). She also did not allow the fact that she was a stranger from Moab to cause her to fear while she was gleaning in a strange field. Ruth was the "new girl in town," an obvious newcomer, but she was not afraid to walk into a totally unfamiliar situation. Countless single women stay home rather than travel alone into the unknown. They not only miss out on being encouraged by others, but also are not exposed to new relationships when they remain at home tied up by cords of fear and feeling sorry for themselves.

If a single woman allows the fearful prospect of meeting new people and new challenges to keep her at home, she may find herself bored and lonely while all the time missing many satisfying and fulfilling experiences. Don't stay home as a fearful single woman. Take that step of faith and volunteer. Get involved and see what you have been missing. One single said, "Serving the Lord brings such inexpressible joy." People who are not involved in serving the Lord obviously have never experienced this joy; otherwise churches wouldn't have to beg them to get involved. If all the singles in the church just realized their "strategic position," churches would not ever need to ask for help with children, youth, or college students. There would probably be so many available single workers that there would be a "surplus of man power"!

Free to Follow

Are you busy serving Jesus during your free time, or do you waste hours trying to pursue and snag an available guy? Ruth was a widow, but she did not use her time sponsoring pity parties for all unhappy single women to gather and compare the misery of datelessness. When she and Naomi moved back to Bethlehem, Ruth did not waste a moment feeling sorry for herself. She went right to work. Instead of being drained by her discouraging circumstances, she took advantage of them and diligently embraced each day.

Ruth came to the God of Israel after years of living in darkness, but He gladly received her service even though she was a Moabite foreigner. She bound herself to the service of the Lord, interweaving her service with Him like the braiding of a heavy rope. Isaiah 56:6-7 (NIV) refers to a foreigner binding himself (or herself) to the Lord and Him willingly receiving their "diligent" service: "And foreigners who bind themselves to the Lord to serve Him…these I will bring to My holy mountain…."

Are you tightly bound to the Lord, serving Him diligently, or has your relationship and service been unraveling over the years as you continue to be single and not married? Has resentment and self-pity unraveled what used to be a tightly woven labor for the Lord? You must be sensitive to the things and situations that distract you from redeeming your free time. "Whatever might blur the vision God had given [Elisabeth Elliot] of His work, whatever could distract or deceive or tempt others to seek anything but the Lord Jesus Himself she tried to eliminate."[2]

Some singles see the lack of a mate as God denying them something for a more "noble purpose"—*a cross to bear*! Our selfish nature tends to focus on what we do not have rather than on what we do have—free time—that can be used for others and ourselves. Is your life on hold until you have someone to hold?

Sitting in a restaurant across from a beautiful blonde, as the woman's personal story began to unfold, the listener was somewhat overwhelmed. Here was a very attractive woman who had put her life with Jesus on hold after her world fell apart. She had been married for a few years, and trying to conceive a child, when she heard her single best friend was pregnant. What irony: her unmarried friend was with child and she remained childless. The irony turned into a trauma when this married woman found out that the father was her own husband. Can you imagine the devastation caused in this beautiful young woman's heart? Have you experienced such a crushing emotional blow? The stunned listener began to cry out for wisdom concerning this tragedy. Jesus reminded the listener that God is not intimidated by trauma. In fact, Psalm 34:18 says, "The Lord is near to the brokenhearted, and saves those who are crushed in spirit." This brokenhearted woman had put her life on hold after her husband divorced her. Such a response is understandable, but that day in the restaurant this now single woman decided to take her broken heart, her empty arms, and her loneliness and give them to Jesus. In exchange, Jesus taught her how to resist feeling sorry for herself and how to stop living in the arena of bitterness. After she made the choice of recklessly abandoning herself to Jesus as Lord, she was free to serve Him. This once brokenhearted single woman has been transformed into a fearless servant of the Lord. In fact, she became a missionary to Quito, Ecuador.

Have you also put your life on hold? Do you have an excuse for not serving Jesus?

A Full Place Setting

A former college friend remained single longer than any of us ever expected. She had dated incessantly in college, so we assumed if any of the girls would marry, it would be Donna. Ten years after her graduation from college, she was not married. Someone asked what helped her to be so satisfied as a single woman. Her immediate response was, "A full place setting." She had lived for several years eating her meals on paper plates while her good china and flatware were snugly stored in her hope chest. Then the Lord showed her that she did not have to wait for a "mate" to bring beauty to her private world. She unpacked her china and silver and began not only to entertain others in style, but also to daily set out china and crystal for herself. (One Wednesday night at church Donna sat in front of two people who were to become her future in-laws. They did not know each other at the time. On the way home from church, the future father-in-law remarked that he thought Donna would become his daughter-in-law. He was absolutely right. This satisfied single woman has someone sharing her china and crystal today, but her feelings of satisfaction did not come because of a husband. She found satisfaction by serving the Lord.)

Some women put their lives on hold, each waiting for some guy to come riding into her life on a white stallion. They have no china, no decent furniture, and no pictures on the walls—none of the little extras that make a house inviting. They make minimal investment in what they hope is a temporary condition. Their lives reflect a "paper plate" mentality. They cannot comprehend fullness and satisfaction without a man. These precious women have settled for the "generic" version of life. How unlike Jesus' statement in John 10:10, in which He said He came so we might have a more abundant life. Do you believe that the abundant life is only for the married woman? Do you think that a woman with a husband, two children, a nice home, and two insurance policies is more satisfied with life than you are? Life is satisfying only when you diligently serve the Lord, whatever your circumstances.

Enviable Singleness

Singleness is an enviable condition. An unmarried woman has something that a married woman gives up on her wedding day: extra time for Jesus. Too many young women waste valuable years as they wait for life to begin—after marriage. They rarely realize the priceless free time they waste, until it is gone. Have you neglected some mission or ministry opportunities because you feared prolonging your unmarried state?

A young woman heard about this enviable condition and wrote a letter asking Jackie whether she should pursue a doctorate. (She continues to count more birthdays as a single than she had anticipated.) Jackie enthusiastically encouraged her to immediately get her degree. As a single woman, she diligently hit the books without neglecting a mate or a child. Her single state served as the perfect qualification for the pursuit of a doctorate. This is not to say that a woman can't pursue her dreams after she is married, but she will have a much higher price to pay and often the pursued dream turns into a nightmare!

If you love serving Jesus, please do not waste any of the free time you have. Do not consider yourself too unhappy to help anyone else. Self-centeredness will rob you of the joy of serving. Satan, who is effective at distracting you from God's best, wants you to continue dreaming about how "one day" you will get involved in ministry. He wants to sidetrack you from making a lasting investment. Too many women foolishly believe his lies. Therefore, they lose sight of opportunities to get involved in any form of outreach to others. Unsatisfied and unfulfilled, they sink deep into the quicksand of "maybe next year."

Many have embraced the ultimate deception, "Poor me." An excerpt from a single friend's letter exposes this self-pitying lie: "As is usually the case, as soon as I stopped asking what was in it for me and began asking what I was meant to give, things began to improve, beginning with my attitude. I continue to grow and be greatly strengthened in my relationship with God one-on-one and to seek out where I can serve those around me." This single woman is a classic beauty. She has learned how to use her free time for Jesus rather than sit home writing melancholy poetry.

Unrelenting Pursuit

Undistracted and unrelenting describe different facets of the word *diligence*. The Lady of Diligence embodies these terms. A verse that describes her attitude toward ministry and service is First Corinthians 15:58 (NIV): "Therefore, my dear brothers, stand firm. Let nothing move you. Always give yourselves fully to the work of the Lord, because you know that your labor in the Lord is not in vain." Do these terms describe your attitude and approach to using your free time for Jesus? Let's examine how diligence affects every aspect of your service and ministry for the Lord.

Diligence and the Ministry of Teaching

Have you been diligently pursuing truth for years, but not giving out as much as you have taken in? Are you involved in a regular Bible study where you give, maybe even teach? Almost as dangerous as neglecting the Word is the habit of taking it in but not putting it into practice. "Impression without expression can lead to depression." Do you keep attending church, Sunday school, Bible studies, seminars, and retreats—taking yet never giving? Take advantage of this time in your life when you can be involved in teaching without so many encumbrances. Maybe you've considered leading a discipleship group. Hesitate no more; go for it! There is no time in your life more perfect than now. Maybe you have toyed with the idea of teaching a Bible study. Do not delay. The future may hold more distractions that would continue to keep you from your goal.

Diligence and the Ministry of Encouragement

How many times a week do you find yourself in a position where someone has shared a need with you and you want so much to respond with wisdom and grace? Isaiah 50:4 (NIV) says, "The Sovereign Lord has given me an instructed tongue, to know the word that sustains the weary. He wakens me morning by morning, wakens my ear to listen like one being taught." Do you have a hard time responding to such an early morning wake-up call? Rising early to develop the tongue of a disciple will open a door of ministry to those who are weary, whether they are at work, at church, or even at the grocery store. Your very words will be a ministry of healing and encouragement. "The tongue that brings healing is a tree of life, but a deceitful tongue crushes the spirit" (Prov. 15:4 NIV). Such predawn training will give you the privilege of becoming God's garden hose in a land of many thirsty people.

Diligence and the Ministry of Prayer

Do you have a prayer partner? Or do you only have someone with whom you have regular pity parties? If you do not have a prayer partner, ask the Lord right now for such a gift. A prayer partner can help you pray for others. Of course, this prayer partner needs to be a female, one who can encourage you to keep God's perspective on your commitment to being all God wants you to be, whether married or single.

"A prayer partnership serves as one of the greatest assets for accomplishing the deepest and highest work of the human spirit: prayer."[3] Praying regularly with someone (or a small group) is such a vital part of your service to God. To intercede on behalf of someone else's need is a privilege. When you intercede with a partner, the "duet" of harmony before God can

change your world. Matthew 18:19 (NIV) describes this harmonious duet: "Again, I tell you that if two of you on earth agree about anything you ask for, it will be done for you by My Father in heaven." That little verb *agree* refers to harmony. Do you have someone with whom you can prayerfully approach God in harmony? Rather than searching for a life-partner, look for a prayer partner. Together you can participate in God-given prayer projects. Together you can discover how you can take your concerns for others and turn them into prayer projects.

Diligence and the Ministry of Service

It is doubtful that there could ever be a better time to serve Jesus than this "moment" of singleness. Rather than wasting precious moments fantasizing about an earthly lover, take advantage of your free hours each day to serve the Lord of Heaven. If you are frustrated and distracted, rather than fruitfully serving Jesus, then ask Him right now to adjust your vision.

As Ruth diligently worked at what she could, God sent her a man to protect and provide for her. God will do the same for you if that is His plan. Is there a ministry opportunity you should be working with? Why not consider a short-term mission trip? Don't worry about that certain guy you have had your eye on for a while. If he is God's best for you, he will be there when you return. Your single state may not be permanent, but it definitely is not to be a comatose state until your Prince Charming arrives and whisks you off to his castle. Single women are not "Sleeping Beauties" waiting for their prince to fight his way through the thorns and past the wicked witch to finally kiss them awake. That is an illusion often used by the enemy to defraud women.

Is there an opportunity of service that you have avoided because you can't give up your "post on the castle wall" looking for your knight in shining armor? Is there an application for a summer ministry waiting for you to fill out? Such a chance may come again next summer, but then it will be even harder to respond to the prospect of serving, for time brings more and more distractions. As you get older, you assume more obligations and responsibilities that demand your time and attention. Such distractions will make serving Jesus even more difficult. Have you given Jesus full reign over your time?

Limitless ministry opportunities exist for the Lady in Diligence. These ministries are available right this moment. They do not demand a Bible college education. The only requirement is a single woman who desires to use her time wisely in ministry.

Diligence and the Ministry of Writing

This ministry requires pen, paper, and a willing heart. Much of the New Testament was originally written as letters to believers. An encouraging letter or postcard can be read and re-read. So often a person will think about writing someone a letter, but the thought never becomes action. You may ignore the inward suggestion because of a busy schedule or a resistance to writing. A personal note, though serves as oxygen to the soul of the recipient. "He who refreshes others will himself be refreshed" (Prov. 11:25b NIV).

If you are not comfortable writing a full letter, or your schedule does not permit such a ministry in writing, then purchase some pre-stamped postcards and try to send them regularly to different people who need a refreshing word. The Lord wants you to be involved in the lives of those around you and writing is one of those opportunities.

Diligence and the Ministry of Listening

A ministry of listening is available right now. When someone is grieving, your presence provides more power than words. When someone is burdened, you may want to just listen and silently pray rather than verbally give the solution to the problem. Being content to listen to someone today is a gift you can give. A listener provides a healing audience for someone who is hurting. When Jackie's sister died, listeners who allowed her to share the loss and cry freely were God's greatest source of comfort. Being content to listen is a gift you can give to someone today.

Lady of Diligence

It may take a gentle touch to minister to the spirit. It also may require just being with the person, whether standing for hours in a hospital hallway or sitting by a sickbed. Sometimes even the greatest songs or truths are not the appropriate thing during a crisis. "Like one who takes away a garment on a cold day, or like vinegar poured on ~~soda~~ a wound, is one who sings songs to a heavy heart" (Prov. 25:20 NIV). This ministry requires not seminary training, but a loving, listening heart.

Diligence and the Ministry of Hospitality

The ministry of hospitality is not producing a demo for the Parade of Homes or a feast featuring Julia Child. Simply cooking for others is a significant ministry, especially during illness or bereavement. Casseroles and cakes can be such a blessing to a new mother, an elderly neighbor, or someone emotionally devastated by a death in the family. What a way to share the love of Christ with someone who needs to see Christianity in action.

Please do not limit your ministry of hospitality to candlelight dinners for the man of your dreams. Think how a beautiful, candlelight dinner for a group of single women, or even high school girls, could minister to them.

Diligence and the Ministry of Helps

This ministry requires time, but it is invaluable. Helping others with the "dailies" of life is a gift that breaks their exhausting monotony. Helping a friend get her apartment ready for special guests, or helping her move into a new place, leaves the recipient grateful. Mere physical labor may seem so insignificant in comparison to church visitation, but the Word of God speaks clearly to such a misconception. "Whether, then, you eat or drink or whatever you do, do all to the glory of God" (1 Cor. 10:31). Maybe a friend needs a ride to the airport during rush hour, or maybe she needs her oven cleaned, or even her laundry done. These duties can all be done unto the Lord. "Whatever you do, work at it with all your heart, as working for the Lord, not for men" (Col. 3:23 NIV).

Non-Newsy Works

For those of you who are diligently going after Jesus and the privilege of serving Him, here is a very special reminder. Sometimes you will be called to do some monotonous work that will not make the headlines. It may frustrate you because it doesn't seem very "impressive." Consider the reality of all the non-newsy things Jesus did during the majority of His life (30 years), before He began His formal ministry. What more humbling work could Ruth have done than gathering leftover grain for the survival of her mother-in-law and herself? Richard Foster brilliantly penned this thought, "If all of our serving is before others, we will be shallow people indeed."[4] Jesus spoke clearly about the constant public display of our service. "Everything they do is done for men to see..." (Mt. 23:5 NIV). The next time someone asks you to help out in service that is monotonous and non-newsy, don't hesitate. The King records such works (see Mt. 25:34-35). Teaching Bible studies, going out on evangelism teams, mission trips, and even prayer groups—all these are priceless opportunities to serve, but they are not the only avenues. Serving in the preschool department at church, going to kids' camp, and even cooking in the kitchen for a junior high banquet are all honorable services that the Lady of Diligence can embrace with respect.

Look at your schedule and decide how some of your free time that was wasted yesterday might be redeemed today. Allow no more room in your schedule for "pity parties." Such wise use of your free time will give you the gift of "no regrets." Your future service will be focused and no longer distracted.

Free hours,
Not wasted by me,
using my free time,
To serve only Thee.
Realizing how temporary free time will be
Never to regret a missed opportunity,
For others to be blest,
Through yielded me.
JMK

Becoming a Lady of Diligence

Determine what may have kept you from being more involved in ministry by seeing which of the following four characters you identify with the most.

JEALOUS JENNY: Do you focus on the gifts others have been given and, therefore, never find your own niche in ministry? Have you unwisely compared yourself with other women? (1 Cor. 4:7; 12:7; Rom. 12:3)

PRIMA DONNA PAULA: Do you want to serve God on your terms? Do you want to write the script and have the leading role? (Jn. 4:34; 7:16,18; Mt. 23:5)

FEARFUL FRANCES: Do you fear what others think? Are you afraid of becoming too involved and being labeled a fanatic? Do you hesitate to be a Lady of Diligence because you feel so inadequate? (Prov. 29:25; 2 Tim. 1:7; 1 Thess. 5:24)

DOUBTING DORIS: Faith is believing what God says about you. Do you long to become more involved in a number of ministries, but feel your faith will fizzle before you finish? Have you struggled with serving the Lord in the past, so you doubt yourself today? (Part of ministry is learning, so don't let yesterday's struggles prevent future successes.) (1 Jn. 4:4; 2 Tim. 1:9; 1 Tim. 6:12)

I'm not really identifying with these four... But I do identify with the mentality of not getting involved to be "available" and waiting just in case.

To get involved in any ministry demands a sacrifice. Have you allowed your self-centeredness to dominate your daily schedule? Why not go through your checkbook tonight and see how many checks were written for things concerning others? (2 Sam. 24:24; Phil. 2:3-4; Mt. 19:29)

I am often selfish with my time and self-centered with my spendings

Lady of Faith

Faith...
a fruit whose blossoming aroma
Inspires one to victory,
and sustains one after loss.
JMK

If you are spouse-hunting, we have heard that Alaska, Montana, and Florida have an abundance of men. Proportionately, women most outnumber men in the Northeastern states.

Are you panicked because you are residing in one of these male-sparse states? A recent statistic from the National Census Bureau states that the percentage of single men in Palm Beach has increased by 47 percent since 1980. Palm Beach, Florida—where the boys are! (Sounds like an old movie from the 1950s.) Do you suddenly have the urge to relocate? Don't start packing yet.

An article in *USA Today* stated: "The Census Bureau reports today that for the first time since the early 1900s, the USA's male population grew faster than the female in the 1980s."[1] Are you breathing easier? Such a statistic does not alleviate your need to be a Lady of Faith. The existence of more single men does not mean exemption from the often trying process of waiting for God's best by faith.

One friend assumed that by going to a big Christian college, she would inevitably find Mr. Right. Considering that she was from a very small town where more livestock lived than people, her strategy for finding a spouse seemed quite logical. She completed her four years and returned home without her MRS. degree. Where do you think she found her mate? You guessed it, back in her very small hometown. Her father invited her to come and watch their church baseball team, and guess who showed up on the opposing team? Mr. Right, a guy she had met at youth camp more than a decade earlier. You know the rest of the story. Her logic did not find Mr. Right. She returned to a hometown barren of many males, and God, who is not limited by our circumstances, delivered her mate from way out in "left field." God did not honor her logic, but He did honor her faith in Him to meet her needs.

Do you presently live in a town or city where you need "eyes of faith" in relation to the prospects of a mate? Do you attend a church where the "pickin's are slim"? Let's take a closer look at two contrasting attitudes toward one's circumstances.

Where the Boys Are

Think back to how the love story in the Book of Ruth began. Three widows, Naomi with her two daughters-in-law, Orpah and Ruth, have just been through the painful experience of losing the men they loved. Just facing each day without their mates required much faith because of the difficulty in providing for one's own needs. Naomi, being a Jewess, made the decision to leave Moab and return to her hometown in Israel (Bethlehem). Her two daughters-in-law had become young widows, so she encouraged them to return to their families where they each might find another husband. Naomi's suggestion appeared very rational. Naomi knew that they (being Moabites) had a better chance of finding husbands in Moab than in Israel. "...Go back, each of you, to your mother's home. May the Lord show kindness to you, as you have shown to your dead and to me. May the Lord grant that each of you will find rest in the home of another husband" (Ruth 1:8-9 NIV). Would Ruth have ever found a Christian husband to be united with if she had also returned to Moab?

Naomi lovingly pointed Orpah and Ruth in the direction of possible prospects. She actually encouraged them to go in a direction where they could *see* how they might each find a husband. Orpah followed Naomi's advice and chose logical sight for future direction. She gave Naomi a kiss good-bye and headed "where the boys are." Such "choices" are often based on logical sight and do not need even a mustard seed of faith.

Many single women spend their free time searching for the same kind of location chosen by Orpah. They attend schools because they can "see" the prospects. They join churches based on apparent ratios of men to women. They go to seminars, retreats, and conferences looking for the man of their dreams, only to demand a refund for the nightmare they often find (the ratio of women to men typically registered at retreats being seven women to every one man).

Some women have changed churches because they were in a "no prospective mate" district. Others avoid churches under-stocked with available men. Can you relate? Some single women serve only one term on a mission field and never return because the ratio of available men to women shrinks even smaller on the mission field than in their home church. A single woman serving as a missionary wrote: "Well, here I am in a no-hope situation. There is only 1 single man to about 50 single women." On what are these women focusing—on the situation or on the Sovereign One?

Chance Rendezvous

A woman who takes the route of Orpah (sensual, logical sight) often invents ways for a "chance rendezvous" with the man of her dreams. You can see her loitering in the very area that Mr. Right regularly frequents, hoping that he might finally notice her and the romance will begin. This sounds more like a Harlequin romance. Such a young woman might sing in the choir, not because she wants to make a joyful noise unto the Lord, but because she wants a weekly chance to sit near the prospect (single man) that her "sensual sight" has focused upon. Such impure motives for such a noble cause! Proverbs 19:14 says, "House and wealth are an inheritance from fathers, but a prudent wife is from the Lord."

If the Lord wants to give you a man, He does not need your clever "chance rendezvous." This is not advocating that you avoid men completely and expect the Lord to "UPS" His choice to your front door. You need to participate in activities that involve men and women, but be sensitive to your motives whenever you find yourself in the presence of "available men." Consider this Scripture whenever checking your motives and your pulse! Proverbs 16:2 (NIV) says, "All a man's ways seem innocent to him, but motives are weighed by the Lord."

You can prevent disappointing moments if you check your heart whenever you go to a singles' activity. Much preparation (like taking a shower, putting on makeup, styling your hair, doing your nails, and choosing the perfect outfit) precedes one's attending such an activity, yet so little heart preparation does. The gal with sensual sight can become so obsessed with finding her guy that she neglects her inner self. Orpah's style (logical sight) tends to become the norm, but Ruth offers an alternative to this vain search for Mr. Right. She demonstrates what it means to be a Lady of Faith.

Eyes of Faith

Orpah's example of going after the available men could have influenced Ruth to return to Moab, the home of her parents and the gods of her youth. Ruth, however, remained with Naomi and her God. Ruth certainly must have considered the probability of remaining single if she went with Naomi. Even though it promised no prospects of a husband, she chose to follow Naomi and her God back to Bethlehem. Ruth chose to trust God with her future. She looked not with sensual sight, but through "eyes of faith." Even though Ruth was young in her faith in the God of Israel, she chose to trust with her heart for the future her eyes could not yet see.

Lady of Faith

The International Children's Bible describes faith in this way: "Faith means being sure of the things we hope for. And faith means knowing that something is real even if we do not see it" (Heb. 11:1). This childlike expression of such an abstract quality can become a daily reality in the life of the Lady of Faith. Your hope cannot be put in some dreamed-up future. It must be in the God who knows your past, present, and future, and loves you enough to give you the best.

Are you in what seems like a "no-hope situation"? Maybe you are attending a church that requires you to exercise faith to even open the door and go in, since every man there is either married, engaged, or the age of your baby brother. Instead of becoming fearful during this trying situation, look to the Lord through "eyes of faith." To do so brings God great pleasure. Hebrews 11:6a says, "And without faith it is impossible to please [totally satisfy] Him…." Your daily use of "eyes of faith" brings Jesus such satisfaction.

Do you long to please Him? Then reconsider your circumstances and realize that what seems to be a hopeless situation (no prospects on the horizon) is just the flip side of the view through "eyes of faith."

Sometimes in an attempt to be a Lady of Faith, one can get sidetracked trying to hurry the "male order delivery" process.

One must admit that it is more likely a woman would find a godly man in a church, at a Christian college, or in local Bible study. These are obviously good places to find Mr. Right, but the assumption of finding him can result in disillusionment. Hundreds of wonderful single women live and breathe in all the right places, but they remain single.

You may wonder, "How can I be a Lady of Faith when I feel so insecure deep in my heart that God will deliver the goods? What if I have faith in God and end up being 98 and unmarried?" Of course, you would never outright admit that you're not sure you can trust God. That would appear too ungodly! But there's that sneaking fear in the back of your mind: "If I really give up my search and have 'eyes of faith,' God might not give me what I desire, like a husband, a home, and children." God knows when your heart aches for these precious things. But He also knows that these earthly things will not make you secure.

To be sure, your gnawing fears are very common. The enemy knows how common these fears are and he feeds them by adding a few lies like, "If you give your desire to the Lord, He will send you to outer Bufelia where all the men are three feet tall," or, "If you give all your desires to the Lord, you might get married, but you'll definitely not want to take pictures of your fiancé for your friends to see."

"Can I really trust God with all my hopes and dreams? How will I meet Mr. Right if I have eyes of faith? Doesn't God need any help in developing my dreams? What about needing to be in the right place at the right time? How will I meet Mr. Right if I'm not out and about where he might be? I feel the urge to make a mad dash to the next party or to attend the college with the most available men." Such anxious thoughts are based on fears, not faith. "Faith does not eliminate questions. But faith knows where to take them."[2] You may say you have faith and are just being practical. Are you? What is the opposite of faith? Fear. Who knows that better than the enemy? At the base of his being is the desire to trick you into missing God's best. Satan wants you to believe the lie that cripples faith: God cannot be trusted.

In order to have "eyes of faith," you may have to use a spiritual eye wash to remove the debris that the enemy has dropped into your eyes. The Lady of Faith will have times when her secure eyes of faith begin to blink into an anxious twitch of insecure, sensual sight. She can admit her insecurity to her heavenly Fiancé and He can calm the twitching eyes. Spending some quality time in the Word is the best "eye wash" for "eyes of faith."

Romans 10:17 says, "So faith comes from hearing, and hearing by the word of Christ." A Lady of Faith may have to spend dateless weekends in male-saturated churches. She can only be content in this trying situation if she has her "eyes of faith" properly focused on the ultimate relationship—with her heavenly Bridegroom. Datelessness is a common type of debris that irritates the "eyes of faith," but the eye wash treatment—quality time with Jesus and reading His Word—is always effective.

Lady of Faith

Divine Encounter

In contrast to the manipulated "chance rendezvous" of the single woman Orpah, Ruth had a divine encounter that affected not only her marital status, but also biblical history. That first morning in Bethlehem, Ruth happened to stop in a field belonging to Boaz. Interestingly enough, the same day, Boaz "just happened" to visit that very same field where Ruth was gathering the leftover grain. Their meeting was not an accident nor the product of female maneuvering. Instead it was the work of a sovereign God.

God providentially directed Ruth to the field of Boaz. You find this divine encounter in the second chapter of Ruth, verse 3: "...and she happened to come to the portion of the field belonging to Boaz...." The verb *happened* in Hebrew means "chanced upon." This leaves no room for manipulation. She had a chance and her chance transported her into the center of God's will and right to Boaz's field. Boaz was wealthy and available. Ruth did not "have plans" when she chanced upon his field. Ruth's "eyes of faith" led her to the exact spot where she would meet her Mr. Right, Boaz, whose name means "pillar of strength." (Contrast the meaning of his name to that of her first husband, Mahlon, which means "weak and sickly"! God rewarded Ruth's faith with a husband who was a "pillar of strength.")

If Jesus wants you married, He will orchestrate the encounter. You have nothing to fear except getting in His way and trying to "write the script" rather than following His. Jesus does have your best interest at heart. He desires to bless you by giving you the best. Sometimes what you perceive as the best is nothing more than a generic version. Consider His wisdom and love in comparison to your own wisdom and self-love. In whom are you going to trust—all Wisdom and Everlasting Love or little ol' finite you? Ever since the Garden of Eden, women have often felt they could and should know as much as God. Much pain in our world has resulted from dependence on our wisdom rather than on our Father's.

Meeting Across Continents

A beautiful airline stewardess left her secular job and went to Germany as a missionary. Her "eyes of faith" sometimes twitched as the reality of no prospects, especially English-speaking ones, continued to loom before her while she diligently served the Lord. At a Bible conference, she met a single guy who served the Lord on the other side of the world. He was an unlikely candidate according to sensual sight and basic logic, but a long-distance courtship began and they eventually married. Today they serve the Lord together in the Philippines.

Your circumstances and geographical location do not threaten God's will and purpose. Just as God brought Eve to Adam, Rebekah to Isaac, Ruth to Boaz, and someday the Bride of Christ to Himself, He will one day bring Mr. Right to you if you are to be married. This is true regardless of your unique situation. Your location or your occupation may not make you very accessible to available godly men, but these roadblocks do not handicap God. Time and time again, we have had the privilege of watching God bring a wonderful, godly guy into the life of a Lady of Faith. He seems to suddenly appear out of nowhere.

One young lady faithfully attended her church for years. Often she needed reminding that "he's just not here yet." God brought her Boaz from across the country to where she was in Florida. This single woman had developed better than 20/20 vision in relation to her "eyes of faith." Many tears of faith had washed away the debris that often caused her to doubt if she would ever get married. She used those times of doubting to grow in faith as she turned to God who orchestrated the future blessing for her.

God brought His best for one woman all the way from Escondido, California, to Kenya, Africa, where she was serving her Lord. She was not anxious about the absence of available men. After a broken engagement and a couple of years of less-than-satisfying dating, Vivian had volunteered to go to Kenya, Africa, to teach missionary kids. Just before she left for Kenya, she attended a Bible study where she met a precious Christian guy named David. Had she not been leaving for Africa that week, they might have had time to become better acquainted. Frustrated by the reality of meeting such a fine Christian guy just before leaving to go halfway around the world, Vivian followed the Lord to Africa with "eyes of faith." Little did she know the script God had written. Halfway through her first term on the field, a construction team arrived from the United States to do some work for the academy where she taught. Guess who was part of the team? You got it: David. He and Vivian not only got acquainted, but they also married right there in Kenya. Just as Jesus brought David to Vivian, Jesus can bring your life-mate to you, no matter where you live.

The ultimate demonstration of Ladies of Faith are the single women who have lived the ten principles in this book—and who themselves continue in a state of singleness. They have not numbed their longing to be married; instead, they have embraced their Lord so tightly that they face their prolonged singleness with peace, not bitterness.

One woman named DeDe has allowed her heavenly Bridegroom to sustain her through more than 40 years as a single. She has never stopped desiring a husband and children, but they are not the focus of her life. Her focus is on the "daily bundle" God gives her. Her "daily bundles" are specific assignments to love and encourage the people in her world. Instead of having her own baby wrapped in a bundle, the Lord gives her someone else's child to love and encourage (she is the vice-principal of a Christian school). Rather than having a husband to wrap her arms around, she has teachers to give hugs and thoughtful notes to during their demanding and draining days. This Lady of Faith has not only pleased her heavenly Bridegroom, but also been a blessing to the Bride of Christ.

Have you hesitated about taking a new job or even going to a foreign mission field because you might miss Mr. Right? Have you passed up opportunities to serve in another Sunday school department because you might miss meeting the man of your dreams? If you are trying to orchestrate the "divine encounter," you might be setting yourself up for a disappointing crash. Wherever you are, whatever your circumstances may be, whether divorced, widowed, or single and getting older every day, be assured that God has not lost your address or your file. He knows exactly where you are and what you need. Remember, God has already taken care of your greatest need—your salvation—and as Romans 8:32 reminds us, "He who did not spare His own Son, but delivered Him up for us all, how will he not also with Him freely give us all things?"

You make the most important decision in life, giving your life to Jesus Christ, "by faith." The second most important decision concerns your life-mate. This decision also demands the element of faith. Waiting for one's life-mate and then saying "I do" to him demands secure faith, like Ruth's faith in the God of Israel.

Before you read any further, if you have been full of doubts and anxiety in reference to your future mate, take a few moments to confess your doubts to God and ask His Spirit to develop in your life this quality of faith. Your faith during the "waiting period" pleases God.

Don't fear or resent the waiting periods in your life. These are the very gardens where the seeds of faith blossom. Whenever circumstances stimulate you to deepen your faith, don't resist them; instead embrace them willingly. Elisabeth Elliot said in *Passion and Purity* (a must-read for those who are having an anxiety attack during their extended waiting periods):

> "I do know that waiting on God requires the willingness to bear uncertainty, to carry within oneself the unanswered question, lifting the heart to God about it whenever it intrudes upon one's thoughts."[3]

Whenever the "unanswered question" captures your mind, or you are overtaken by the restlessness of singleness, take a moment to commit that care where it belongs. As First Peter 5:7 says, "Casting all your anxiety on Him, because He cares for you." This intruding anxiety about your lack of a life-mate is not reality, but rather a weakness that the Greater Reality is capable of handling. Just go to Jesus as soon as the intruder arrives. Such a practice will only enhance your life as a Lady of Faith. Many single women have not recognized that the trying, frustrating waiting period is the perfect classroom for the Lady of Faith. Don't skip class! Embrace those dateless nights and, by faith, rest in His faithfulness.

Becoming a Lady of Faith

Go through selected Psalms and circle the words *trust* and *rely upon* in red. Notice David's trust in God.

This exercise will strengthen your "eyes of faith." What are two other ways to strengthen your faith?

Through prayer, and watching to see how God answers them, and by reading accounts of people who's faith was rewarded.

Can you see the parallel between a strong devotional life and the Lady of Faith? Read Romans 10:17.

By reading God's Word and studying it, I can learn what He has to say about my life, and read the promises he has made to me.

Can you see a parallel between your own journey of faith and your daily quiet time with God?

As I learn more from God's Word, the more I learn to trust Him, because He has proven Himself trust-worthy time and time again.

Read through Hebrews 11 and underline all the verbs. Then go back through and confess, "By faith I can _____," filling in the blank with the verbs from each verse.

Is there anything you can think of that you can't do by faith?

The obvious answer after reading that passage: NO.

_____

_____

_____

Can you trust God to sovereignly bring you together with a Boaz?

Absolutely! Easier said than done at times, because of my sinful, doubting flesh, but my heart knows that I can trust God.

What causes you to struggle in your walk of faith?

I'm human! I still fight my flesh like everyone else. I also am distracted easily by my present circumstances instead of looking past them to see the bigger picture.

Explain how you tend to manipulate your rendezvous with men and/or how you can allow God to be your heavenly dating service.

Instead of getting involved in activities with chasing guys as my motive, I can ask God to change my heart and motives, and stop worrying about guys and let God take care of it.

Can you see how an extended period of singleness serves as a great opportunity to develop into a Lady of Faith? Explain.

Yes, I can. I can grow into a Lady of Faith by completely surrendering my love story to Him, and letting Him take care of it all, while I in the meantime focus on serving Him.

Lady of Virtue

"Providing lasting pleasure,
potential beyond measure,
the rarest of treasure,
a reputation of virtuous character."
JMK

One of life's most costly and beautiful objects is born out of pain and irritation—the pearl. A tiny piece of sand slips into an oyster's shell and begins to rub against the soft tissue, causing irritation. In response to the irritation, the oyster produces a hard substance. This substance eventually develops into one of the world's most beautiful jewels—a lovely luminous pearl. In fact, the greater the irritation, the more valuable the pearl!

Like the oyster, Ruth experienced many irritations or trials in her young life. She grieved the deaths of her father-in-law and husband. She bravely faced the turmoil of change in the direction of her life as well as a move to a foreign land with a bitter mother-in-law. When she arrived in that strange land, the trials did not end. She was immediately thrown into a new working situation among total strangers with new customs. Through all this stress, her new faith began to wrap itself around the painful situations. The by-product was a pearl from the washbasin of Moab.

Many single women view themselves as ugly oyster shells lying on the beaches of life, beset with the trials and problems that come with not being married. To make matters worse, they compare their crusty exterior to all the beautiful seashells around them and wonder how any man could ever give his attention to them.

If you are one of these women, be encouraged. Don't view the trials of singleness as irritating grains of sand to be discarded as quickly as possible. Realize that God has them there to create something beautiful in you. James 1:2-4 says, "Consider it all joy, my brethren, when you encounter various trials, knowing that the testing of your faith produces endurance. And let endurance have its perfect result, that you may be perfect and complete, lacking in nothing."

God is using the sands of singleness to make you perfect and complete. He's developing pearls of character in your life. He knows that whatever you use to "catch" a guy, you must also use to keep him. If you attract a guy with only your looks, then you are headed for trouble, since looks don't last. As time goes on, we all end up looking like oysters. Therefore, what you look like on the inside is far more important than what you look like on the outside.

Consider again our Lady in Waiting. What enabled Ruth to catch Boaz's attention? Was it her gorgeous hair or beautiful eyes? No! The answer is found in Boaz's response to her question in Ruth chapter 2.

> *Then she fell on her face, bowing to the ground and said to him, "Why have I found favor in your sight that you should take notice of me, since I am a foreigner?" Boaz replied to her, "All that you have done for your mother-in-law after the death of your husband has been fully reported to me, and how you left your father and mother and the land of your birth, and came to a people that you did not previously know"* (Ruth 2:10-11).

Boaz was attracted to the virtue and character displayed in Ruth's life. A woman of virtue is irresistible to a godly man.

Lady of Virtue

At a singles conference, one pastor's wife spoke of her life as a child. She grew up with a harsh alcoholic father. He left the family without a penny when she was a young teen. Her outward appearance was very plain and she could not afford fancy clothing, makeup, or expensive hairstyles. She had very little time to socialize because she had to work to support her family. Instead of feeling bitterness over the rejection she had experienced or frustration over her lack of material possessions and free time, she trusted God to take care of her. She developed a strong prayer life and asked God to make her beautiful. She worked hard and grew strong in faith, believing that God would provide all she needed.

Her testimony was stirring, but the real climax came the next day as her husband spoke. He said, "My wife's character is what caught my attention. Her inner beauty was irresistible. Now, thirty years of marriage and half a dozen children later, I am more attracted to and in love with her than when I first met her." This lady gained her knight's attention with lasting godly character. Today their marriage and ministry remain strong and blessed because of the qualities she allowed God to develop in her while she was single.

An ugly oyster shell is an unlikely place to find a lovely gem, but Isaiah 55:8 says, "For My thoughts are not your thoughts, nor are your ways My ways…." You may see an ugly shell, but God sees the beauty He is creating in you. Are the sands of singleness causing you bitterness right now, or are you allowing these trials to change you into a pearl? The Lord wants you to be a Lady of Virtue—a costly, beautiful pearl for all to admire.

The Body Beautiful Trap

The world has convinced many Christians that the only way to get a man's attention is through a gorgeous body. Hollywood has sold the lie that a woman will never marry the man of her dreams if she is not pretty enough or slim enough or tall enough or if she does not have high enough cheek bones! Most dateless women think their condition is the result of the "reflection in the mirror." Consequently, women spend millions of dollars every year believing the myth that physical beauty is mandatory for marriage.

Proverbs describes how a woman with no character got a man's attention. Some of the descriptives used for her include the following: smooth tongue, captivating eyes, persuasive and seductive speech, a mouth smoother than oil, and flattering speech (see Prov. 5:3; 6:24-25; 7:21). The techniques used today by the modern woman are as old as the first woman who ever snared a man's soul. The whole emphasis is on the superficial, external aspects of a woman—aspects that fade with every passing day. Many women's magazines glorify this woman's techniques rather than expose her bitter end. Marriage based simply on outward beauty can lead to immorality and ultimately, divorce when an even more attractive body comes along.

The Word of God very clearly warns women not to fall into "the body beautiful trap." "Your beauty should not come from outward adornment, such as braided hair and the wearing of gold jewelry and fine clothes" (1 Pet. 3:3 NIV). Although braided hair and gold jewelry are not wrong in and of themselves, real beauty is not found on the outside. This verse does not advocate homeliness as proof of godliness. Some women are under the misguided perception that to be holy, one must look homely. This is not true. Women should seek to look their best. This verse simply challenges you to not devote all your energies toward painting the outside, thus neglecting the enduring qualities that need developing on the inside.

The key to beauty is found in First Peter 3:4 (NIV): "Instead, it should be that of your inner self, the unfading beauty of a gentle and quiet spirit, which is of great worth in God's sight." This kind of beauty can only get better the older it gets. As Jackie once said, "If a man chose me for external beauty, his destiny would be hugging a prune. But, if a man chooses me for my internal beauty, his destiny will be unfading beauty even in the twilight years of marriage, because of Jesus."

When you look at the virtuous woman of Proverbs 31:10-31, you will see God's picture of a beautiful woman. There are 20 verses describing her. Only one verse mentions her outward appearance. If you were to spend 1/20 of your time on outward physical beauty and the other 19/20 on developing the other qualities God describes as beautiful, such as wisdom, kindness, and godliness, you would become the excellent woman Proverbs 31:10 says a man should try to find.

Remember what King Solomon said in Proverbs 31:30 (NIV) about the external emphasis of charm and glitz? "Charm is deceptive, and beauty if fleeting; but a woman who fears the Lord is to be praised." There are many women who fear pimples, wrinkles, flabby thighs, and crow's feet, but very few women who really fear the Lord. With which are you attractive to men: the snares of Proverbs 5, 6, and 7, or the beauty of First Peter 3:4?

Fit for a King

When you picture the perfect man for you, what is your prince like? Do you see a man devoted to God? A man of character—teachable, loyal, faithful, gentle, and kind? What kind of woman do you think this godly man desires to marry—a shallow woman or a woman full of charm who knows how to dress and capture other men's attention? Is this the one he imagines he will one day want to spend the rest of his life with—the mother of his heirs? No way!!

To marry a prince, you must first become a princess. To marry into royalty, you must be appropriately prepared. Even Diana, the Princess of Wales, had to go through a period of "waiting and preparing" before marrying Prince Charles. She had to learn how to properly act, dress, and speak so she would honor the royal family. Is it any wonder that a heavenly princess must prepare inwardly for the calling to which she will give her life? As you set your attention on developing godly character, Christ will change you into the beautiful princess He created you to be.

Ruth is not the only biblical example of a Lady in Waiting who developed into God's virtuous pearl. Consider the story of the lovely Rebekah in Genesis.

Lady *in* Waiting

The girl was very beautiful, a virgin, and no man had had relations with her; and she went down to the spring and filled her jar, and came up. Then the servant ran to meet her, and said, "Please let me drink a little water from your jar." And she said, "Drink, my lord"; and she quickly lowered her jar to her hand, and gave him a drink. Now when she had finished giving him a drink, she said, "I will draw also for your camels until they have finished drinking." So she quickly emptied her jar into the trough, and ran back to the well to draw, and she drew for all his camels. Meanwhile, the man was gazing at her in silence, to know whether the Lord had made his journey successful or not. When the camels had finished drinking, that the man took a gold ring weighing a half-shekel and two bracelets for her wrists weighing ten shekels in gold, and said, "Whose daughter are you? Please tell me, is there room for us to lodge in your father's house?" She said to him, "I am the daughter of Bethuel, the son of Milcah, whom she bore to Nahor." Again she said to him, "We have plenty of both straw and feed, and room to lodge in" (Genesis 24:16-25).

The "pickin's were slim" in Rebekah's shepherding community. Worse than that, she worked full-time for her father tending sheep! As you read her story though, there is good indication that Rebekah was doing more than "just waiting." Look at the endearing qualities she developed for her unknown knight (Isaac).

Genesis 24:15-16 shows that she was a hard worker with a "jar on her shoulder" serving her dad's sheep. She also was *"a virgin, and no man had had relations with her."* She had not settled for second best in her wait. She had been under her father's authority and in her father's home serving his interests. Her respect for others showed in her kindness to a stranger in verse 18: "…'Drink, my lord'; and she quickly lowered her jar to her hand, and gave him a drink." This was no slow, lazy woman, but one with the character quality of genuine care for someone in need. She had character like "Ruby" in Proverbs 31:20: "She extends her hand to the poor; and she stretches out her hands to the needy."

Rebekah did not stop after one act of kindness either! "…I will draw also for your camels until they have finished drinking" (Gen. 24:19). Rebekah had initiative and served without even being asked. She was not being manipulative with her service either. This was not a plan to get a man. She was not initiating service and working with such gusto for the reward of a young man's attention. She was treating a smelly old traveler and his dusty cantankerous camels special because that was her character! She was attentive to the needs of those around her and sought to meet them. She didn't offer them a sip of water, just doing a halfway job—she waited until they were finished drinking. Look at her diligence in verse 20: "So she quickly emptied her jar into the trough, and *ran back* to the well to draw, and she drew for all his camels." She was a gracious, giving woman, as Genesis 24:25 says: "Again she said to him, 'We have plenty of both straw and feed, and room to lodge in.' "

The servant had found a wife for his master's son completely on her virtuous character. She wasn't even in Isaac's neighborhood trying to meet him. She was busy with her father's sheep, but God brought them together. When the servant made his intentions known and wanted her to leave with him in Genesis 24:54-57, Rebekah knew she had been in the Lord's school of preparation, and she was ready. Her answer was, *"I will go"* (Gen. 24:58). Are you becoming a virtuous woman that a man may need as a helpmate? Are you using these days to develop godliness in order that, if asked, you will be ready? Whether you marry or not, every woman should seek the virtues of Christlikeness.

Rebekah's story closes with the perfect ending to a love story. "Isaac…lifted up his eyes…. Rebekah lifted up her eyes, and when she saw Isaac she dismounted….Then Isaac brought her into his mother Sarah's tent…and she became his wife, and he loved her…" (Gen. 24:63-64,67). God rewarded this virtuous woman's wait with her dream come true. The wait was worth it. Isaac loved the woman who waited for him.

If Rebekah had not developed godly character, would Isaac have been so attracted to her? Perhaps for a time, but within marriage, the real man and woman comes out. That can be a wonderful or a horrible experience.

God desires that every man and woman develop their inner lives so that through the passing years and fading of outward beauty, their love still deepens and grows. Are you developing into a woman who will be able to live "happily ever after"?

To Tell the Truth

So there are two ways to get a man to notice you. The first way, "the body beautiful trap," is to get his attention by how you look on the outside. This is a snare because looks don't last. They are superficial. The second way is what caused Boaz to notice Ruth and Isaac to be drawn to Rebekah. A Lady of Virtue is noticed because she has gained admiration for her godly character. Be truthful. Which approach best represents you? Take the following test. Check the items in each column that describe you most often. Score each total of qualities on the two lists to see if you are developing inner or outer beauty most diligently.

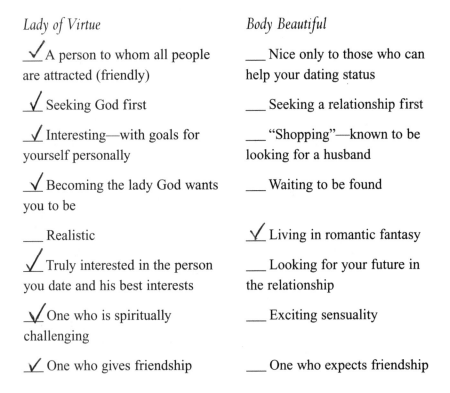

Lady of Virtue	*Body Beautiful*
✓ A person to whom all people are attracted (friendly)	___ Nice only to those who can help your dating status
✓ Seeking God first	___ Seeking a relationship first
✓ Interesting—with goals for yourself personally	___ "Shopping"—known to be looking for a husband
✓ Becoming the lady God wants you to be	___ Waiting to be found
___ Realistic	✓ Living in romantic fantasy
✓ Truly interested in the person you date and his best interests	___ Looking for your future in the relationship
✓ One who is spiritually challenging	___ Exciting sensuality
✓ One who gives friendship	___ One who expects friendship

Lady of Virtue

(?)✓ One who communicates verbally   ___ A wallflower

✓ Committed to trusting God   ___ Clinging to a guy

✓ Prepared for lasting friendships   ___ Playing games

___ Open to other friendships   ✓ Possessive

✓ Secure in the Lord   ___ Insecure without a "dream man"

✓ Building positive qualities in yourself   ___ Wanting him *now*

___ Trusting God   ✓ Trusting in schemes and plans to catch a man

✓ Patiently waiting   ___ On the hunt

Score yourself: __13__   Score yourself: __3__
(total qualities) __16__   (total qualities) __16__

How did you do? Are you allowing the Holy Spirit to use the sands of singleness to create in you priceless pearls of virtuous character?

Stringing Together a Pearl Necklace

The qualities Ruth and Rebekah displayed do not come from the jewelry store; neither are they activated the day someone places an engagement ring on your finger. Virtue is developed over time as you allow God's Spirit to do a special work in your life.

It is the Holy Spirit, not you, who produces the godly character you seek. These pearls of character are listed in Galatians 5:22-23 as "...love, joy, peace, patience, kindness, goodness, faithfulness, gentleness, self-control...." As these qualities develop, your life will become like a beautiful necklace strung with the pearls of godly character.

Galatians 5:19-21, however, describes some "beads" with which many singles choose to adorn their lives instead. They are "...immorality, impurity, sensuality, idolatry, sorcery, enmities, strife, jealousy, outbursts of anger, disputes, dissensions, factions, envying, drunkenness, carousing, and things like these...." If you desire to be a Lady of Virtue, these beads cannot belong on your necklace. If you see that you have a bad bead in your strand of pearls, it must be removed and replaced with the character quality that pleases God.

To remove the bad bead, confess the sin that developed this unattractive quality. Be honest with yourself and don't cover over or excuse the sin God shows you. Be specific. For instance, instead of saying, "Forgive me for all my many sins," say, "Lord, I have been envious of _____. Forgive me for dwelling on what You have given *her* instead of thanking You for what You have given me." After specifically describing the bead that detracts from your inner beauty, then receive God's forgiveness. His Word says, "If we confess our sins, He is faithful and righteous to forgive us our sins and to cleanse us from all unrighteousness" (1 Jn. 1:9). You no longer need to feel condemned or guilty because "As far as the east is from the west, so far has He removed our transgressions from us" (Ps. 103:12).

Once you have received God's forgiveness, ask the Lord to cleanse you from whatever caused the sin in the first place. For example, envy often results from comparing yourself to others or from an ungrateful heart. This deeper problem must be changed if envy is to be decisively overcome. If you do not cleanse your heart of these deeper issues, you will find yourself always on your knees asking forgiveness because of a continual struggle with the sin of envy.

One deals with these deeper issues through the power of God's Holy Spirit. He provides the needed power to take care of the deeper issues that produce bad beads. Galatians 5:16 speaks of this when it says, "...walk by the Spirit, and you will not carry out the desire of the flesh." How does one walk by the Spirit and tap into this pearl-producing power? Three portions of Scripture make it clear.

The first, Ephesians 4:30a, says, "Do not grieve the Holy Spirit of God. " You grieve or hurt God's Spirit when you choose to think, say, or do something that offends God. To tap into pearl-producing power, you must first decide to live a life that will please your Lord in all respects. From the time you wake in the morning until you go to bed at night, set your heart's desire on exalting Him.

The second verse is found in First Thessalonians 5:19. It says, "Do not quench the Spirit." To "quench" gives the word picture of throwing water on a fire. When God's Spirit prompts you to do something, give expression to that impression. Don't douse it with cold water by ignoring His leadership. For example, He may prompt you to perform an act of kindness, or caution you not to say something you are about to say, or lead you to encourage a friend who may be hurting. Whatever it is, seek to obey the Spirit of God in you on a moment-by-moment basis.

Finally, to tap into pearl-producing power, Ephesians 5:18 says, "...be filled with the Spirit." To be filled, something must first be empty. To be filled by the Spirit you must be empty of yourself and full of God. You give the Holy Spirit complete and total control of your life. When you became a Christian, you received all of the Holy Spirit. To be a virtuous woman, you must let the Holy Spirit have all of you.

There are many imitations of a true pearl, but with years, the shiny pearl paint cracks and wears off and all that is left is an unattractive bead hanging on a string. God's Spirit, however, produces true inner beauty, as you confess your sin, avoid displeasing God's Spirit, obey even the slightest of His promptings, and give the Holy Spirit full control of your life. Pearls of godly character take time to develop, but how blessed is the woman adorned by them.

You can settle for an imitation necklace of fake pearls by trying to simply cover over ungodly character, or you can allow the Holy Spirit to use the sands of singleness to create the real thing. If you want a cheap imitation, a modeling or charm school will be sufficient for what you seek. But if you want genuine pearls, you must allow the Holy Spirit to perform a special work in your life. Determine to string a lovely pearl "necklace of virtue" as a treasure for your Lord.

The Pearl

In every oyster there lies the ability
to produce something rare.
Truth like a grain of sand will produce
the pearl that is hidden there.

Young woman you are often mocked and scorned.
And told you never should have been born.
You want to run away, to hide your hurt.
Your heart is wounded, bleeding and torn.

God makes not mistakes
every life is special,
every life is planned.
Seeds can sprout in sand.

Open yourselves up to the Spirit of God
Grow in grace and maturity
Be what He wants you to be
Your beauty your strength lies deep within you.

Young woman, young girl,
open yourselves up to God.
Allow Him to reveal your pearl.
Sylvia Hannah

Becoming a Lady of Virtue

Study Rebekah in Genesis 24 and write out all the character qualities you find. Which of these do you need to develop? Pick one of these qualities and describe how you will specifically work on making it real in your life.

Rebekah's qualities: Kind, compassionate, hard working, willing to go the extra mile, obedient to God. When I see someone who needs help, I can help them and then go the extra mile to do something extra for them.

What books have you read dealing with the virtues/disciplines of a godly woman? In contrast, how many magazines have you read that deal with external glamour? What good books can you begin to read that will help develop your own personal godliness?

Bible, this book, Authentic Beauty, Brio, Everything Counts

Pick out a picture of a woman who, according to magazines, "has everything." What features do you see? What appeal has been used? What is dangerous about comparing yourself with pictures like that?

Magazine pictures aren't real! Computer programs change imperfections to perfection, making the reader think the unreality is real.

Read Proverbs 31. In prayer admit, "Father, You don't choose to zap me into completion. So today I choose to cooperate with the Holy Spirit as You make me a Lady of Virtue. From my Scripture reading, show me one quality from Proverbs 31 that I need to develop." (For example: discipline, thoroughness, graciousness, giving, diligence.) Pray over this quality for a month before moving to something else.

Self-discipline when it comes to getting in the Word daily.

Examine the "necklace" you are stringing by checking it in the light of Galatians 5:16-24. How many bad beads do you see in your necklace? Confess these sins and ask God's Spirit to control you in these areas. Get with a godly friend who will pray for you weekly until the bad beads are replaced by quality pearls.

Doubt, unkindness, anger, jelousy, laziness, lying, wrong motives, pride, unthankfulness, not honoring my parents

Chapter 5

Lady of Devotion

In the receiving line at her younger sister's wedding, many guests greeted Brenda over and over with teasing remarks. She heard comments such as, "Always a bridesmaid but never a bride. When is it going to be your turn? The only girl in your dad's home still unmarried!" Though these well-wishers may have been speaking out of fun or even compassion, their speech was not wise. The barrage caused its damage. It is hard enough for a single woman to keep her focus where it should be without friends making insensitive comments. How much better it would be for the Lady in Waiting if she were encouraged to pursue her undistracted devotion to the Lord Jesus Christ, instead of being made to feel like she does not quite measure up. If Jesus had been one of the guests, He would have surely commended her for productively using her single time to its fullest.

Much too often people view a single woman as though she should be pitied rather than envied. Nothing could be further from the truth. A Lady in Waiting has the advantage of being able to develop her love relationship with Christ without the distractions that a husband or family inherently bring to one's heart.

This has been God's plan from the beginning. He tenderly created woman to love Him and to experience the blessedness of fellowship with Him. In those first days, Eve communed with God in indescribable fellowship and oneness. When God came to walk in the cool of the day, there was no fear; only love. Eve had only positive feelings about God. She loved Him and knew He loved her. She enjoyed Him and devoted herself totally to His pleasure.

God still desires to know and be known by women today. But because sin entered the world, we no longer have a clear picture of the true God. "Satan's first attack upon the human race was his sly effort to destroy Eve's confidence in the kindness of God."[1] Satan lied to Eve about God's character. *"Indeed, has God said...?"* (Gen. 3:1) Satan has continued to lie to Eve's daughters. As a result, fear has often alienated women from the One who loves them as they need to be loved. Deep within a woman's soul remains the longing for the gentle embrace of the God Who Is, not the god that the enemy has craftily devised.

Boaz spoke of Ruth's devotion to God when he said, "May the Lord reward your work, and your wages be full from the Lord, the God of Israel, under whose wings you have come to seek refuge" (Ruth 2:12). Ruth chose to cling to Naomi's God as her own even though her mother-in-law had drawn a negative, harsh picture of Him. "She said to them, 'Do not call me Naomi [pleasant]; call me Mara [bitter], for *the Almighty* has dealt very bitterly with me. I went out full, but the Lord has brought me back empty. ...the Lord has witnessed against me and the Almighty has afflicted me?' " (Ruth 1:20-21).

Would you be devoted to a God like Noami's? In Naomi's bitterness, she no longer referred to God as "the Lord" as she had in verses 8 and 9, but with a title that can cause one to feel alienated and insignificant—"the Almighty." Though Ruth clung to Naomi as a mother, she did not accept her mother-in-law's view of God for herself. "If we think of Him (God) as cold and exacting, we shall find it impossible to love Him, and our lives will be ridden with servile fear."[2]

Your past experiences, present circumstances, or your parents' devotion or lack thereof may cause you to have an incorrect view of God. But nothing and no one can give you a clearer picture of the true God than slipping under His wings and discovering for yourself who God really is, the refuge for which you long. He desires for you to come again "into the garden" and walk with Him in complete fellowship. This is the fullness of devotion.

As a single, you have a wonderful opportunity to use your time to maximize your fellowship with God. When you love someone, you give them your heart, the center of your being. God asks for no less. He desires a totally devoted heart. Deuteronomy 6:5 says that you are to love Him with all your heart (deepest devotion), your soul (what you think and what you feel), and your might (your strength and energy).

Many women today are devoted, all right! They have devoted themselves to developing a love relationship, but not with the Lord. They erroneously seek for love in sensations and promises. The world's version of love is something they want to "fall into." Meanwhile, "true love" escapes them. True love can only be found in undistracted devotion to Jesus Christ.

To love Him like this, you must know Him intimately. Paul expressed the desire to "know" God in Philippians 3:10. In Greek, this *know* means "a knowledge that perfectly united the subject with the object."[3] Paul was desiring to know God intimately. Second Peter 1:3 says that everything pertaining to life and godliness is yours "through the true *knowledge* of Him." Peter and John in Acts 4:13 were identified as uneducated men, but the people observed their confidence and devotion to the Lord and marveled. In the King James Version of Scripture, the people exclaimed that these men "knew" Him, or that "they had been with Jesus." This "knowing" has the same depth as the term in Genesis 4:1 when Scripture speaks of the intimate relations Eve had when she "knew" or "had been with" her husband. It is a personal, intimate knowledge. Do you have a devotion to God that causes people to marvel at how intimately you know Him? Do you know God in a way that causes Him to be an intimate, personal part of your being as you may desire a husband to one day be?

As a woman, you have been created with a desire to be known—not just in a physical or general way, but deeply known and intimately loved. If you are hoping a man will one day fill your heart's desire for intimacy, you will be disappointed. God knows your deep longings for intimate love. Only He, the Lover of your soul, can fill this need completely. Your heavenly Father tenderly created you with needs that only God can fully understand and fulfill. As you come to know who He really is, He will meet your needs for love.

Your heavenly Father is incapable of doing evil. He loves you, and forgives and completely forgets confessed sins and grievances. Is this the God you know? You may think you know God, but your responses to God will betray you. If you retract in fear, try to hide things, give excuses when you do something you feel God would not like, then it shows your knowledge of God, like Naomi's, is incorrect. God is not supersensitive, selfish, or temperamental.

Do you ever have a feeling of guilt that you are not doing enough to please God, hanging over your head? Do you feel like the scale of expectations is tipping heavily in the negative and you must balance it? Do you feel like you could never do enough to pay for your inability to be perfect? Then your view of God is incorrect. God is not hard to please. He takes delight in His creation and quickly notices every simple effort to please Him (see Ps. 103:11-14).

Do you feel like God requires too much of you? Do you feel like God denies you the things you need most? If you do, then you don't really know God. Psalm 103:8-14 destroys these wrong assumptions about God. Have you lived with lies about God for too long? Get to know Him.

God wants to do you good and not evil. Jeremiah 29:11 says He wants to give you a future and a hope. Has your wrong picture of God been invented by the enemy in order to rob you of a true knowledge and love of God? Do not be deceived as Eve was in the garden. Get to know the One your heart truly desires to love. To love God, you must know Him intimately, personally, and devotedly. This does not require immediate entrance into a convent; you get to know Him by seeking Him.

Seeking True Love

Seeking God is very similar to developing a friendship. You talk a lot, you listen, you write each other letters, you think about each other, you find out what the other likes and does not like, and you try to do things that please that person. The more you spend time together, the more intimately you know your friend. And the more intimately you know your friend, the greater your love will be. It works the same way with your relationship with God.

Jeremiah 29:12-13 promises that a woman who diligently seeks God with all her heart will find Him. Your heart is the key to devotion to God. To find God, you must seek Him with your whole heart. A halfhearted search is not sufficient. This means you cannot seek God while you do your own thing.

Is God demanding too much to require that you seek Him with all your heart? No way! Think of it this way. Mr. Right comes over one day and begins to speak of his devotion to you. He says what you have been waiting to hear: "I love you. I give you my heart completely. For 364 days of every year, I will devote myself to you and you only." But then he adds, "However, *one* day each year I want to date others and see what I have missed. Don't worry, you can have *all* the rest. Will you marry me?"

What would your response be? Would you want this kind of devotion? Would it be selfish of you to deny him his heart just one day a year to give to others? No! Absolutely not. You would want his total love and devotion. You would want his heart all 365 days a year. Similarly, giving Christ your heart means you are not free to give it away to other things or people that come into your life (in idolatry). You can't give a part to relationships that delight you in this world and still seek God with a *whole* heart. You cannot keep a part of your heart for something that may seem better if it comes along. Devotion to the Lord Jesus Christ is giving everything or nothing at all. Your devotion to Christ must be a serious commitment to His Lordship. Christ loves you and is completely committed to you. Wholeheartedly devote yourself to loving and enjoying Him in return 365 days a year.

If you are to know God intimately, then you must seek Him, not only with a whole heart, but also with a clean heart. When you think of the word *bride*, you probably first imagine a beautiful, clean, pure woman in white.

No grime or dirt mars the image of purity. As a Christian you are part of the Bride of Christ. Any grime or dirt of sin will mar your image before Him.

The Lord's fiancé must have a clean heart. You must clean up any blot of sin that may arise between you and your heavenly Sweetheart. Sin causes God to back away from a person. It is disgusting to Him; He will not abide with it. Picture a couple deeply in love. He loves to be near her—so near he can breathe the fresh aroma of her sweet breath! What love! He hates onions though, especially on his beloved's breath. It really turns him off. What do you think she does before she sees him if she has eaten onions? Well, she wouldn't want the sweetness of their fellowship hindered, so she brushes away what offends him. Not only does she brush, but she also "Scopes, Close-ups and Gleems." She doesn't want to offend her love! She wants nothing to come between them. Sin is far more repulsive to God than even onion breath is to a sweetheart. If you want your devotion to God to be complete, don't merely brush at sin lightly. Get in there and confess it, clean it up, and clear it out. Be rid of it. If you notice you have spiritual halitosis during the day, take care of it immediately. Let Psalm 51:10 be your prayer: "Create in me a clean heart, O God...."

Many seek God, but only for His hand. They don't want God as much as they want something from God, such as a man, happiness, or a family. This impure search for God is limited to what you can get. It is more of a self-love than a God-love. This seeking will end in misery, not in the union of love you desire. God cannot be used like your credit card. He knows your motives. To grow in your knowledge of God, you must seek God correctly, which means you must also seek God with a pure heart.

A woman with a pure heart for God does not focus on what He gives, but delights in who He is. She seeks God's *face*, not just His *hand*. Would you want someone to say he loves you just so you would do something for him? To find God, you must seek Him with pure motives. Seek Him for who He is, not just for what He can do for you.

Have you ever tried to develop an intimate relationship with Jana Jabberbox? She's the gal who has lots to say and loves to hear herself say it. You try to say something when she takes a breath—which isn't often—but she keeps right on talking. She never listens. It's a one-way conversation, and you are left out. Even when someone is very special to you, you do not get too excited with a steady monologue. Listening is an important part of developing a closeness with someone else. If you want to get to know the Lord, you must seek Him not only with a whole, clean, and pure heart, but also with a listening heart.

As you spend time with God during your daily devotional time, learn to listen to Him as you read of His love and thoughts about you in the Bible. Think about what He is saying to you personally. Sit silently and write what impressions come to your listening heart. As you read and study His love letters, the Bible, you begin to see what He really thinks of you and what wonderful plans He has for you. As a result, your devotion grows and grows.

To find God you must seek Him with a whole heart, a pure heart, a clean heart, and a listening heart. Hebrews 11:6 (NIV) says that He "rewards those who earnestly seek Him." Does this describe your growing relationship with the Lord?

Singleness does not have to be a curse. Single gals do not have to wear long faces and be pitied until they are finally married. Quite the contrary! Singleness puts you in an advantageous position because, more than likely, you have much more time to seek the Lord now than you will ever have if you marry.

An Advantageous Position

Married women wrestle constantly with having to balance the physical and emotional demands placed on them. All women must learn to balance their priorities, but the single woman's heart is not sent in different directions by the needs of a husband and children.

Before the sun rises, a mother of young children may gingerly creep down the stairs and dig under the pile of unanswered letters and school assignments to find her Bible. "Ahhh! A few moments of undistracted time," she whispers as she opens her Bible. To her chagrin, from the top of the stairs she hears, "Is it morning yet?" She puts her Bible down and whispers for the little early bird to come quietly down. She encourages him to sit with his favorite book, turns to find her Bible, and begins to read (while Junior makes animal noises reading beside her). Suddenly, from upstairs comes the sound of splashing. "Oh no—Mommy! I missed the potty and it got on me!" Up the stairs she races to free the soggy victim, mop the floor, wake the school-age child, and get breakfast for everyone.

Her husband needs a button on his shirt, help finding his keys, and dinner an hour early. The kids need an arbitrator, a chauffeur, a nurse—and their P.E. clothes to be washed immediately. She sorts her way through piles of unwashed clothes cluttering the bedroom, trips over toys in the hall, and shovels aside newspapers and coloring books to collapse on the couch for a minute, only to be roused by screams from the children as the day's first civil war breaks out. Phone calls and drop-in visits continue to interrupt her day at every turn. It is midnight before she finally gets to the dirty dishes…and where is her undistracted time for devotion? If she was a wise Lady in Waiting and used her singleness to develop her devotional life, she has resources that allow her to commune with God during the wildest of days. A wife/mother may find her day beginning early and ending late, often before she has had any uninterrupted time to seek her heart's True Love. A single woman can choose to cherish the single time instead of feeling unhappy with it.

The Word of God illustrates the advantageous position of the single woman in relation to the affairs of life. "…An unmarried woman or virgin is concerned about the Lord's affairs: Her aim is to be devoted to the Lord in both body and spirit. But a married woman is concerned about the affairs of this world—how she can please her husband" (1 Cor. 7:34 NIV).

God says the unmarried woman has the advantage when it comes to her devotion to the Lord. An unmarried woman can give the Lord what a married woman rarely can—undistracted devotion. The time to develop a consistent devotional life cannot wait until you marry. Many single women waste valuable years as they wait "for life to begin"—after marriage. Ask any wife, even without children, and she will tell you her own juggling routine. A married woman struggles to have time alone with herself, much less time alone with God.

Becoming a Lady in Waiting, devoted to loving, knowing, and seeking God, will not come cheaply. You are the one who determines the depth of your relationship with God. He does not have favorites. You must choose to pursue the Lover of your soul—your heavenly Fiancé.

A single woman, one who chose to take advantage of her singleness, wrote the following poem:

The Single Gift

How blessed you are, you single one,
Don't talk of care and woes.
You've got too much to be thankful for,
Oh what, you'd like to know.

It's no mistake, no misdirection
Of God's perfect plan
That you've not found your special lady
Or you, that certain man.

God loves you so and has much more
To give than you've ever received.
That He's giving His best to you right now,
You really must believe.

His best is Himself, do you have it in full
Or only a bit on the side.
No man can meet your needs like God,
Nor can a lovely bride.

If your life's not complete, you know that Jesus is
And your life He will fill
If you'll only put Him first each day
And live to do His will.

He's gifted you for undistracted
Devotion to the Lord.
There should be nothing that can interfere
With Him and prayer and the Word.

Unless you let down the guard of your heart
And let others take His place,
Then you'll lack joy and peace and hope
And not experience His grace.

So give your heart right back to God,
Let Him keep it safe for you.
And when it's better than His best,
He'll make your one into two.
Donna L. Mihura

God has given you a precious privileged time. Don't waste a day of it! You will never have it again. These days can be treasure-finding days in your Kingly Father's chambers. As you linger at the window ledge searching for a glimmer of your knight's shining armor, don't miss the jewels your Father has for you to adorn yourself. Will you grow cold and bitter at the window sill, or will you hold your royal head high, glowing in your Father's love and attention. The choice remains with you, dear princess. Your Father will not force you to turn from the window, but He longs to fellowship with you. Come into His chambers, delight in His Presence. May you be found in Him—a Lady of Devotion.

Becoming a Lady of Devotion

Read Deuteronomy 30:11-20. What are the benefits of devotion to Christ? What are the results of living a life not devoted to Christ?

The benefits include life and blessings, and the consequences of not devoting one's life to Christ include death, destruction, and curses.

What warnings does God give about your heart in Deuteronomy 11:16 and Deuteronomy 30:17? What gods seek to distract your heart?

To not be drawn to worship worldly gods. Some include myself, money, posessions, status, favor in another's eyes, personal gain, education, pleasure, etc...

How did David seek God in Psalm 63? What was his reward?

He sought God with his "whole being" (v. 1), and he found God to be a source of refuge and protection.

How is your heavenly courtship progressing? How can you make it better?

I'm starting to grow in my knowledge of God, and thus closer and closer to Him by studying His Word.

Have you come to a place where your relationship with Jesus is beyond comparison with any earthly love?

I've never had an "earthly love", so there's nothing really to compare it to.

Does your daily devotional relationship with Jesus satisfy you from the top of your head to the bottom of your toes?

Yes, I'm completely content and satisfied.

Are you following hard after Jesus, or every eligible guy?

I often stray, but God's training me to follow hard after Jesus.

Read Song of Solomon 6:1. Does your love relationship with Jesus cause your friends to seek after Him as the Shulammite woman's praises did her friends? Why or why not? What can you do differently?

Jenna has been deeply impacted by my walk with Christ, so it has, but I could be so much more verbal about what I have in Jesus.

If you have never spent a consistent devotional time with God before now, begin by reading a Psalm a day. After reading the Psalm, write answers to these three questions in a notebook:

_____

_____

_____

What does this passage say about me?

_____

What does this passage say about the Lord?

_____

How can it apply to me?

_____

Lady

in

Waiting *Chapter 6*

Lady of Purity

No one was surprised when Tim and Susan began dating. They seemed just right for each other. They could talk about anything and had the same ideals for a strong Christian dating relationship. After a year of steady dating, Susan realized how deeply she loved Tim. She wanted to be his wife. She began to show her affection for him in different ways. They began to kiss and touch a little. She felt this was all right. She rationalized that she was in control of the situation and intended to remain pure until they married.

Marriage? Well, Tim had not actually made any kind of commitment, but she felt in her heart that he soon would.

Their little kisses and touches became more involved, but they always quickly asked forgiveness of each other and God when the petting became intense. After several months of these heavy petting sessions, Susan began to feel Tim had become distant. She then began to think that she may not have adequately assured him of her love. Maybe he was having second thoughts about her. She feared she might lose him—but she couldn't! He was the one.

Susan purposed to do whatever it took to keep him. She wondered if she had acted old-fashioned. After all, she just knew they would marry one day. Maybe he just needed to know the depth of her commitment to him.

Gradually, their relationship became more and more physical until one evening, Susan gave Tim the gift she had vowed not to open until her honeymoon night. She had imagined how strong and pure this moment of intimacy would make their love. Certainly this would cement the deep love they had for each other. It didn't.

Tim's face was no longer gentle. Susan felt as if he were a stranger. Her heart died within her. They were together, yet further apart than they had ever been. As he rose to leave, he said nothing. Instead of cementing their love, this one act of physical affection destroyed it. Susan longed to take her treasure back. She longed to start the night over. Unfortunately, the harsh reality had only just begun.

Tim and Susan are fictitious names, but this is a true story—and not just for this one young lady. It is true for hundreds of women who want to do what is right, but who unwisely give away their gift of physical purity too early. The gift is a treasure that can be rewrapped and given again, but never again for the first time.

We live in a day of blatant sexual impurity. A woman who marries, still a virgin, has become the exception, not the rule. Statistics say 80 percent of all unmarried women have given away their virginity by 20 years of age.[1] The Ruth of our biblical story, like us, also lived in a society of rampant moral decay. Ruth's story occurs during a time of year when sexual promiscuity would be at its height in the small farming community of Israel. "Immoral practices at harvest times were by no means uncommon and, indeed appear to have been encouraged by the fertility rites practiced in some religions."[2]

In this promiscuous society Ruth was a Lady of Purity, even in the midst of a potentially compromising situation. Ruth 3:7 says, "When Boaz had eaten and drunk and his heart was merry, he went to lie down at the end of the heap of grain; and she came secretly, and uncovered his feet and lay down." At a glance, you may read this and picture the beginnings of an X-rated scene in Ruth's story. But you must realize that Ruth was acting according to the customs of the time. She was not slinking into Boaz's bed to seduce him. In obedience to her mother-in-law's instructions, Ruth quietly lay at his feet for him to notice her, thus symbolizing her subjection to Boaz as her nearest of kin. This would give him the opportunity, if he so chose, to take legal action for the well-being of Ruth and her mother-in-law. (A woman had no form of social security and very few rights in that culture without a man.) This was not a brazen act of seduction, but an act of obedience to God's plan for her provision in that day. One thing is certain. When she left to go home, she walked away as a Lady of Purity.

Although the customs of Ruth's day may be difficult to understand, the temptations to compromise physically are not. Unfortunately, many women have been snared by the devil's deceptions and robbed of their innocence. How does today's single woman safeguard this special treasure and, like Ruth, go home at night a Lady of Purity?

Deadly Deception

Remember how the serpent deceived Eve by causing her to question God? He caused her to believe that God wanted to deny her something good, not provide her with something better. The enemy wants you to believe that if you wait to have sex, you will miss out on some of the delights of life.

Godly women must avoid basing their comprehension of the pleasures of sex on what commercials advertise, magazines glamorize, or books sensationalize. These are all full of the enemy's propaganda. Today's society seeks ultimate pleasure with no pain. But following society's example usually brings just the opposite. Look to your heavenly Father, your Creator, for the truth. God gives true sexual fulfillment to the lady who waits for this gift. God intended for you to enjoy the fulfillment and pleasure of sex within marriage only. The wonder and joy of this intimate act is maximized through purity before marriage.

Ask any woman of God who waited and she will tell you with eyes aglow that it was worth the sacrifice of denying her desires for a time. Look at that woman's marriage. Most likely the romance between her and her spouse still burns in a delightful love affair. Compare this real-life situation to the illusions in just one half-hour of "true life" romance on the television in an episode of "As the Stomach Turns" or "Body Watch." Have those actresses and actors (who, by the way, never scrub a toilet or break a nail and who always seem to be in their evening gown attire) found true fulfillment? They should "Ah! Yes—the delights of sex." Do not be deceived. Sex is special! Not sensuous sex, but satisfying sex in your Creator's way and time.

Why Wait?

Since sex is desirable, why not have sex? Why would God want to limit your pleasure with someone for whom you feel affection but haven't married? Have you ever been dieting but treated yourself to a huge piece of rich chocolate cake with fudge icing to celebrate some special occasion? Cake is good. Cake is desirable. The more cake, the more pleasure. But cake, in the midst of a strict diet, can really make one sick! The pleasure of a big, luscious piece of cake depends on the right timing, just as the pleasures of sex do.

God wants you to be a Lady of Purity because He wants to protect you from the consequences that sex before marriage brings. These consequences can be physical, emotional, relational, and spiritual. Let's look at these a little more closely.

Physical

Have you ever secretly opened a Christmas gift before Christmas Day and rewrapped it, putting it back under the tree? How thrilling and exciting it was when you saw the surprise. But what about the "big day" when the gifts were supposed to be opened for the first time? Where was the excitement when you opened your gift? The gift did not seem quite as special because it had already been opened for the first time. Each woman receives one "first time." God desires for your precious gift to be given to a committed lover who will cherish, keep, and protect you in marriage. God wants you and your gift to this man to be treasured and cherished, and trampled and conquered. Song of Solomon 8:4 (NIV) says, "...Do not arouse or awaken love until it so desires." God wants to protect you from losing your virginity.

God also wants to protect you from the sexually transmitted diseases that could affect not only you, but also your future husband. One young single cried the night she discovered that she had contracted genital warts. She grieved over the realization that when her future knight in shining armor proposed to her, she would have to disclose the fact that she carried an infectious disease. This grieved her more than the fact that genital warts are incurable. Not only could you or your husband personally incur irreparable physical damage, but also transmit these infectious diseases to your future children.

God also desires to shield you from an unwanted pregnancy. Although precautions exist, pregnancy always remains a possibility. A rushed marriage, adoption, or abortion only complicate the consequences.

Judy, a wonderful Christian girl with a promising future, looked forward to graduating from high school. To celebrate this special occasion, she went to a party with a great-looking guy. She decided a few drinks that night would be okay. She didn't want to seem "different" in front of her date. His invitation to go off to a secluded room made her feel uncomfortable, but the evening was so special and her date was so kind and tender and romantic.

In the following months, Judy tried to deny the physical changes she was experiencing. Bible College would start soon, so she blamed them on the stress. God had forgiven her for going all the way that night—surely He would not have allowed her to get pregnant. It would ruin all her plans.

Only after her mother noticed her condition did Judy go for a doctor's appointment. Unfortunately, it confirmed the worst of her fears. Judy would soon be a mother. Regardless of how sorry she was and the fact that God had forgiven her, the consequences of that one act changed her life forever. God wanted to protect Judy physically, but He left the choices up to her.

God desires to shield you from the negative physical consequences of premarital sex. He wants to protect you from sinning against your body. First Corinthians 6:18 (NIV) says, "Flee from sexual immorality. All other sins a [woman] commits are outside [her] body, but [she] who sins sexually sins against [her] own body." "He wants you to be free from an addiction to premarital sex. Passionate physical exchange is a short-lived high. As with drugs, you keep wanting more intense highs."[3]

Emotional

God intricately and delicately formed women with emotional characteristics that differ from men. A woman cannot separate her emotions from her physical state. If a woman's emotions could be separated from her physical state, she would not struggle with PMS. The man who touches your body, also touches your emotions. God made you that way, and He desires to protect your heart from being ripped apart by any man. You cannot make love to a man and remain emotionally untouched, no matter how hard you try. Therefore, if God knows that the man you think you love cannot care for your heart, He does not want you to give him any part of your body. You cannot give one without affecting the other! How your heavenly Father longs to keep your emotions safe and to guard you from feelings that threaten to wreck your emotional well-being.

God wants to protect you from the devastation of condemnation. The devil loves to get you down, to make you feel unworthy, thus making you unable to glorify God or stand before others. He enhances this tactic when he can whisper in your ear, "Some Christian you are. How can you witness to Jane?...She may have heard...You can't be a missionary; you compromised, remember?...Condemned...Condemned...Condemned."

If your emotions lied to you, causing you to give away your treasure to the wrong man, haunting fears may also begin to plague you. "Will he still respect me? Will he still love me? Why is that all he wants from me right now? What if I'm pregnant? Will anyone else find out? What if my parents find out? How can I face them? If we break up, what if the next man I date finds out?" Day and night these fears can play on your mind and emotions. God wants to protect you from these emotional traumas.

After premarital sex, there will usually be some lurking doubts. Would he have loved me without my body? Would he have married me if I hadn't gotten pregnant? Will he be attracted to someone better-looking after we're married? Most overwhelming are the doubts of God's love for you and, possibly, doubts of your salvation or your ability to ever again have a morally pure relationship.

You can be fully forgiven and cleansed by Christ, but damaged emotions take time to heal. The Lord doesn't want you to suffer these hurts. You are precious to Him. That's why He sets loving limits on your physical relationship and emotional attachments.

The emotional burdens of condemnation, fear, and doubt are often compounded with many other emotions such as resentment, bitterness, depression, and mistrust. God created you with emotions that can be overwhelmed by sexual promiscuity. Let Him protect your heart.

Relational

A woman has a depth of soul that desires an intimate friendship, apart from anything physical, with the man she loves. She desires to be known for the woman she is, not just for her physical body. A couple who chooses to remain physically pure gives all their time and attention to knowing one another on a deeper mental and emotional level. Once passion is introduced into the relationship, it is difficult for the man to stop and be satisfied again with just developing the friendship. The man becomes distracted by the physical. This is why so many women enjoy the relationship until the "friendship" changes to "dating." Something is lost when physical passion begins.

You cannot give double messages. Either you want him to know the you on the inside or the you on the outside. If you encourage your date to play with the bow on your package, he will want to untie the ribbon and unwrap the gift. Don't distract him with the bow. Allowing sex to enter into a relationship before marriage will almost always result in the loss of an intimate friendship with the one you desire to know you for you.

Premarital sex also brings a consequence that remains hidden until you marry. Mistrust and disrespect surface after the wedding cake has been eaten and "postmarital insecurity" begins. When a couple becomes involved sexually before marriage, they massage their consciences with the rationalization that they will marry anyway, so their lack of self-control doesn't matter. This is where they are wrong! Lack of self-control before marriage is *fornication*. Lack of self-control after marriage is *adultery*. The seeds for adultery are planted in the "hotbeds" of fornication. A woman subconsciously wonders, "If he did not exhibit self-control with me before marriage, how can I be sure that he will not give in to temptation during marriage when an attractive younger woman comes along?" A young man who cannot control himself before marriage does not suddenly become a man of self-control because he wears a wedding band!

Two other very real relational consequences deal with your present and future families. Think of your parents' shame about your sexual choices. Also, what about your future children? One day you may face your children's knowing that you did not set an example of purity for them to follow. What will you say if they ask the question, "Did you and Dad wait?"

Finally, should you not marry the man who opened your gift first, you take memories of him into your marriage that flash back to haunt you. God wants you to have the joy of saying to your knight on that special wedding night, "Here I am, clean and pure, emotionally and physically. No one has touched the treasure of my love. I kept myself for you."

God knows that a woman has much more to offer than a body. He knows that the dynamic relationship a woman has with a man is more than a physical experience. God intended for man and woman to enjoy not merely sexual intercourse, but a love that the physical relationship merely enhances. This love remains even when there is no physical culmination. Sometimes physical contact distracts a couple from developing and enjoying communication. If you want the friendship to be knowing who you each are, don't distract each other with early or inappropriate physical contact.

Spiritual

Passion makes it difficult to see that God also set physical limits to protect you spiritually. Hebrews 13:4 (NIV) very clearly says that "Marriage should be honored by all, and the marriage bed kept pure, for God will judge the adulterer and all the sexually immoral." God judges the sin of immorality. It feels awful to be separated from your Lord by the guilt of sin.

Actions speak louder than words, and this is especially true regarding premarital sex. It is difficult to share Christ with one who knows your reputation. Your actions can also cause weaker brothers and sisters to stumble. One night of passion can totally destroy a reputation you have built over a lifetime. "The spiritual side of sex is often overlooked. Even many Christians are not aware of the profoundly spiritual nature of their sex lives. A person will feel acute spiritual pain and separation from God when engaging in sex outside of marriage, but may not even realize how spiritually beneficial and unifying sex is within marriage."[4]

God does not intend to deny you pleasure. He protects you so you might enjoy physical health, emotional stability, relational intimacy, and spiritual blessings. If you marry, He wants you to grow more in love with your husband with each passing year. He wants you to live in complete trust of one another and spend a lifetime in love instead of the consequences of a fleeting night of uncontrolled lust.

Guarding the Treasure

How then does a Lady in Waiting guard her purity? Once a man has a woman's heart, her body is not far behind. That is one reason Proverbs 4:23 says, "Watch over your heart with all diligence, for from it flow the springs of life." To walk in purity, a Lady in Waiting must first guard the key to her heart. This does not imply that your relationships with men are robotic and free from feelings. It means that you focus on growing in friendship, not romance.

Here is how Debby guarded her purity while dating.

"I asked the Lord to help me remember not to take my heart away from Him and give it to a boyfriend too quickly. To keep this commitment, I decided I would pray before accepting any date. Before going out, I would pray again, this time asking that my thoughts and actions during the time together would not center on encouraging him romantically, but building a friendship and encouraging his love for the Lord. At times, when I felt flutters of romance rising and my heart trembling, I would ask the Lord to renew my strength and reset my focus; I would picture myself kneeling in new commitment.

"I enjoyed friendship-building 'dating' more after deciding to let God protect my heart. The only man who was given the key to my heart was the man I married. When we were engaged, I gave him a small red velvet box with an antique key inside to symbolize that I was giving him my heart to care for and cherish as the Lord had done before I met him. I am grateful that now Bill cherishes me as a priceless treasure and views the key to my heart as a privileged possession. An added bonus is that marriage is full of the 'extra special' romances that I denied myself before I met my husband."

Don't let your heart be given away too easily. If a man says he loves you, you don't have to echo the phrase. To men these three words can mean all kinds of things, like "I lust for you" or "I want you to kiss me." Or maybe he just can't think of anything else to say at the moment! But what did that "I love you" do to your heartstrings? Gradually those "I love you's" can trap you emotionally and lead you on physically. To guard the key to your heart, make a commitment to say you love someone only if you love him with a committed love, not a casual love feeling. You will remain much more in control of your friendship. Real love will have time to blossom and grow without those three words. Guard and save them to be whispered when God reveals it is time. What a gift to tell your fiancé, "You are the first person I have ever said this to: 'I love you.' " Give meaning to those precious words, and you may use them and hear them with fondness through many happy years of marriage.

There's a second step you can take to guard your purity. It's a radical statement, but save all your kisses for your future husband. One woman who made this decision said, "Early in my dating, I tired of giving a kiss at the door for a hamburger, coke, and fries. What would I have to give next for a steak dinner or a night on the town? After I was married I realized the decision not to give my kisses freely to my dates had an added bonus. For every kiss I denied dates at the door, the man I married received my kisses 'with interest' in our years of marriage. It was worth waiting for kisses—so they would be full of meaning—for years."

A woman's kiss or embrace is not just another way of saying thank you! A kiss should say something more intimate. If so, do you want to say intimate things to every guy you date? All the kisses you give before marriage and all the kisses you give after marriage express the love that belongs to one person: your knight.

If you remember to whom your kisses belong, you won't be so quick to give them away. If you think you may be dating Mr. Right, give your friendship time to grow before you give the "fringe benefits." He will appreciate them and respect you much more if you wait.

Realize that a kiss starts physical contact and once you get started it's hard to turn back from passion. Determine what you mean with a kiss. Let it reveal your heart, not "rev up" your hormones. One lady put it this way when asked why "friends" have trouble becoming friends again once they start dating: "Once you start having sex, that's about the only thing you have in common."

A third practical step is to make your decisions and choices about what you will and will not do with a date *before* things become hot and heavy. Here are some examples of "dating standards" that many godly women have made. They will help you resist the pressure to "open the gift" too early. (You can find more in Chapter 9.)

I will date only growing Christian men. (You will most likely marry a man you date. This is important!!)

I will concentrate on the friendship—not romance. (Don't be tricked!)

I will not spend time with him at home when we are alone.

I will not give kisses and hugs freely.

I will not lay down beside a man.

Don't set standards "as you go." Emotions can be tricky. You must make wise choices before the "flutters" and "heartthrobs" become so loud you cannot hear yourself think. Write them down and read them often! Commit them to God regularly in prayer.

During a Bible study, one Lady in Waiting made this point about "dating."

"Before Jesus became Lord of my relationships, I accepted our society's idea of dating as the time for a man and woman to be alone together. This time usually was devoted to romance and involved a measure of physical involvement—gradually accelerating if the dating continued. As I became closer to the Lord, I began to see dating from His perspective as a time for friendship-building without a need for promises of love or giving physical affection. As I spend time in group situations instead of one-to-one dating, I can really see the character of the guy friends I am spending time with. Doing things with groups also guards our purity, but doesn't limit our friendship-building and communication. When I do spend time with a guy, I don't refer to it as dating any longer. I talk about 'friendship-building' founded on Christ—the One who holds my heart and guides the friendship."

Too many women think that if they give a man what he is longing for in terms of physical satisfaction, they will inevitably win his love forever. Hundreds of women have lowered their standards sexually and gone further than they knew the Lord wanted in hopes of hanging onto the guy they were spending time with. It's a lie. Don't believe it!

Women are easily turned on by words. Most men know this. Another way to protect your purity is to stand on guard when you hear "sweet talk." Don't let any of these lines cause you to surrender.

If you love me...

I have never felt such love before...

Just try it once...

Lady of Purity

I won't get you pregnant...

I want to spend the rest of my life with you...

Since we're going to be married anyway...

Nobody is still a virgin at your age...

What we do in private is no one else's business...

If we only go so far and not all the way, it's okay...

They are doing it, and they are Christians...

If you won't prove your love, I'll find someone who will...

You are too old-fashioned...

Do it now so we will be prepared for marriage...

It will never happen to us...

You can't believe any of these. They have been said before, the gift has been opened, and the lady left in an emotional heap labeled "conquered." These words have trapped many ladies—beware! When you catch yourself rationalizing what you are doing and assuring yourself you are in control, make a second check. You'll be glad you did. A godly man will not pressure a woman verbally, but will cherish her with his declarations of love and take her home before they have to regret any violation of their purity.

What If It's Too Late?

You do not have to make the same mistakes many have made. But if you are reading this "after the fact" and are dealing with the guilt of the lost gift, do not be discouraged. Although it is true that there is only one first time, God is the God of the first-time experience. Let Him heal your broken heart through forgiveness. Agree with God that you have sinned and leave the sin before Him. Then guard yourself from entering into that sin pattern again. Learn a valuable lesson, but do not continue to beat yourself with condemnation. Jesus paid for those sins at Calvary. Do not continue to allow yourself or the enemy to defeat you with remembering a sin once you have confessed it to God and those you have offended. There may be consequences of your sin, but you do not have to live with the guilt of it.

God is the God who forgives and forgets. Jeremiah 31:34 says, "...for I will forgive their iniquity, and their sin I will remember no more." One of God's greatest abilities is that He forgets the sins of those who belong to Christ Jesus, "I, even I, am the One who wipes out your transgressions for My own sake; and I will not remember your sins" (Is. 43:25). Let this be your motto: "...but one thing I do: forgetting what lies behind [as God does] and reaching forward to what lies ahead, I press on toward the goal for the prize of the upward call of God in Christ Jesus" (Phil. 3:13-14).

Even though you have been freed from the guilt by confession, do not use it as an opportunity to continue in sin or to leave yourself open to temptation. Continue to choose freedom over sin's mastery. Lay aside every encumbrance and the sin that so easily entangles you and run with endurance the race set before you (see Heb. 12:1). How? Fix your eyes on Jesus (not on your sin, the past, or even yourself). Jesus is the Author and Perfecter of your faith (see Heb. 12:2).

There is one last response that brings complete freedom. You must forgive and forget the sins of those who sinned against you. Jesus is very clear in Matthew 5:21-24 about what to do with anger toward a brother. But how do you do it? First choose to forgive your brother with your heart and then God will help you work through the emotions that may remain. You will not be free of the hurt if you harbor bitterness. A quick way to ruin a beautiful complexion is to hold on to an unforgiving, bitter attitude.

If you have opened your gift too soon, do not be kept from beginning new again. Accept God's forgiveness and refuse to feel like damaged goods. God has better in store for you. You, dear Lady in Waiting, are a treasure. The enemy attempts to deceive you when he offers to delight you by his ways and means. Don't lose sight of the value of what you have or of who you are. Don't allow the flickering pleasures of an evening of "making love" destroy a lifetime of "lasting love."

Becoming a Lady of Purity

Second Samuel 13:1-19 is a painful story of rape, but note the reaction of the man who got what he wanted. After his sexual thirst was quenched, what was his response toward the woman for whom he lusted? How did he feel toward the woman? Why?

After Amnon raped Tamar, he hated her even more than he had loved her (v. 15).

How can a young woman stay pure? (Ps. 119:9,11)

By learning the Word of God and applying its teachings to your life.

How do friendships affect your purity? (1 Cor. 15:33)

Spending excessive amounts of time with people who disregard purity can cause you to diminish your standards.

Write out a specific list of ways you will guard your purity as you build relationships with the opposite sex.

no physical contact beyond holding hands; not spending time together in a private, unsupervised environment; not laying down (even on a couch) together

Is striving to be pure too hard? (1 Cor. 10:13) List some of the ways of escape God has given you.

avoiding potentially compromising situations altogether, fleeing when a situation gets "too hot" (and no, it is never beyond what we can bear)

Write out what a kiss means to you. What are you wanting to say when you kiss a man? Is there any other way to say this? How could adding physical affection to a friendship limit communication-building?

To me, a kiss is the ^(mild) physical expression of deep affection (saying "I truly love you" with your lips^(instead of words)). Physical affection distracts a couple from the process of developing communication skills and getting to know each other for who they really are.

Lady of Security

"I still can't believe it!" one friend exclaimed. "I had a date with the perfect guy! I spent days searching for and finding a gorgeous outfit, I had my nails done, and my hair looked better than it ever has. I took a whole day off work to get ready and left in plenty of time to get there. The 150-mile drive to pick him up was nothing. I could have flown I was so excited. I tried to calm myself down the whole drive, but could not help thinking how right we were for each other, how beautiful our relationship and future would be. We went to a very romantic setting. I can't believe it! I was ready, willing, available. Everything was perfect except for one problem. It turned out that he was gay."

This single woman diligently and faithfully "went after her man," only to find disappointment and pain. Ruth, our epitome of a "Lady in Waiting," had a totally different approach.

> Then he [Boaz] *said, "May you be blessed of the Lord, my daughter. You have shown your last kindness to be better than the first by not going after young men, whether poor or rich. Now, my daughter, do not fear. I will do for you whatever you ask, for all my people in the city know that you are a woman of excellence"* (Ruth 3:10-11).

Ruth—single, young, and widowed—must have experienced the lonely longings for the warmth of a husband. But she lived in victory over the desire to "man hunt." Instead of "going after the boys," she sat still and let God bring her prince to her. She was a Lady of Security.

Feelings of Insecurity

Why do women tend to "go after the guys"? Why do women experience difficulty being still and waiting for the man to initiate and develop the relationship? You find the answer in one word: insecurity. An insecure woman has her world centered on something (marriage) or someone (Mr. Right) that can be lost or taken away. Insecurity keeps a woman from experiencing consistent joy even within a relationship because a man cannot provide security, only God can.

Insecurity causes you to cling to a relationship. You feel a lack of confidence unless you have a man. When he is not with you, you fear he will not come back or call again. You want him to make a commitment so you will not lose him. You want all his time and attention. All your dreams, plans, and goals revolve around him. Insecurity in a relationship can cause jealousy and bickering. It makes you lose your confidence when he looks at another woman. You want to know his plans and with whom he spends his time. You don't want him to be around other interesting or attractive women; you feel threatened when he is.

Insecurity can cause you to be demanding and have unrealistic expectations of your relationship. When he hurts or disappoints you, you can be upset for days. You live with the fear of doing the wrong thing and losing him. You constantly feel the need to "define" your relationship and talk about your love for each other. You feel that you must show your love for him in greater and greater ways.

Insecurity fills the relationship with frustration and worry. You think, "I can't live with or without him!" You find yourself scheming to keep him.

Lisa even told her boyfriend she was pregnant so he would make a commitment to marry her. Her well-devised plan backfired as she had to go deeper and deeper into the lie when her new husband discovered she was not. She felt she would experience happiness and security only when he was hers. Instead her scheming caused guilt, making her feel alienated from him. His anger toward her for being married before he felt ready resulted in great difficulty in their relationship.

Believing a Lie

Why do women feel they have to go after men? Many women have believed a lie. They think, "I must get the best for myself because God may not give it to me." What do you think would have been the outcome of Ruth's life if she had chosen to believe this lie? Would she have returned home with Orpah and married one of the local guys? Would she have followed Naomi to a new land, but taken control of her own destiny in choosing a mate to care for herself and her mother-in-law? With these poor choices, her life of blessing and joy found in Boaz would not have happened and we would have missed the blessing of a book such as Ruth.

Ladies, God gives you the choice between His plans and yours. In the midst of her circumstances, Ruth could not have possibly seen that a man like Boaz would one day be her prince. Neither can you with your limited perspective see who or where your prince will be. Only God has all things in view. Are you trying to control your own life? Are you making plans for your life that only God should make? Don't settle for less than God's best. Surrender the terrible burden of always needing life on your terms. Don't look back one day and regret that you made your "life mate" choice from a limited perspective because you longed for the security of a relationship. God can and will give you His best if you wait for it.

Secure Love

Women tend to struggle with insecurity because of the unique way God created them. God made every little girl with the need to love and be loved by her earthly father. God designed His world with a picture of a family as the theme. The father protects, loves, and cares for his wife and their children. The ideal earthly father models the gentle, nurturing love of the heavenly Father. Many young women in our society did not have a father who followed God's design. This God-given need for a father's love caused a deficit in their lives.

Karen described it this way.

"I never really felt loved the way I needed to be. I wanted someone I could love and who would love me in the deepest way. I met and dated a wonderful man. He was a Christian, good-looking, popular, and best of all, he loved me. A deep wonderful friendship with him flourished for almost two years. I wanted to be his wife, but he was not making any move toward a commitment. I was a 21-year-old virgin. I wanted to keep him so badly that I knew I was willing to do anything. I did not intentionally plan to compromise my high standards, but I felt if I were intimate with him, it would show my deep commitment to him and I would be able to keep him.

"As a child I wanted my dad to really love me, but I never seemed to gain his love. I thought this man could fill that need for love that I felt. I was wrong. I lost both my virginity and my closest friend with one act. I believe if I had dealt with the insecurity in my life, I would have seen clearly that no man could meet the heart-felt need for secure love I wanted."

As a little girl, you may remember feeling the desire to be cherished, loved, and accepted by your daddy. If he failed to show that love to you in God's way, perhaps you continued to search for a man who would. No man, not even a husband, can fill the need you have for secure love. Only Jesus who "is the same yesterday and today, and forever," will never disappoint or fail you (Heb. 13:8).

Turn to your heavenly Father now. Pour out to Him your heart's longing to be loved. See His arms open wide and His empty lap ready to embrace and hold you near. He considers you dear. He longs to give you satisfying love. Perhaps He does desire to give you a man to love also. But the man you marry cannot meet your need for security. Only God's love brings security.

Lady of Security

Manipulation and Maneuvering

When you see a woman going after the guys, you probably don't immediately say, "Yes, I see that she really is insecure!" Insecurity dwells in the
heart. What you see outwardly is a woman's age-old ability to manipulate
and maneuver. When a woman manipulates a situation, she feels personal
satisfaction because she believes she is in control.

At one college, a new student arrived who was one of the most attractive guys ever to arrive on campus. In fact, whenever he walked by, the air
would move because of all the gasping women. When he walked into the
dining hall, the females would suddenly stop talking. (That alone was a
miracle!)

Linda, who worked in the Dean of Men's office, had a myriad of females
ask for his class schedule. Why would his class schedule be significant?
Such information offered a chance for a "life-changing" experience. These
silly women would find out his daily schedule and, as soon as their classes
ended, would *run* to wherever he would most likely be walking, and "just
happen" to be standing on the corner as he passed. Daily, these committed
manipulators "just happened" to see him after English literature and then
"just happened" to see him after World Civics. Such a schedule definitely
kept these gals in peak aerobic condition as daily they frantically tried to
arrive in his personal hemisphere.

Manipulation and maneuvering can also take the form of serving as a
"surrogate (substitute) helpmeet." Many women want to marry as badly as
they want to go to Heaven. They long to care for a man, so they run around
trying to find at least a "generic" version of the real thing. These precious
(but deceived) women constantly look for a man with a need and pounce on
that need in hopes of eventually winning the affection of the man. Any male
in need irresistibly attracts them.

Once, a single man at a conference mentioned his need for some name
tags, and a mob of women scurried to get tags for him. It was like a race, or
a spring sale at the mall! One typical surrogate overheard that a man needed his house cleaned because his parents were coming for a visit. The young

man had little time to do it himself because he had been so busy helping at his church, so he made his need known. This "Martha" decided to help the needy man, but didn't check her motive. She assumed that he would appreciate her help so much that he would repay her with some extra attention, perhaps even a date. At the same time, she knew that one of her female friends at the church also had a need, yet Martha would not lift a finger to help her catch up domestically.

What is the difference? Women may find more pleasure doing for a man than a woman because the potential "payoff" seems more valuable. She envisions surrendering her "surrogate" apron for an engagement ring. A wise woman once said, "Do not do for a brother that which you would not do for a sister." Brownies often are baked for the best-looking and most desirable guys, but seldom for the average Joe. (How all these guys stay slim is a miracle—except for their constant running from all the aggressive, manipulative women.)

A "manipulator" may hear of a female friend who needs help and callously allow her to do without it. But if one handsome guy even slightly alludes to his desire for something to drink, she may "crawl across broken glass" to get him a cool drink, all the while quoting Scripture about giving a cup of cool water to him who is thirsty. Allow God to use you to minister to brothers and sisters equally with no ulterior motives. In the beginning, Ruth ministered not to a desirable man, but to a bitter widow—her mother-in-law, at that!

Another form of maneuvering is to become the guy's "mom." Insecure females all too often deceive themselves into thinking that because they do so much for a particular young man, they will surely win his love. *Wrong!* It is easy for a man, whether he is young or old, to let a woman sacrifice for him. Why? Most men are used to the sacrifices of a woman. Good ol' mom has been sacrificing for him since the womb. Sure, the young man will say, "Thanks," but young men do not marry their mothers! When a woman does something really nice for a certain guy, he usually does not spend the rest of the day thinking about her unselfish service (he may be accustomed to receiving). The woman may begin to feel used.

Some women prepare meals, sew on buttons, and wash the guy's clothes—all the things a mom would do—assuming all this is practice for their future together. Inevitably, the man she has served so unselfishly may fall for a girl who can't bake or sew and thinks you take all clothes to the dry cleaners that "fluff and fold."

Elisabeth Elliot says she is often asked the question, "What can I do to get him to notice me?" Note carefully the advice she gives.

"My answer is 'nothing.' That is, nothing toward the man.

"Don't call him. Don't write a little note with a smiley face or a flower or fish under the signature and put it in his campus mailbox. Don't slide up to him in the hall and gasp, 'I've just got to talk to you!' Don't look woebegone, don't ignore him, don't pursue him, don't do him favors, don't talk about him to nine carefully selected listeners.

"There is one thing you can do: turn the whole business over to God. If he's the man God has for you, 'No good thing does He withhold from those who walk uprightly' (Ps. 84:11). Direct your energies to obedience, not to nailing the man. God has His own methods of getting the two of you together. He doesn't need any help or advice from you."[1]

Notice the word *nothing*. Maybe this little dose of reality will help you constantly check your motives whenever relating to a guy.

Motive Check

This is not to say that you cannot do nice things for a man; it is simply a warning to check your motives. A woman with selfish motivation mentally plots the next maneuver to capture the attention of the man of her dreams. Before you go to another activity to spend time with the available guys, as you check your hair and makeup and teeth, give yourself a thorough "heart flossing." Ask the Lord to reveal any impure motive that resides in your heart. Before you bake one more thing for a brother or purchase one more book or meaningful card, be very careful to check your motive and honestly respond to whatever the Lord shows you. You can save yourself many tears and much frustration if you are just willing to do a regular "motive check" on your heart.

To keep your motives pure, check them daily. Proverbs 16:2 (NIV) says, "All a man's [woman's] ways seem innocent to him [her], but motives are weighed by the Lord."

Manipulation and maneuvering can be deadly. If you maneuver to get a man, you will have to maneuver to keep him! This is not implying that there is no work involved in a good relationship, but there is a huge difference between working and maneuvering. You recognize the difference between the two by discerning your motive. Refuse to be a member of the M/M (Manipulation and Maneuvering) Team!

Quitting the Hunt

To quit the hunt and stop "going after the guys," you must first avoid maneuvering and manipulating. Ruth did, and God can give you the grace to do it too. Believe that God will take care of you regardless of your circumstances. Don't put your own devices to work. You can only see the outward man from today's perspective. God sees men's hearts from the perspective of eternity. With His perspective, He can see much better what you need. Trust Him and let Him show you His dependable love for you.

Second, you must put your security in Christ. He longs for you to be secure in His love. He wants to protect, lead, and love you. To develop security, give your heart and emotions to the Lord. Debby remembers a specific time in her life when she pictured herself before the Lord. In her mind's eye she imagined His loving, kind, Father's face. She pictured herself bringing her broken, lonely heart to her heavenly Father after yet another love bubble had been burst. Debby specifically gave the Lord her love life that day. She prayed:

"Father, my heart is fragile and delicate and easily broken. I have tried to find one who will cherish me, without Your view. My heart has been broken and my emotions bruised. I ask You to take and guard my heart. I will choose not to entertain thoughts and emotions of love which cause me to give my heart away too readily. I will come quickly to You when I start feeling like I am in love. Please hold the key to my heart and emotions until a day I can give it to the man You have prepared for me."

Debby has often said what a difficult turning point this was for her. She wanted to trust the Lord with this precious area of her life, but had nagging feelings that she might never again have the giddy, delightful feelings of love. As she dated, she spent time in prayer before and after dates to make sure her heart and emotions were still in the Father's hands. Many times she feared she would never feel those "heart leaps of love," but instead would just marry one of the "nice" guys she had dated.

One day, as she was praying, she realized she had come to really care for a man named Bill in a special way. They had been dating for several months and the temptations to let her emotions run wild were very real. Instead, she wrote this in her journal:

"I feel as though I really care for Bill in a deep way. You know what is best for me, Father. I have given my heart to You and my emotions, too. I will wait for a clearer indication that he is my knight in shining armor, than just how I feel. You will not allow my heart to be broken again if I leave it with You. I trust You to keep me calm and waiting on Your best timing."

A formula she wrote in her prayer journal to help her keep perspective was this: ***With Jesus first and my boyfriend second, I will have lasting peace and security.***

All this may sound like a good idea, but how do you begin? To build security into your life, spend time in God's Word. Proverbs 1:33 says to listen to God and live securely. As you do, you will find out what God is really like—what His character is—not just what you think or have heard He is like. You will be surprised at how differently He sees you than what you have thought. Read through the Psalms and write down the many promises

He has made to you if you are a believer. Psalm 16:11 (KJV) says, "Thou wilt show me the path of life [married or not]; in Thy presence is fulness of joy [His presence, not marriage, brings joy]; in Thy right hand there are pleasures for evermore." (What more could a girl ask for?)

By spending time in God's Word, you will also learn what God thinks of you. In First Peter 2:4, God says you are choice and precious to Him. He calls you precious, honored, loved, and His redeemed one in Isaiah 43:1-6. Isaiah 43:7 says you were created for His glory. You are very special to God—so special that He has plans for you: "plans for [your] welfare and not for calamity to give you a future and a hope" (Jer. 29:11b).

The New Testament is also full of God's thoughts of you. You are accepted (Rom. 15:7); you are not condemned (Rom. 8:1); and you are His child (Jn. 1:12). (By the way, the female child of a King is a *princess*. Act like the valuable princess you are, and plan to be treated as royalty.) You also are the temple of God (1 Cor. 3:17). He is your adequacy (2 Cor. 3:5) and He leads you in His triumph (2 Cor. 2:14). His love letter to you, the Bible, is full of all the wonderful things He says about you.

Do not allow insecurity to motivate you to maneuver or manipulate your relationships. Instead of hunting for a husband or boyfriend, concentrate on becoming a woman of excellence (Ruth 3:11). As a Lady of Security, wait for your heavenly Father to bring about His perfect plans for you.

Learning to sit still,
Resting in His will,
Confident to abide,
With Him by my side,
Resisting manipulation,
Waiting only for His stipulations.
JMK

Becoming a Lady of Security

Look at the things most important to you, the things on which you spend the most of your time and energy (e.g., appearance, money, career, family, friendships, dates). If these were taken away, how would you be affected? Security is basing one's life on that which cannot be taken away. Are you building your life on what makes you secure or insecure?

I'm trying to learn to build my life more on secure things, but there are many things that I've built my life on that are insecure.

Do you find yourself manipulating for friendships with guys? **Proverbs 4:23** exhorts you to watch over your heart. Write out ways you can respond when the temptation to "scheme" for a date comes your way.

Yes, I do that a lot. I can pray for God to change wrong motives I feel to do things and attend events.

Meditate on **Colossians 3:1-3**. How could these verses help you the next time you feel insecure and want to take future matters into your own hands?

It can serve as a reminder to look to God when I'm doubting Him, because I know that He is in complete control of my life, and everything else as well.

What can a Lady in Waiting do with her feelings while she waits? List them from Psalm 37:3-7.

She can trust God with her feelings, find her joy in Him, commit her life to God and trust Him to lead her through her life, and wait patiently for God's timing.

In your journal confess any times you sought to manipulate a person or situation. Seek to put your security in your King and ask His Holy Spirit for help.

Going to New Tribes to help (and for other reasons), going to church and youth group and volleyball to see the guys I liked.

How would having your security in the Lord and not in whom you are dating affect you if the dating relationship ended? Could you be grateful for a friendship even without the promise of a future? Being secure in God's forever love (see Heb. 13:5) allows a woman to build relationships for friendship, not merely romance for a future.

By being secure in God, when a relationship would end, the disappointment and hurt would be much less, because I would have my security (and thus my contentment) in Him

Lady of Contentment

You have just returned home from a great single's retreat where you once again surrendered your frustrations as a single in exchange for God's peace and contentment. As you listen to your answering machine, you hear a certain voice. The most sought-after bachelor you know asks you for a date next weekend. Do you remain calm and give your expectations to the Lord? Or do you jump back in your car and head to the mall to register your china and look at some wedding gowns? Would the prospect of a date with the most eligible bachelor in town cause you to experience the "Pre-romantic Stress Disorder"? Or would you surrender your expectations to Jesus?

For a single woman to experience genuine contentment while soloing in a "couples' world," she must avoid the ditches of discontentment. She needs to learn the mystery of contentment and its power over the restless torture of desire.

The Torture of Desire

It has been said that suffering is having what you do not want (singleness), and wanting what you do not have (a husband). As a single woman, you would probably scream "Amen" to such a description of suffering. You know what it is like to get up each day knowing that you do not have what you want—a husband. How do you cope with such a longing?

Longing for what you do not have is a universal condition. It is not limited to singles. It is true that the longing for a husband can be satisfied on your wedding day, but that longing is soon replaced by desires and expectations about the marriage relationship that may not be satisfied in a thousand lifetimes. If you are presently discontent as a single woman, you can count on being dissatisfied as a married woman in the future.

The mystery of contentment often seems to escape the understanding of the single woman. She assumes that her circumstances justify her condition and give her permission to remain dissatisfied with her life assignment. Not having learned how to lay down the terrible burden of always wanting life to be on her terms, she continues to struggle with the torture of her desires. The restlessness caused by her desire for what she does not have makes waiting seem an impossible task. In fact, to the discontented woman, the word *wait* probably compares to a "cuss" word in her mind. A Lady in Waiting finds her capacity to wait for God's best to be rooted in contentment.

The Capacity to Wait

Circumstantially, Ruth had the perfect excuse to be discontented. Widowed at a young age, her circumstances provided the perfect breeding ground for self-pity and bitterness. In fact, her mother-in-law changed her own name from Naomi (pleasant) to Mara (bitter) to signify her discontentment. Yet Ruth chose to cling to the God of Israel, whom she found to be trustworthy even in difficult circumstances.

Contentedly facing each day's task, Ruth received the attention and blessing of the most eligible bachelor in town. Then Naomi told her that Boaz was a candidate for being their kinsman-redeemer (see the levirate law in Deuteronomy 25:5-10). This simply meant that the Mosaic Law allowed Boaz, as the closest kin, to redeem the childless widow and keep the family name alive. The law could even require that Boaz marry Ruth. Can you imagine finding the most eligible bachelor and saying to him, "The law requires you to marry me before my thirtieth birthday?"

Naomi instructs Ruth to approach Boaz and ask him if he would be their kinsman-redeemer. This episode is covered in chapter 3 of the Book of Ruth. Boaz's response to Ruth's request is precious. "And now, my daughter, don't be afraid. I will do for you all you ask. All my fellow townsmen know that you are a woman of noble character" (Ruth 3:11 NIV). Can you imagine any man saying to you, "I will do for you all you ask"? His willingness was directly related to the character he had noticed in her responses to life and God.

Ruth returns home with the good news. Naomi, however, does not immediately respond by taking her daughter-in-law to the mall to look for a wedding gown. An anxious and discontented woman would think that a willing and interested bachelor is enough motivation for ordering wedding invitations. But for the Lady of Contentment, this would be inappropriate behavior.

Noami's response to Boaz's willingness may have put a damper on most single women's racing heartbeat. "Then Naomi said, 'Wait, my daughter, until you find out what happens. For the man will not rest until the matter is settled today'" (Ruth 3:18 NIV). Who has to *wait*? The woman must wait. Who is the one who will not rest? The man, Boaz, will not rest.

Wait

Such an assignments is not to cause suffering, but prevent it. Women experience so much needless pain when they run ahead of God's format. Naomi knew that there may exist an even closer kinsman who would qualify to redeem her and Ruth. (In fact, there was a kinsman closer than Boaz whom she did not know about, but he would be disqualified by a former pledge.) Naomi did not want Ruth's heart to race ahead into disappointment in case the circumstances did not go as assumed.

Ditches of Discontentment

Being single can be difficult enough for a woman, but the heartbreak from being "led on" by a man can dangerously lead to a ditch of discontentment. Some women are so emotionally scarred from falling into such a ditch that it literally takes them years to recover and rediscover the capacity to trust any male in their life.

Why some males are unaware of their capacity to defraud is still a mystery. "And that no man transgress and defraud his brother [sister] in the matter because the Lord is the avenger in all these things..." (1 Thess. 4:6). To defraud is to excite physical or emotional desires that cannot be righteously fulfilled. Since many men do not realize how their actions defraud their sisters in Christ, single women need to be aware of common situations where a guy might lead a woman on. When aware of such techniques, a single woman can avoid unnecessary heartbreak and more effectively keep a rein on her emotions.

One way a guy may lead a woman on is by the unwise things he may say or do. A wonderful single guy started a letter one day with the words *Dear Sunshine*. When asked who this "Dear Sunshine" was, he said it was his nickname for a girl at college. He came up with this affectionate nickname for her one evening while they stood on a hill overlooking the school as the sun was setting. When asked if they were dating he replied, "Oh, no, we are just friends and there isn't any future for our relationship." He was encouraged to stop calling her Sunshine because it would defraud her emotionally. But, like many men, he had a hard time understanding that calling her Sunshine might cause her to dream about being the "sunshine" in his future after they graduate.

A second way a man might defraud a woman is by ascribing to an unwritten code that has been distributed by Hollywood and swallowed by most of Christianity: friendships with the opposite sex must be romantic and must not establish any emotional boundaries. What Hollywood advocates is like body surfing on the crest of an emotional wave. To establish boundaries seems like an attack on love. Ironically, limits protect real love and leave no room for painful defrauding.

Ken and Jackie established some specific guidelines for their dating relationship in the areas of leadership, communication, and purity. Classmates (even Christians) thought their goals and guidelines would prevent their friendship from blossoming and surviving. Contrary to popular opinion, they have been building on those guidelines for the past 20 years—and romance thrives in their relationship.

In a McDonald's commercial, a guy presented clear guidelines for him and his date. Just before the couple gets to the car, the guy makes one last remark, "I want you to realize that this is just a date, not a commitment and not a proposal." The girl just smiles and continues toward the car, enroute to McDonald's and a movie. Now, you may feel his style is just too honest, but such clear communication prevents much misunderstanding between a man's actions and a woman's interpretation of his behavior.

Another way a guy may defraud a woman is by emphasizing the future potential of the relationship rather than focusing on the present opportunities for the friendship to grow. This way of defrauding incites feelings in a woman that cannot be properly fulfilled at that time. This creates emotional turmoil for many women, making it difficult to wait with contentment. Postpone talk of a future together, marriage, or what kind of home you want, until engagement. Do not encourage talk of things that "might be," but rather encourage words and actions that develop the present friendship.

The Eleventh Commandment

Keeping in mind these common ways that women can be defrauded by men, realize that a single woman can sabotage her own contentment by defrauding herself. A single woman can defraud herself as effectively as can her male counterpart. Protect your contentment by adopting this "Eleventh Commandment": Thou shalt not defraud thyself.

Women defraud themselves by confusing ministry with matrimony. A guy tries to help a girl grow spiritually, and she sees his care and interest as leading inevitably to marriage. Another guy and girl work on a ministry team together and their spiritual intimacy is confused in her mind with romantic intentions.

Misread intentions between males and females put them on a collision course. The crash can be avoided if the Lady of Contentment would keep in mind that her emotions must be submitted to the facts: ministering together is a privilege as a believer, not an automatic marriage opportunity. Daily, throughout the world, women's hearts are broken because they allow their emotions to run ahead of commitments. Women, young and old, seem to resist controlling their emotions. As a result, they end up emotional cripples, angry at the men who failed to live up to their emotional fantasies.

A most innocent gesture can produce the most elaborate fantasy. A man sends a single woman a thank-you card for her vital help in some project or ministry. What is her response to this kind gesture? She laminates the card, anticipates a future with him, and allows her expectations to run rampant.

Counselors are constantly helping men and women properly interpret their relationships. Nancy had been in counseling for more than a year because her heart had been broken and her emotions devastated through defrauding. She told her counselor how she had deceived herself in her relationships with men.

As a new Christian, Nancy joined a large Singles Ministry where she became very attentive to the various needs of the Singles Director. She did all the special things that a "mom" often does for her son, or a woman does for her boyfriend. Not only did she attend to his practical needs, but she also was an inspiration to him as she grew by leaps and bounds in the Lord. She unselfishly gave him every spare moment she had, helping him with the many needs he had as the leader of such a huge singles group. If he needed someone to counsel a woman, he always called on her. If a speaker needed a ride to the airport, he called on her. She was a 24-hour crisis line at his disposal. To the undiscerning eye, it all seemed innocent—a very dedicated new Christian enthusiastically serving her singles director. But the lack of discretion on the part of the minister, coupled with her own spiritual immaturity, made a deadly combination. She confused ministry with matrimony and defrauded herself.

After a Christmas trip together where they shared many deep emotions, she went to Israel for a month. When she returned, he greeted her with the shocking news that he had become engaged while she was away. Did he ask the woman who had worked faithfully by his side to share his life and ministry? No. He proposed to a sweet, but less-involved member of the singles group. Needless to say, this devastated Nancy. This is not an isolated incident. The number of single women defrauding themselves seems to have grown to epidemic proportions.

To heed the Eleventh Commandment, you must consciously resist doing another good deed for a man in your life until you know the motive behind your "unselfish" gesture. How many gifts have you already given to some guy in your life because you sensed that the relationship had future dating potential? How many ministries have you participated in because of the chance to be seen by him? How many times have you volunteered to help a brother when you knew you would not be so willing to help a sister in Christ?

The easiest way to break the Eleventh Commandment is to play the "surrogate wife or mother" in relation to a brother in Christ. You pick a worthy recipient of your time and attention, then you tend to any special needs you find out about in the guise of unselfish giving. There are single women who wash the guy's clothes and clean his apartment, but haven't even been on their first date with him. You might as well wash his car also. What this single woman does not know is that doing good deeds for a man does not win his love. Why? Most of the time, he is used to a woman waiting on him. Remember good ol' mom?

A dedicated Christian should do good deeds, but when you limit your service to the men in your group, it will ultimately backfire. You can end up feeling bruised by your own self-defrauding when you realize the man has taken your special gestures of service for granted.

One summer, as a member of a traveling drama team, a single woman gave herself unselfishly to a particular guy in the group. For ten weeks, during every free minute, she helped him study to pass his ordination exam, which required pages of memorization. At first, all the help she gave him really impressed the other team members. But as time went on, it became obvious to everyone, except him, that her feelings for him had changed from sisterly love to romantic affection. Was anyone to blame for the pain that came at the end of the summer? If both had more discernment, maybe they could have acted more wisely in their friendship so she would not have been defrauded.

When the tour was over and everyone went their own way, he gave her a hearty hug and big "thank you"—and off he went to his ordination, which was followed by his marriage to a girl from back home. What happened to the one left behind with the big "thank you"? She learned a hard lesson, but she was emotionally devastated. She carelessly allowed herself to give her heart away. She gave hours to someone in the hope of reciprocation, but she ended up empty-handed with only a painful memory of giving so much and getting so little. Her motive was wrong. She defrauded herself through unchecked emotions.

Prenuptial Fantasies

An important method of limiting your own self-defrauding is through daily discipline over "prenuptial fantasies." Such fantasies may provide you an escape from monotonous reality, but these moments are dangerous. They will aggravate your struggle for contentment because they are not innocent daydreams, but an attack on your godly contentment. You may be so used to daily fantasies that you might not even realize when you begin daydreaming again about your prince.

Often a single woman's struggle with contentment can be traced back to her fantasies more than to her frustrating circumstances. Just think for a moment about three words from Second Corinthians 10:5 (KJV): "Casting down imaginations." Fantasizing about a future with a guy you have been watching in Sunday school or at work is nothing more than your very active imagination. What should you do when you start daydreaming about a guy you've never dated or even formally met? You must take your thoughts to Jesus and leave them in His capable hands. This daily discipline of taking your fantasies to Jesus is the foundation for your future as a contented woman, whether you are married or single. Right now they are just prenuptial fantasies, but when you are married, those fantasies about other men could continue.

Lack of discipline in the area of "casting down imaginations" may result in self-defrauding and needless discontentment. Sally did not develop this discipline and was hurt needlessly. She went as a counselor to a national youth convention and met a sharp Christian guy from her home state. They enjoyed chatting between seminars and after she returned home, he began calling her long distance. After each phone call she would dream and talk to her friends about their potential together. She thought about his being younger, but refused to let her fantasy be spoiled by something as insignificant as age. She allowed the fantasy to move into vivid living color after every long distance phone call. Then her dreams turned into a nightmare. During one of their delightful conversations, he asked her a favor. "Would you mind if I come and visit you during spring break?" That sounded exciting to her, but then he asked the second part of his favor. "Would you mind if I bring two friends?" She assumed he meant two guys he had been discipling, but to her surprise their names were not Bill and John but Sarah and Becky. After she picked herself up off the floor, she very politely told him that such a plan would not work. When she hung up the phone she felt angry and betrayed that he apparently wanted to use her home (three blocks from the beach) as a vacation spot. Maybe the guy was insensitive to her, but her hurt was multiplied because she had chosen to spend the preceding days and nights daydreaming about their potential relationship. Her pain and anger could have been reduced if she had exercised some discipline in relation to prenuptial fantasizing about this guy.

Friends too often participate in the development of one's prenuptial fantasies. After only one date with a wonderful man, a girl will share the details of the evening and her friends will not only share her joy, but also foster excessive imaginings by asking questions like, "Do you think this is the one? Could this be the Boaz you have been waiting so long for?" We not only need the discipline of monitoring our own fantasies, but we also need friends who will remind us not to run ahead of God's timing. Such monitoring of our emotions and accountability between friends is so helpful for the Christian single woman.

Spiritual Monitor

When a friend excitedly calls to tell you about the evening she has just spent with a special man, you often know before she gets two paragraphs into her telling of the evening where she is going—fantasy land. As she begins to tell how he is a friend from her past who recently became a Christian and is suddenly back in her life, be careful. As she rattles on at 100-miles an hour, it would be easy to say, "Maybe your Boaz is finally here"—but don't. Remember wise Naomi and avoid defrauding your friend. By enthusiastically building false hope in a situation that could be here today but gone before her next paycheck, you can easily help a friend to defraud herself. To help her monitor her reactions, point out that one long distance phone call from a male friend is not reason enough to take him home to meet her parents. Encourage your friend, instead, to wait until she sees how the friendship develops.

Your monitoring may not be appreciated at first, but the fruit of such counsel will be sweet. This is not to suggest that you cannot share a friend's joy about a wonderful date with a godly man. But a gift greater than simply sharing her joy is to encourage your friend not to run ahead of the relationship through prenuptial fantasies. Many tears have been shed over relationships that never materialized except in one's dreams.

At a girls' night out, a single woman shared how she used to resent spiritual monitoring from her mom in relation to her fantasies. She used to dread her mother's calm and reserved response to her dramatic presentation of the date she had with the man of her dreams. Her mom, a vivacious woman, seemed so restrained and even a little cynical when responding to her daughter's "bubbly babbling" about Mr. Right. How could such an outgoing, positive, and uplifting mom be so reserved when responding to the dreamy-eyed chatter about the arrival of the man worth waiting for? Did her mom have information of which the daughter was unaware? Had she hired a detective to follow the man of her daughter's dreams and find incriminating information? Of course not! This mom, like Naomi, was extremely wise in monitoring her own response so her daughter would not get excited and distracted by a prospect who might never become a reality.

How refreshing to hear about a wise mom who helped her daughter not to deceive (defraud) herself. Too often moms innocently focus on the famine their daughters face in relation to dating. Instead of encouraging her daughter to use her free time for Jesus (i.e., to be a Lady of Diligence), mom and daughter analyze and re-analyze her dateless state and head for the mall to soothe the emptiness. Not everyone has been blessed with a "spiritual monitor" in a mother, but we can learn from this one's example and we can be spiritual monitors to the single women in our lives.

How can you begin to be a spiritual monitor? The next time a friend is bubbling over with joy after a date with a wonderful guy, pray for your capacity to share her joy; then pray for the courage to speak the truth about surrendering her dreams to the Lord and not running ahead of Him in her expectations. The spiritual monitor knows the importance of surrendering her own expectations to the only One who can be trusted with her desires and dreams. She can encourage others to surrender their own prenuptial fantasies in exchange for the truth in Psalm 62:5 (KJV): "My soul, wait thou only upon God; for my expectation is from Him."

Did you expect to be married by now? Or did you expect to be married forever, and now you are divorced? These expectations mean that you need God's tender loving care and the encouragement of a spiritual monitor who will regularly remind you not to run ahead of the Lord in your relationships with men.

Two women took the challenge to be spiritual monitors to their dearest friend, who was dating Mr. Wonderful. These friends had to consistently resist fanning the fire of their friend's enthusiasm. They monitored their responses and limited their reactions to what was reality and not hopeful fantasy. Because this single woman had waited quite a long time for her

Boaz, it would have been easy for her to run with the simplest amount of attention received. But since her best friends monitored their lips and resisted chatting incessantly about them being the perfect couple, she was free to respond properly to her boyfriend. Unmonitored chatting can lead to major defrauding.

Ironically, the same close friends who help to accelerate the prenuptial fantasy may be the ones who must comfort the lone lovebird when Mr. Right asks another girl out and no more history is to be made with him. Her disappointment will be in direct proportion to the degree that she and her friends responded prematurely to a relationship that will last only in her memory. The next time a friend shares the details of an exciting evening with such a hunk of a guy, don't overreact. Instead, say to her, "I am thrilled that you had a great time. I am so glad you shared your excitement with me. Now do yourself a favor and before you close your eyes to dream tonight, prayerfully commit Mr. Wonderful to Jesus." You will be a true friend and a spiritual monitor for her.

Thousands of needless tears,
Produced by careless cheers,
Assuming that Boaz is finally here,
When the arrival of her prince is not even near...
JMK

If you do not have a spiritual monitor in a close friend, then ask the Lord to help you find such a friend.

The Mystery of Contentment

Whether married or single, in prison or shopping at the mall, the key to your enjoying this moment deals with your inner contentment. When your happiness in life is based on "your terms," it is a terrible limitation that will result in a hollow gladness. Singleness does not produce lack of contentment any more than marriage provides contentment. Lack of contentment is the result of the terrible burden of wanting life on your terms.

Lady of Contentment

Married women complain about their lack of contentment as often as single women do, if not more. Both groups of women need to develop the quality of contentment. Paul the apostle, while living in a dark, damp dungeon, wrote of the mystery of contentment that does not depend on circumstances. He described the secret as a "learning process" to which he willingly submitted rather that resisting the conditions.

*Not that I speak from want; for I have learned to be content in **whatever** circumstances I am. I know how to get along with humble means, and I also know how to live in prosperity; in any and every circumstance I have learned the secret of being filled and going hungry, both of having abundance and suffering need. I can do all things through Him who strengthens me (Phil. 4:11-13).*

Whether married or single, one must learn that it is Jesus who strengthens you to walk in the most dismal or delightful of circumstances. True contentment is learned. You are not born with it and you cannot buy it at one of Kmart's blue-light specials. Your classroom for learning is your daily life. Every shattered dream or unfulfilled expectation serves as a perfect opportunity to learn contentment. These circumstances are your classroom assignments for learning the mystery of contentment. Learning contentment will require complete dependence upon Jesus, for difficult circumstances without the strength of Jesus can rob you of potential contentment. Do not be deceived into thinking you do not need Jesus' strength to face the good circumstances as well as the bad. When the sun is shining with no clouds in sight, you may assume that you can securely bask in the sunshine without any prospect of rain; however, this full feeling can easily breed a tendency to ignore Jesus. *"Otherwise, I may have too much and disown you and say, 'Who is the Lord?'"* (Prov. 30:9a NIV)

Stop Arguing With the Umpire

Do you now see the incompatibility of anxiety-filled singleness and contented godliness? Are you ready to rid yourself of the ditches of discontentment that have robbed you of so much peace and joy?

Defrauding by a man, a friend, or even oneself, will aggravate your lack of contentment; however, the source of your lack is not defrauding or even frustrating circumstances. Your lack of contentment is because of *pride.* Pride can be described as an excessively high opinion of what one deserves. When a single's life is not moving in the direction she wants (husband, career, children, house, etc.) the arguing often begins. With whom is the single woman arguing? It is none other than the umpire, the arbitrator: Jesus. "Let the peace of Christ rule [arbitrate, umpire] in your hearts..." (Col. 3:15).

The struggle with the Umpire is not limited to the single women up to bat! Every woman who has descended from Eve must learn to trust the call of her heavenly Umpire. The trouble from the beginning was a woman not listening to the Umpire, but reaching out for a life on "her terms." Why would a woman argue with such an all-wise Umpire? "Pride only breeds quarrels" (Prov. 13:10a NIV).

Consider a very poignant verse that brilliantly reveals the war in all of us. "What causes fights and quarrels among you? Don't they come from your desires that battle within you? *You want something but don't get it...*" (Jas. 4:1-2 NIV). Honestly face any struggle you may have with your pride-driven desire to have life on your terms. Exchange your pride for Jesus' strength so you may accept whatever assignment the Umpire has for you from this moment forward. Dating is not a reward or a prize for living for Jesus. A Friday night without a date is often a night of "being spared" by an all-wise Umpire.

My soul finds rest in God alone... (Ps. 62:1 NIV).

Becoming a Lady of Contentment

Do you have a spiritual monitor? Are you a spiritual monitor? (Read Proverbs 28:23 and Hebrews 3:13.) Are you intimidated by the prospect of this role in a friend's life? Why?

Not really, because a true friend would see that I'd been acting as a monitor out of genuine love for her.

118

Review the methods of defrauding by a guy and by yourself. (Read First
Thessalonians 4:6.)

*By leading a woman on with his actions and/or
words, by allowing a woman to go out of her way
to do things for him without thinking about her feelings etc.*

A contented woman has the ability to lay down the terrible burden of
always needing life on her terms. Are you a contented woman? (Read
Judges 21:25, Luke 1:38, and Matthew 26:39.)

*I think for the most part, I am content with
my life. I can't truthfully claim to be 100%
satisfied with my life, but I try to be content with
all of the things God has already blessed me with.*

Pride is an excessively high opinion of what one deserves. Do you struggle with pride's control of your desires? (Read Proverbs 13:10, 16:18,
29:23; Jeremiah 5:3; and James 4:1-2.)

*Yes, I constantly catch myself thinking prideful
thoughts, and then I have to remember that Jesus
is the only thing I can boast in, because it is He who
has blessed me with the things I try to boast in.*

Does toe-tapping, nail-biting, "I'm a quarter past 30 years old" thinking
rob you of contentment? What limits God from acting on your behalf?
(Read Matthew 6:27, Isaiah 30:18, and 64:4.)

*Not really, I'm only 16. When we wait for God
and His timing, He will act on our behalf
with His best.*

Lady of Conviction

On the eve of her wedding day, Cindy, a Lady of Conviction, wrote the following poem to her bridegroom:

Dear Sweetheart,

For many years I sought to find my most perfect mate, But all that ever resulted from my search were shattered dreams, a broken heart and what seemed to be an endless wait. I wanted to find God's very best, But first He had to teach me that in His loving hands, I must solely rest.

So, one evening I prayed "God, just as you put Adam to sleep until the perfect one for him, he was ready to meet; so put me and my desires to sleep until I too am ready to know the one you have chosen for me."

From that time forward God gave me a peace. And although others came into my life God protected my heart and spared me from more strife. Then when God knew that in His hands I had placed my heart, He brought you into my life and I was history from the start.

My dear friends who know me well perhaps see tomorrow as a miraculous day. For they have known me and all my picky ways. Once while in the dorm, A.M. came into my room and asked me just exactly what I was looking for in a man. I ran to my diary and pulled out a list of 30 qualities I was looking for and on which I would insist.

As I read each trait one by one, Dear A.M. looked at me, she was very stunned. After pondering the list she said with a nod, "Well, Cindy, looks like you'll have to marry God." Well, God you are not, but my heaven on earth you are. God heard my prayers and answered them In the most perfect way with you.

I have no unanswered questions, no doubts, no hesitations, no reservations.

You are my Prince Charming, my knight in shining armor, my gift from the sea, my gift from God.

Cindy Jordan Feldewerth

Does it seem too unrealistic for today's woman to set her sights on a knight in shining armor? Was Cindy just an idealist who got lucky and found a man that satisfied her list of "30 traits"? A single friend (a modern Ruth) wrote a letter in which she admitted that her high ideals often made her feel like the "Lone Ranger." She said, "So often I meet women who don't want to go the deeper, more radical route of separation from our culture in seeking after God's standards." Do we lower our standards because we seem out of step with all our peers? Does the woman in Proverbs 31 seem obsolete? Maybe for the "cosmopolitan" woman she is obsolete, but not for the Lady of Conviction. God has the best in hand for those who seek Him.

Ruth's choice to wait for God's best resulted in her union with a Boaz rather than a Bozo. Ruth not only married a man who was a "pillar of strength" (Boaz), but she also was blessed by the privilege of bearing a son (Obed) who would be part of the lineage of Jesus Christ. Ruth's wise choices resulted in her experiencing God's overwhelming goodness.

Damaged Goods

Ruth did not allow the past influences of a heathen culture to keep her from setting new standards and making wise choices for her life that would honor God. Ruth could have allowed herself to remain within a destructive family cycle that moved against God's standards. She could have given up on a godly life style by assuming she was doomed as "damaged goods." But she didn't. She chose, instead, to break her family's sin cycle and establish a new godly cycle.

After becoming a Christian, Jackie found herself ashamed of her lack of a proper upbringing. She says this:

"I knew I had been forgiven for the past, but I often wrestled with the feelings of being damaged goods. I found myself envying other girls who were from godly homes and great heritages, spiritually. Whenever I would be introduced to a wonderful Christian guy, I would immediately think, 'I'm not good enough.'

"This was exactly how I felt when I first met my husband. He had asked Jesus to take control of his life at the young age of eleven. He went to church faithfully; he never smoked, drank, or fooled around sexually. His high standards were very intimidating to me. Throughout the years of our friendship, I knew he would never date me because of my imperfect past and ungodly family. Was I in for a surprise! As I continued to make choices to break the ungodly influences of my past, the Lord was working on bringing Ken and me together as a team for His glory. Like David I thought, 'Who am I, O Sovereign Lord, and what is my family, that you have brought me this far?' (2 Sam. 7:18b NIV)"

Ungodly cycles can be broken. Your destiny is not something that is left to chance or fate; it is the product of wise choices.

Destiny—Chance or Choice?

Do you think your ideals and standards are too high? Do you feel the pressure to compromise and settle for the generic version of life? Ruth lived in an era that was exactly like modern America. Judges 21:25 describes the era in which she lived: "In those days there was no king in Israel; everyone did what was right in his own eyes." We too live in a culture where it seems that no one fears God and people just "do their own thing."

You, like Ruth, will be greatly affected by your choices. Ruth's wise choices allowed her to break a godless family cycle and begin a new cycle that the Word of God triumphantly records. God has not changed—and neither have men. The high standards in God's Word are not irrelevant, but completely applicable to finding God's best for your life. Choices, guided by your convictions rather than by chance, determine your destiny. How wise have your decisions been in the past in regard to relating to and dating men? Have you made some poor choices that you can see were the result of your own lack of proper convictions in the areas of love, sex, and dating? Your present choices will affect the rest of your life in this delicate area that is often a collision course—male/female relating.

You cannot make good choices without proper, biblical convictions. Don't carelessly leave your dating/relating standards to chance. Too much depends on your decisions in this area. A stanza from the song "Guard Your Heart" by Jon Mohr captures this warning:

> *The human heart is easily swayed*
> *And often betrayed*
> *At the hand of emotion.*
> *We dare not leave the outcome to chance;*
> *We must choose in advance*
> *Or live in agony*
> *Such needless tragedy.*

From the beginning of time, God has shown His own people exactly what course they should take to avoid needless tragedy. A passage of Scripture that clearly states the reality of our own choices of happiness or

misery is Deuteronomy 30:15-20. Remember that the media, music, literature, teachers, and peers often oppose the godly choices that you might want
to make.

Standard-Bearer

May we go back to the basics for just a moment? What is a conviction
and how does one develop biblical convictions? A conviction is a standard
that serves as a springboard for your choices. Consider where your standards, in the area of relating and dating, originated. Are your standards
based more on Hollywood's terms of love and romance, or have you allowed
God's Holy Word to shape your perspective?

The Lady of Conviction gives the Lord permission to renew her mind on
a daily basis. She spends time searching the Word of God for standards that
will guide her safely to God's best. She has made a significant choice as a
godly woman. She has surrendered her mind to a new persuasion: God's
perspective on love and romance. The convictions that she establishes,
based on the Word, allow her to resist being squeezed into the mold of this
world. She is a non-conformist in a biblical sense, as in Romans 12:2 (NIV)
which says, "Do not conform any longer to the pattern of this world, but be
transformed by the renewing of your mind. Then you will be able to test and
approve what God's will is—His good, pleasing and perfect will." Notice
the words test and approve; your convictions (whether Hollywood-based or
Bible-based) gauge your ability to "test and approve" the relationships
you've had or will have.

If you want to live by God's standards for love, sex, and dating, you
must prepare yourself for the inevitable resistance that "standard-bearers"
face. When you live by your convictions, many of your friends will consider you unrealistic. Some of your girlfriends may even think you are
stubbornly opinionated. Facing such opposition from the people you love
is not easy, but the Lord will give you the grace to refuse to compromise.
A true standard-bearer wants to be a vanguard in a movement. Through
Jesus' strength, you can stand firm, unwavering, as you wait for His best.
The woman without the high ideals that the Word of God sets forth, leaves

her choices to chance. She will tend to end up with a Bozo rather than a Boaz because she cannot measure accurately the man behind the "makeup."

Since most biblical convictions are in opposition to all the propaganda from Hollywood, relatively few, even among Christians, hold to these standards. This harsh reality is revealed throughout the Word. James 4:4-5 (Phillips) says, "You are like unfaithful wives, never realizing that to be the world's lover means becoming the enemy of God! Anyone who chooses to be the world's friend is thereby making himself God's enemy. Or do you think what the scriptures have to say about this is a mere formality?" When you pass up dates with certain guys because you know they do not measure up to God's standards, then you have taken seriously your commitment not to oppose God. If your friends pressure and oppose you, ask the Lord for the strength to be more concerned with being His friend and not His enemy through compromising standards.

In America, government agencies regulate the standards of the food that you consume on a daily basis. For example, meat is subject to federal regulation of its grade, weight, and quality. How much more significant than ground beef (even prime rib) is the man with whom you hope to share the rest of your life? Such consideration and evaluation cannot be obtained through a glance or chance encounter at the "meet" counter. A lifelong relationship demands the highest standards of regulation. There are men breathing on this planet today who can handle such scrutiny and be found "worth waiting for."

Avoiding Bozos

What is a Bozo? A Bozo is a guy whose outward appearance is a façade. It is hard to discern who he really is because of the "makeup and costume" he wears. What he appears to be physically, socially, and even spiritually is just a performance. A Bozo is a counterfeit of a Boaz.

It is possible to avoid such a clown. Your standards and convictions will help you recognize the difference. The remainder of this chapter will accentuate the genuine Boaz. Concentrating on the real thing will make the Bozos more apparent.

Before any girl accepts her first date, she should have established in her heart and mind a biblical alternative to Hollywood's dating style. As a pre-requisite to every date, you should examine your motive (elaborated in the chapter on contentment). Are you going out with this guy because you haven't had a date in years? Are you going out with someone who may not really be a Christian because you think a date—even with a Bozo—is bet-ter than no date at all? Many women spend time with guys who do not real-ly care for them. They would rather waste an evening with a Bozo than face another lonely night in a dateless condition. Some women even give up their biblical convictions in order to get a date with a certain guy. Do you feel as though you allow your dating schedule to determine your personal worth? Many single women are prisoners of the world's dating syndrome. They equate their self-worth with how many dates they had last month.

Have you dated more Bozos than Boazs? If your answer is yes, you may need to develop higher ideals. A very attractive and popular high school girl was challenged to develop a list of biblical dating standards and to put them into practice. She carried a copy of those standards in her wallet for five years. Thus she dated more Boazs than Bozos because her convictions helped her clearly see the type of guys with whom she was relating and ulti-mately dating. Do you carry God's standards for dating in your heart as well as in your wallet?

One Auburn University graduate left school with not only a diploma but also a very specific list of the qualities she was looking for in a future mate. See if her list contains any of the qualities you are looking for in Mr. Right:

Spirit-controlled Christian (Eph. 5:18).

Jesus is #1 in his life, not just an ornament (Mk. 12:30).

Broken; understands how to rely totally upon Jesus (Phil. 4:13).

Ministry-minded; wherever he is, he is available (1 Cor. 4:2 NIV).

Motivator; man of vision, concerned about lost souls (Rom. 10:14).

Sensitive spirit; in tune to the needs of others (Gal. 6:2).

Understands the awesome responsibility of a husband to his wife (Eph. 5:25-31).

Humble enough to be a disciple (teachable) and able to disciple others (Mt. 28:19-20).

Man of prayer; he knows the key to success is his private time with God (Col. 4:2).

Family man; he desires to have children and raise them properly for God's glory (Prov. 22:6).

Clear standards for dating and relating will guard you against compromise and making wrong choices out of sudden emotion rather than a God-directed will. These guidelines for your dating friendships will keep God as your focus rather than allowing the guy to become the focus (idol). Clear standards coupled with accountability to a sister in Christ will help you walk in the convictions you establish. To guard you against haphazard meetings or just the "WF's" (weird feelings) in your heart, you need standards for which you will be accountable.

A disclaimer that we would like to include at this point is not to simplify the reason so many women are attracted to Bozos. The issue of standards is most relevant, but may seem simplistic. We acknowledge that some women find it difficult to raise their standards and change their patterns because they are still entangled with the past. Unresolved conflicts with a father, a brother, or an ex-boyfriend may overshadow and control the attraction to Bozos. In this case we suggest a possible date fast, a period of time during which you refrain from accepting another date until you can sort out some of the unresolved conflicts from the past. This method has been used by many single women who have been entangled with old dating patterns. During the "date fast," they find time to search for new ways of relating and dating biblically.

If you have already spent time with the Lord establishing dating/relating standards, then you will receive affirmation through the following material.

Lady of Conviction

If you have been letting your dating routine be controlled by chance rather than biblical choice, consider not accepting another date until you have nailed down your convictions. Too much is at stake.

Once you have set dating standards and understand the significance of a constant motive check, (daily bringing the flutters in your heart to the Lord), you are ready to consider other guidelines for successful dating and relating.

Wedding Day Chains

"Here comes the bride all dressed in…chains!" Hey, wasn't that supposed to be "all dressed in white"? The last word in the chorus was changed to "chains," not because the bride is marrying a member of a motorcycle gang, but because she made the unwise choice of marrying an unbeliever. The chains symbolize what she has to look forward to as a believer married to an unbeliever. The Word of God speaks clearly about a partnership with an unbeliever. A common verse used for this conviction is Second Corinthians 6:14-17, but you find a more poignant message for the one who wavers in this conviction in Joshua.

> But if you turn away and ally yourselves with the survivors of these
> nations that remain among you and if you intermarry with them
> and associate with them, then you may be sure that the Lord your
> God will no longer drive out these nations before you. Instead, they
> will become snares and traps for you, whips on your backs and
> thorns in your eyes, until you perish from this good land, which the
> Lord your God has given you (Joshua 23:12-13 NIV).

One would be foolish to disobey God in the area of marrying an unbeliever.

When a single woman experiences a prolonged period of datelessness, loneliness tempts her to compromise her conviction concerning dating a growing Christian. Her dateless state may pressure her to surrender to the temptation of dating an unbeliever. She may justify such a date in the guise of being a witness for Jesus. Many single women have been trapped emotionally with an unbeliever when it all began with "missionary dating."

Ponder this: Every unbelieving marriage partner arrived as an unbeliever on the first date. As trite as it may seem, every date is a potential mate. Avoid dating an unbeliever.

Many women want so desperately to date that the only qualification they have for the guy is that he goes to church. Every Sunday churches have people attending to appease God or to satisfy a religious urge. You must set a higher standard and resist dating a guy who is not growing in his intimacy with Christ.

The Man-Worth-Waiting-For

How would you describe the ideal man? A group of sharp women were asked to describe a "Man-Worth-Waiting-For," and all of them immediately replied: spiritual leader. One woman expounded on this quality in her unique way: "I want a guy who enjoys talking about Jesus in such a way that it reveals his obvious, bursting love for Him." Too many guys want to talk about Jesus for 60 seconds and their car or job or latest toy for the rest of the evening. One woman shared a verse that she thought his life should reflect, "Psalm 73:25: "Whom have I in heaven but You [the Lord]? And besides You, I desire nothing on earth." Do such spiritual men exist? Yes, but they are exceptions and not the rule. Their appearance requires waiting on the part of the recipient.

Before considering the specific qualities found in a Boaz, one should deal with certain physical stereotypes. Whether you have been looking for a guy who is a bronzed, blue-eyed blonde ("B.B.B.") or is tall, dark, and handsome ("T.D.H."), you need to surrender your desires to the Lord. Everyone has certain preferences. But such a mind-set needs to be given to Jesus. Too many single women have missed wonderful treasures in godly guys because the treasure was not encased in a B.B.B. or T.D.H. The Lord will probably not require you to date a guy who repulses you physically. But you need to be open to guys who do not fit your desired stereotype. Too often a guy may satisfy your eyesight, but leave your heart empty and still longing. Remember, after a few years that bronzed, blue-eyed blonde can be transformed into a pale, bald guy with bifocals on those gorgeous eyes.

A famous actress told a Christian psychologist that her five husbands had all been attractive outside (they were all B.B.B.'s or T.D.H.'s), but rotten on the inside. How many women, after the honeymoon is over, feel like they married a stranger? How many newlyweds are disillusioned by their mate's behavior within a few months of marriage? Most marriage counseling problems have their roots in personality problems—not physiques.

The Book of Ruth gives not only the story of a Lady in Waiting, but also the profile of a Knight in Shining Armor. From the first mention of this man Boaz, you begin to notice special qualities that distinguish a Boaz from a Bozo.

You want to marry someone for the qualities he possesses now, not for the qualities you hope he will develop. The most common mistake made by marriage partners is marrying someone they intend to change. Since it is nearly impossible to change a person, you will want to set standards of dating, or of building friendships, with men who are characterized by the qualities below. A single woman can sidestep a lifetime of tragedy by seriously considering these characteristics in a prospective steady date.

Puts the needs of others ahead of his own. This man accepts people just the way they are, loving others even when his love is not returned. He will continue to love someone because of his commitment to that person, not because of how he feels.

Do nothing from selfishness or empty conceit, but with humility of mind regard one another as more important than yourselves; do not merely look out for your own personal interests, but also for the interests of others (Philippians 2:3-4).

Rejoices in his relationship with Christ. You don't have to ask this man if he is a Christian. His joy in the Lord is evident in his life.

*These things I have spoken to you, so that My joy may be in you,
and that your joy may be made full* (John 15:11).

Maintains proper relationships. This man seeks a good relationship
with everyone—from his friends to his parents. He listens to differing
perspectives without feeling threatened. He has the strength to back off
from a fight. He works to forgive wrongs done to him and seeks to make his
own offenses right. He will not hold a grudge.

Pursue peace with all men... (Hebrews 12:14).

Refuses to jump ahead of God's timing. He is not so eager to be something, do something, or have something that he cannot wait on God's timing. He chooses against impulsiveness so he may be in the exact center of
God's will.

Rest in the Lord and wait patiently for Him... (Psalm 37:7).

Seeks to meet the practical needs of others. He is not so self-absorbed
that he cannot make time for the needy. He is interested in the welfare of
others and is willing to give his time, money, and energy for their benefit.

Be kind to one another, tender-hearted... (Ephesians 4:32).

Stands for what is right. He hates anything contrary to God's holy
character. He is known as a man of integrity by those with whom he works.

*There will be...glory and honor and peace to everyone who does
good...* (Romans 2:9-10).

Follows through on his God-given responsibilities. He uses the talents
God has given him and realizes that "he + Jesus = adequacy for any God-
given job." He is neither overconfident nor absorbed with feelings of infe-
riority. He is not a dreamer, wishing for more ability, but a diligent steward
of the talents he has been given. This man is dependable and stays with even
a difficult task until it is completed.

*Now it is required that those who have been given a trust must
prove faithful* (1 Corinthians 4:2 NIV).

Understands the importance of feelings and emotions. Some women may find themselves attracted to a demanding man, assuming that his dominance will be their security. Other women may marry a doormat they can dominate, but inevitably end up despising the man's weakness. A gentle man is the best of both; he takes the initiative to lead but tempers it with gentle responses toward the other's feelings.

So, as those who have been chosen of God, holy and beloved, put on a heart of compassion, kindness, humility, gentleness and patience (Colossians 3:12).

Flees temptations to compromise. This man refuses to be in situations that are sensual, immoral, or impure. He does not entertain friendships that lead to drunkenness or carousing. He avoids talk that could cause strife or jealousy. This man does not allow a temper to control him or anger to destroy him.

Like a city that is broken into and without walls is a man who has no control over his spirit (Proverbs 25:28).

These qualities are not unrealistic ideals. When a man follows Jesus, the Holy Spirit works these into his life. In fact, you can read this list again and match the fruit of the Spirit with the appropriate characteristic. "But the fruit of the Spirit is love, joy, peace, patience, kindness, goodness, faithfulness, gentleness, self-control; against such things there is no law" (Gal. 5:22-23).

None of the men you date will have all these qualities perfected. All of us are at differing levels of maturity. A man of God is one who works toward being conformed to the character of Christ. But be careful when a quality of God's Spirit is completely missing in a man's life and he is unwilling to deal with it before marriage. Realize that if character is absent before the wedding ceremony, it will be missing after the wedding ceremony and cause considerable problems during marriage.

Was Boaz, Ruth's knight, the last man of godly character, or was he just one of many? We are convinced that God still grooms Boazs for His daughters today. This does not mean a guy has to be perfect in order for you to go out with him. It does mean that he needs to be growing in Christlikeness by the enabling power of the Holy Spirit before you start to date him.

Do you want to marry a knight in shining armor? Then set your standards high. To be married to a man who loves the Lord and wants to serve Him is one of life's highest privileges. It is worth whatever wait, whatever cost. Nail down your convictions and refuse to compromise by dating men who are not controlled by God's Holy Spirit. These standards will stand guard over the castle of your heart. Proverbs 4:23 (NIV) says, *"Above all else, guard your heart,* for it is the wellspring of life."

Becoming a Lady of Conviction

Write out your convictions for the kind of guys you will date and the Scripture where you found those qualities. Why did you select these particular convictions?

Guys who are completely on fire for Jesus, who are visibly maturing in their walk with Him, and who will sharpen me in my faith

What is the problem with just dating guys who are good, but who are not Christians? What is the difference between a good man who goes to church and a growing Christian man? What difference would it make in marriage?

His lack of godly principles can corrupt a woman's morals and standards. A growing Christian man doesn't just do the motions, but is genuinely in love with Christ.

If the wait becomes hard and you meet someone who loves you, but has a glaring character flaw, what do you sacrifice if you marry him? Look through each of the characteristics found in the Man-Worth-Waiting-For section and determine what would be lost in your marriage if that quality was missing in your husband and the father of your children.

By making an unwise choice like this, the woman would be sacrificing God's best for a mediocre substitute.

Put a check beside each of the following characteristics that *you* can change in your husband after marriage:

___ Unwillingness to communicate (Prov. 14:10)

___ Dominating ego (Rom. 12:3)

___ Bad temper (Jas. 1:19-20)

___ Argumentative tendencies (Prov. 20:3)

___ Difficulty in apologizing (Eph. 4:32)

___ Bad language (Eph. 5:4)

___ Unwillingness to be involved with church (Heb. 10:24-25)

___ Inability to keep a job (1 Tim. 5:8)

___ Jealousy (1 Cor. 13:4)

___ Self-centeredness (2 Cor. 5:15)

___ Depression (2 Cor. 4:16)

___ Unwillingness to give (2 Cor. 9:7)

___ Always "going with the guys" (1 Cor. 15:33)

___ Wandering eyes (1 Thess. 4:2-7)

___ Lying (Eph. 4:25)

___ Immaturity (Eph. 4:15)

___ Workaholic tendencies (1 Tim. 6:7-11)

What does the Bible say about these qualities in reference to godliness?

These qualities do not display the likeness of Jesus in a man's life, and make for a disastrous marriage and a hard family life.

Lady of Patience

Janis and Linda were long-time friends and roommates. Inside their hall closet hung two sizes of every color bridesmaid's dress imaginable. "Well," they would say, with a laugh, "we have been bridesmaids at the weddings of many friends, but we are still here, holding out for the man God has for each of us!" Linda often added, "One thing I do know, when I walk down that aisle in white I want 'Great Is Thy Faithfulness' to be the procession song."

Although their ability to joke in the midst of their prolonged singleness is admirable, one has to wonder how an older woman can be patient when there appears to be no end to the waiting in sight. Waiting isn't easy when you are young, and it can be terribly hard as you get older.

God demonstrated His faithfulness in a special way to these two close single friends who chose to wait for His best, whether they married or not. He allowed each of their princes to appear within weeks of each other. Linda and Janis rejoiced in the faithfulness of God as they planned their weddings and then participated in each other's wedding ceremony. They witnessed God's faithfulness in marriage as in singleness because they waited on His perfect timing for their future.

Was the wait easy? No. Was the wait worth it? Many years of marriage and six children later, the two friends answer with a resounding, "Praise God. Yes, the wait was worth it!"

Take courage, single friend. You are not alone in your wait; neither are you alone in the feelings and struggles you encounter. Many godly women have waited and won. Many women have lost hope and compromised. Wait patiently and win triumphantly the future your Father has planned for you. It will always be designed with you in mind and is worth being patient to discover.

Ruth was a wonderful example of a Lady of Patience. Ruth did not allow her circumstances or lack of male companionship to cause her to be impatient. Instead she concentrated on developing companionship with her heavenly Father and chose to let Him bring a husband to her if He saw fit. Concern over the ticking of her "biological clock" did not make her fearful of the future. Instead she concentrated on being a lady of character, not on getting a man. She took one day at a time, knowing that God was not bound by circumstances nor her age. She used the wait to become the woman God wanted her to be. At the end of this personal preparation God chose to provide her with a husband. In Ruth 4:13, we see the end to their love story. "So Boaz took Ruth, and she became his wife...."

Why Is Waiting So Hard?

If God is faithful, why is it so easy to lose patience? Why is it so hard to wait? Why is it easier to settle for less than God's best? Fear is a huge hindrance to waiting. You may fear that your biological clock is ticking away and God has not noticed. You may fear, with every wedding you attend, that soon you will no longer have any single friends. You might feel that you better marry this "okay fella" who just proposed because he's pretty good and you fear you may not find another. Or possibly you fear loneliness and a lifetime of eating by yourself and of going to a church filled with people, only to sit alone.

Lady of Patience

Fear is an internal pressure. There are external pressures as well. Society pushes single women to grab for marriage because of a male shortage. Your parents want grandchildren and your cousins want to know, "What's wrong with you?" You feel like you don't fit in with the youth any longer but you can't very well go to the young marrieds' functions at church (where your friends now attend). If that isn't enough, a knowledge of statistics on singleness can finish you off:

> "Marriage patterns in the United States revealed: white college educated women born in the mid-50's who are still single at thirty have a 20% chance of marrying. By the age of 35, the odds drop to 5%. Forty year olds are more likely to be killed by a terrorist than the minuscule 2.6% probability of tying the knot."[1]

How encouraging! The world is attacking a single woman's confidence as the enemy discourages her hopes through fear. These pressures often provoke single women to take more initiative rather than patiently wait for God's best.

Consequences of Impatience

There are grave consequences for the single woman who does not choose to develop patience and wait on God's timing. Society is full of heartbreaking examples. Some end in divorce; others end in an emotional separation that causes the husband and wife to merely live under the same roof. Some leave precious children damaged by the insecurity and fear that an unhealthy marriage produces. The personal loneliness and hurt that these life styles bring is an anguish that is indescribable. God did not intend a woman to have to live like that.

Impatience to find a man can cause a woman to argue about her "right" to date a man who is not godly, maybe not even a Christian. In Joshua 23:12-14 the Lord warns His people not to marry unbelievers. God knows that an ungodly husband will end up being "snares and traps for you, whips on your backs and thorns in your eyes..." (Josh. 23:13 NIV). Many young women argue that they are just dating, not marrying an unbeliever. But think about this—in our society, does anyone ever marry someone he or she never dated? Every date is a potential mate.

Marriage to a non-Christian brings pain to the believing wife. As women, we long to be known and loved for all we are. A man who is spiritually dead can never know the very intimate spiritual part of you that is your heart. He would be blind to much of what you would try to share with him. He could never know and understand you fully.

Be careful when you begin to think that you are "in love" and you "just can't live without him." Think again. Think of the loneliness you will feel when your husband will not attend church with you. Think of the angry bickering that may take place between the two of you because he can never understand the depths of your spiritual awareness and, consequently, your convictions. If you do not think about this now, you may one day think, "Before, I couldn't live without him; now I can hardly live with him." Second Corinthians 6:14-15 is very clear: "Do not be bound together with unbelievers; for what partnership have righteousness and lawlessness, or what fellowship has light with darkness? Or what harmony has Christ with Belial, or what has a believer in common with an unbeliever?"

Please consider a greater consequence than being unhappily married to a man who does not know your Lord. Will you be able to handle the pain of watching your children live with possible rejection by their father, day in and day out? Will you think it is worth the cost when you are the only one who gets up on Sunday mornings to take your dear children to church? Will it be worth the compromise when your children look up at you and ask why daddy doesn't love Jesus? They could even reject the Lord for eternity and live a miserable, ill-chosen life style because of the choice you made to marry a wonderful, but lost, man. Children will often follow their father's example—good or bad. Exodus 34:7 gives a warning you cannot ignore: "...He will by no means leave the guilty unpunished, visiting the iniquity of fathers on the children and on the grandchildren to the third and fourth generations." You are not just marrying a husband, but choosing a father for your children.

Lady of Patience

When you marry, you do not choose blessings or curses for you alone; you choose for the generations after you. If you choose to wait patiently for your knight in shining armor, you will be blessed by the heritage that a prince brings. If you choose to run eagerly ahead of God's plan and marry a man with no conscience toward God, you will reap the life's course he follows, but not alone. Your children's and grandchildren's lives will be directly affected by the man you marry.

Consider the following Scriptures:

All these blessings will come upon you and overtake you if you will obey the Lord your God (Deuteronomy 28:2).

But it shall come about, if you do not obey the Lord your God...all these curses shall come upon you and overtake you (Deuteronomy 28:15).

God warned His people in Deuteronomy of the long-term effect of their choices. Today other countries may not take our children, but there are many bondages in our wicked generation that could hold them.

Your sons and your daughters shall be given to another people, while your eyes look on and yearn for them continually; but there will be nothing you can do (Deuteronomy 28:32).

Have you seen the yearning eyes of a mother as she sees her son on drugs or her daughter living on the streets? There is nothing she can do but look on in pain.

Deuteronomy 28:2, 15, and 32 show that God has always desired to bless His people, but He will not force them to do what is best. In His Word He has often warned us to wait, to be careful, and to trust Him. He will not make us wait. His heart of love begs us to listen and obey so He may bless us and the dear ones who will one day look to and follow us. The words He gave to the children of Israel in Deuteronomy 30:15-20 show the love and concern He has for the choices you make.

...So choose life in order that you may live, you and your descendants, by loving the Lord your God, by obeying His voice, and by holding fast to Him... (Deuteronomy 30:19-20).

You must choose to wait patiently for God's best. If you have seen patterns in your life that show a lack of patience, commit yourself right now to waiting for God's best.

You may pray something like this:

Lord, You are my sovereign God. You know all about me and love me more than anyone else ever could. You know how I feel, what I need, and what my future is. I confess that I have taken matters into my own hands. I confess to being afraid of totally trusting You. Today I commit myself to focus on You and Your love for me. Today I commit to look to You for my future—not to my outward circumstances. Thank You for knowing how weak I feel, but being strong for me and in me. I love You. I choose to trust You.

You may have to repeat this prayer, or one like it, many times when you feel afraid. But Psalm 103:13-14 assures us that He understands and has compassion on us:

Just as a father has compassion on his children, so the Lord has compassion on those who fear Him. For He Himself knows our frame; He is mindful that we are but dust (Psalm 103:13-14).

Developing Patience

Kimmy expressed that her focus was set and patience began in a real way in her life when, during her late twenties, she surrendered her life to Jesus. She said, "I remember telling the Lord, 'I don't care if I ever get married, I just want to love You, please You, and know You.' From that time I had a new peace and power. I got involved by ministering to the youth in my church and found joy in serving others. One girl told me her mother thought I was absolutely crazy, being as old as I was, to spend my time with the youth instead of trying to find a husband."

Kimmy served the Lord faithfully and contentedly alone until years later when Lynn recognized her as the lady God had for him. They were soon married because they had patiently used their waiting time to get ready. Kimmy said, "God didn't supply all my wants when I was single. He changed my wants and supplied all my needs, better than I could have imagined."

One older single woman struggling to be a Lady in Waiting cried out to the Lord as to why He was delaying the coming of her knight. She searched her heart, thinking there must be something horribly amiss in her life for God to spend so many extra years developing her into a princess suitable for her knight-to-be. Her self-image began to suffer as she mentally blamed herself for the delays. Tenderly the Father gave her a verse she could cling to: "Dwell in the land and cultivate faithfulness" (Ps. 37:3b).

She didn't really understand all that it meant, but chose to believe she was being all she should be before the Lord. As she began to dwell upon the positive things the Lord said about her in His Word, like "The King's daughter is all glorious within" (Ps. 45:13a), she was able to reject negative, condemning thoughts and feelings, and choose to be the woman He wanted her to be as a single.

Little did she know that God needed those days to perfect her Boaz. We, as women, are not the only ones who need the days of waiting in order to be perfected for a future life-mate. Her knight had not been a Christian long and in his spiritual immaturity would not have been a proper spiritual leader. He needed time to be founded in the Word and to experience complete freedom over the sins of his past.

When the two of them were finally introduced, she understood why she had to wait. While she cultivated faithfulness before God, her knight had been slaying a few dragons and shining his armor. God did not leave her waiting any longer than necessary. She desired a knight, but patiently waited on God's timing. The two of them now glorify God in a ministry to drug and alcohol abusers.

Wait patiently. Perhaps you are giving God time to prepare, not yourself, but your beloved. Let your heavenly Father accomplish His work thoroughly while your single man is undistracted. Issues settled in a person's life while single limit unnecessary stress and difficulty later in a marriage. Psalm 37:7 says, "Rest in the Lord and wait patiently for Him...." Wait not for a man or a preconceived perfect future, but for Him. Verses 3, 4, and 5 of Psalm 37 give some great action words for the Lady of Patience to follow in order to wait before Him.

Realizing that marriage is not a dream but real life can also help you to wait more patiently. Instead of merely being envious, get with a godly married woman and see the extra load she carries. Look at all she cannot do, instead of the fact that she has a man in her house. Understand that in reality, married life is not constant communication, daily roses, hugs and kisses, breakfast in bed, and sheer bliss. Marriage is every bit as much work as it is wonderful, even in God's way and time. It is good, but don't be deceived into mistaking it for Heaven.

Since no spouse is perfect, learning to live "as one" is not without its tears. Marriage alone is not a cure-all or answer to every heartfelt need. If you think it is, you had better just keep waiting, for that kind of marriage doesn't exist. Although there is a romantic inside every one of us, you must be realistic regarding marriage or the shock could be devastating.

"Another thing that helped me wait patiently." Kimmy wrote, "was a sense of humor. Laugh about 'always a bridesmaid but never a bride.' Joke about opening your own attendant shop because you have so many bridesmaid's dresses. Talk about being single with others in a fun way, not with a 'woe is me' attitude."

Find other single girls and plan activities. Don't just sit at home on Friday night. Go out to eat, or to the movies, and become involved working with children, young people, or senior adults. There are many things you can do to stay busy and keep from becoming impatient.

Developing patience is hard. Getting married ahead of God's timing is worse. God may not work according to your time schedule, but He does have your best interests in mind. One single said, "As a teenager, I had my life all planned out. I would meet my husband at age 19, marry at 21, and start my family at 23. These were my plans, but evidently not God's plans for my life. I am 41 now, but enjoy a wonderful single life."

You don't know what tomorrow holds, but you do know who holds tomorrow. Say this with the psalmist:

O Lord, my heart is not proud, nor my eyes haughty; nor do I involve myself in great matters, or in things too difficult for me. Surely I have composed and quieted my soul; like a weaned child rests against his mother, my soul is like a weaned child within me. O [substitute your name], *hope in the Lord from this time forth and forever* (Psalm 131).

The place of rest that the psalmist found was a result of the choice he made. This quietness of soul did not come naturally to him. He actively chose to take himself out of involvement and quiet his soul (his mind, will, and emotions). He chose to put his hope in God. Are you trying to involve yourself in matters that are too great for you? Can you see into a man's heart? Can you know the future? You know Someone who does know men's hearts and the future. Patiently rest against His chest. He will bring you the peace you need. This attitude of patience is not something that will just happen. By an act of your will you must choose to trust God regardless of what happens. Patiently wait for His best.

Every single woman must at some point come to grips with the fact that not all women will marry. Marriage is not a need, though God chooses to let marriage meet some needs a woman may have. Marriage is not a right, though God chooses to plan marriage for the majority of women. Marriage does not complete a person, though women who properly marry find that marriage rounds out some of their weaknesses. If marriage were a need, right, or completion for women, then all godly women would marry. There are many examples of true, God-honoring women who had no earthly mate but were still Ladies of Patience.

One Lady in Waiting wrote this:

"I believe part of being a Lady of Patience is honestly facing the future. For me that was realizing that I might not ever get married.

"I could handle the thoughts of 'waiting on the Lord,' but to face the reality that it may not be His desire for me to marry was hard to cope with. As I read my Bible, I found Isaiah 54:5. The verse said I was already married to Him. He was my Husband! I was His bride. He wanted me to know Him, my Husband. He wanted me to see myself as His bride, to know His love for me. He wanted to be intimate with me. So I began my walk with my Husband, the Lord Jesus.

"I still desire to get married; in fact, many times I have longed for a husband and even cried for one. There have been times when I thought I had met 'the one for me,' then was terribly disappointed. But I always knew I could go back to my 'Husband' who understood my desire and my hurts. He would encourage me by showing me His love in even deeper ways."

Another single woman named Beverly developed the following Bible study to calm the impatience of her heart.

By Beverly Seward Brandon

Why Do I Want to Get Married?	*How Can God Meet Those Needs in My Life?*
I want to be loved.	"…I have loved you with an everlasting love…" (Jer. 31:3).
I want someone to adore me.	The King has brought me into his chambers to adore me. My lover is outstanding among 10,000 (see Song 1:4; 5:10).
I want someone to hold my hand.	"…I will uphold you with My righteous right hand" (Is. 41:10).

I want to be accepted and valued.	I am accepted in the Beloved (see Eph. 1:6 KJV).
I want a "place," a nesting place that is my own to create and use.	We can rest in the shadow of the Almighty (see Ps. 91:1).
I want help in my days of trouble.	"Call upon Me in the day of trouble; I shall rescue you…" (Ps. 50:15).
I want to share my life—the joys and the struggles—with one person (intimacy).	God will share with me the treasures of darkness and hidden riches (see Is. 45:3).
I want a champion of my causes—one who is willing to fight for me.	"The Lord will fight for you…" (Ex. 14:14).
I want someone to meet my needs.	God is meeting all my needs (see Phil. 4:19).
I want intimacy.	The Lord is intimate with the upright (see Ps. 140:13).
I want someone to help me in my life.	There is no one like God who rides the heavens to help you (see Deut. 33:26).
I want to walk through life sustained and carried. I don't want the whole load of life.	Even to my old age, God will sustain me, carry me, and rescue me (see Is. 46:4).
I want a companion for this life.	God invites us to humbly walk with Him (see Mic. 6:8).
I desire children.	God gives us spiritual children like the numberless grains of sand if we invest in lives (see Is. 48:19).

Beverly's response to this study is: "The Lord, my Maker, is my Husband. Only He can meet the deepest needs of my heart. No man can ever come through for me fully. Only He can. He is what I long for. Only God is enough."

Regardless of what you see or what you feel, God is in full control of your situation. You, Lady in Waiting, can walk in victory by choosing to be patient in your wait.

Don't let your impatient longings rob you of the life God wants to bless you with as a single. Realize you do not need marriage for happiness or a full life. If you are holding onto marriage as a right, relinquish this right so it will not keep you from God's fullest blessings. God knows what is best for you. His timing is perfect and He will take care of His Lady of Patience.

Becoming a Lady of Patience

Write out the things that make you lose patience. Which of these cause your Sovereign God concern? Give these concerns to Him and ask Him to help you trust while you wait. "I will trust while I wait, for my God is never late" is a good motto.

Seeing other girls interacting with boys/boyfriends, thinking/talking about engagements and weddings

Read Deuteronomy 28:1-48. Write on one side of a piece of paper the blessings God wanted the nation of Israel to have as His children. Write on the other side what He asked them to do. What does He require of you?

faith

Read Deuteronomy 28:1-48 again. Write the curses that came from choosing to be disobedient to God. Confess any ways that you have chosen to disobey God's will for your life.

_____

_____

_____

Read Deuteronomy 30 and write down all the tender ways God spoke to His children, trying to help them choose what was best. How can you commit today to remain true to your loving Father and patiently wait? Look at the way He understands how His children feel in verses 11-14.

He said that if they followed and obeyed Him, He would have compassion on them and delight in them.

_____

Make Psalm 27 your prayer and commit it, or another passage, to memory to use on those hard days.

_____

_____

_____

Endnotes

Chapter 1: Lady of Reckless Abandonment

1. Kenneth G. Smith, *Learning to Be a Woman*. (Downers Grove, Illinois: InterVarsity Press, 1972), back cover.

2. Scofield Bible. (New York, New York: Oxford University Press, 1967), p. 51, note on Genesis 35:19.

3. A.W. Tozer, *The Pursuit of God*. (Camp Hill, Pennsylvania: Christian Publishing Inc., 1982), p. 16.

4. Elisabeth Elliot, *Loneliness*. (Nashville, Tennessee: Oliver Nelson, 1988), p. 16.

5. Tozer, *The Pursuit of God,* p. 29.

6. Quoted in Elisabeth Elliot, *A Chance to Die*. (Old Tappan, New Jersey: Fleming H. Revell Company, 1987), p. 117.

Chapter 2: Lady of Diligence

1. John Fischer, *A Single Person's Identity*. (Discovery Papers, Catalog No. 3154, August 5, 1973), p. 3.

2. Elisabeth Elliot, *A Chance to Die.* (Old Tappan, New Jersey: Fleming H. Revell Company, 1987), p. 117.

3. Charles F. Stanley, *Handle With Prayer.* (Wheaton, Illinois: Victory Books, 1982), p. 15.

4. Richard J. Foster, *Celebration of Discipline.* (San Francisco, California: Harper & Row, Publishers, 1978), p. 117.

Chapter 3: Lady of Faith

1. *USA Today*, April 10, 1990, p. 4.

2. Elisabeth Elliot, *A Chance to Die.* (Old Tappan, New Jersey: Fleming H. Revell Company, 1987), p. 117.

3. Elisabeth Elliot, *Passion and Purity.* (Old Tappan, New Jersey: Fleming H. Revell Company, 1984), pp. 59-60.

Chapter 5: Lady of Devotion

1. A.W. Tozer, *The Root of the Righteous.* (Camp Hill, Pennsylvania: Christian Publishing, Inc. 1985), p. 5.

2. Tozer, *The Root of the Righteous,* p. 5.

3. W.E. Vine, M.A. *Vine's New Testament Dictionary of New Testament Words,* p. 639.

Chapter 6: Lady of Purity

1. Nadine Joseph, "The New Rules of Courtship," *Newsweek Magazine,* Special Edition, Summer/Fall, 1990, p. 27.

2. Author E. Cundall and Leon Morris, *Judges and Ruth, an Introduction and Commentary.* (Downers Grove, Illinois: InterVarsity Press, 1968), p. 287.

3. Tim Stanford, "The Best of Sex," *Campus Life Magazine,* February, 1992, pp. 25-26.

4. Stanford, "The Best of Sex," pp. 25-26.

Chapter 7: Lady of Security

1. Elisabeth Elliot, *Passion and Purity,* (Old Tappan, New Jersey: Fleming H. Revell Company, 1984), pp. 59-60.

Chapter 10: Lady of Patience

1. Eloise Salholz, "Too Late for Prince Charming?" *Newsweek,* June 2, 1986.

Lady *in* Waiting
Meditations for the Heart

DEVELOPING YOUR LOVE RELATIONSHIPS

A Word From the Authors

Have you ever noticed the funny way a pigeon walks? His head moves forward, he stops, then he takes a step. I have read that a pigeon's eyes do not focus unless his head is still...therefore, he focuses—then steps. We could learn a lot from this "pigeon walk."

Sometimes our lives seem to get out of control and our hearts are injured and our steps unsure. We lose focus and life comes apart at the seams. This Journal is designed to help us keep focus—step by step and day by day.

Proverbs 3:5-6 are key words to live by with regard to our steps. "Trust in the Lord with all your heart...." How much misdirection and pain could we avoid if we trusted in and were daily assured of our God's awesome love for us? "And do not lean on your own understanding...." What trouble could we avoid if we went to the all-knowing God for daily direction and wisdom instead of fretting, planning, and worrying? "In all your ways acknowledge Him...." This is our focus for each step. And the promise? "He will make your paths straight."

It really doesn't matter how much we "know"—it matters how much we "live." This type of journaling through the years has helped me to live more of what I know. I pray that, as you use this spiritual journey tool, you will catch yourself refocusing before each step.

May God richly bless your "walk" with Him!
— Debby Jones

Thirty-plus years ago, my spiritual mentor shared the secret of her incredible life with Jesus, and I have tried to *live* the secret since she shared it on that memorable summer day in 1972:

"There is no success, no happiness, and no fulfillment in life apart from a consistent, daily growing relationship with Jesus through the Word."

I have watched thousands of women try to find happiness, success, and fulfillment without spending quiet time with Jesus...and I can testify that their efforts have been in vain.

— Jackie Kendall

Helpful Tips for the Lady in Waiting

The purpose of this meditation journal is to introduce you to a fresh and exciting way of enhancing your personal life and enriching your spiritual journey. We have taken some of the most energizing quotes from *Lady in Waiting*, mixed in great motivational thoughts from classic writers of the past, and have come up with a delectable spiritual meal that will satisfy the appetite of the hungry soul.

It is not enough to simply read the individual quotes, write a few words, and then move on to the next page. The authors and the publisher encourage you to prayerfully meditate on these powerful truths. As you do so, this journal can then become a resource that will help promote you to new heights of intimacy with the Lord Jesus and prepare you for deeper levels of relationships.

To Learn His Presence

It is our desire that this journal will help you live in the presence of the Lord every day. It is not intended to simply add new truth to a bag of theological truth that is already full; rather, it is our expectation that it will bring you to a place of new experiences with your God.

It will require that you spend time carefully considering the significance and implications of each individual quote. Let its spiritual vibrations resonate in your heart. Contemplate their spiritual meaning as you apply them to your life, ultimately letting them lead you to a quiet place of prayer and communion with your Divine Lover, the Lord Jesus.

Begin Your Journey

Few of us have the opportunity for quiet meditation and personal contemplation every day. Therefore, the pages are not dated. It is important that you use this journal when you have the time to give yourself to prayer and meditation. It will not help you if you simply make this experience a part of a daily regimen of religious duty.

To begin the journey, it is imperative that you find a quiet place where you can get alone with your journal, your Bible, and your Lord. Read each quote several times, making sure that you have captured the essence of the writer's thoughts. Do not be content with a casual glance before quickly moving on to the next quote. Allow the Spirit of the Lord to enter your thought processes and bring fresh insight. Let the words become a prayer that is formed on your lips.

The practice of contemplative prayer is certainly a lost art in our Western society. We are used to having our spiritual food gathered, prepared, cooked, and delivered to our table by our favorite preachers of the day. This journal will help you break out of this spiritual rut.

You might want to talk to your friends about a quote and get their thoughts and reactions. How about memorizing a portion of the quote so that you can reflect on it during the day?

Come back to these words several times. Do not be satisfied with only one look. Often, days down the road, fresh meaning and application will come to you.

Here are a few reflective questions that will help guide you in your meditations:

What is the main focus and intent of the author's words?

How does this concept apply to my life?

What Scripture verses will lead me into further application of the truth?

What circumstances have I gone through that enrich the meaning of the statements?

Are there any particular areas of my life that need adjustment so that I can move into a new dimension of experiencing the power of this truth?

What is preventing me right now from entering into the reality of this compelling insight?

How can I form the truth of this quote into a personal prayer to the Lord?

Before you begin, start with this quote from Madame Guyon's book, *A Short and Very Easy Method of Prayer*:

> *Meditative reading is choosing some important practical or speculative truth, always preferring the practical, and proceeding thus: whatever truth you have chosen, read only a small portion of it, endeavoring to taste and digest it, to extract the essence and substance of it, and proceed no farther while any savor or relish remains in the passage: then take up your book again, and proceed as before, seldom reading more than half a page at a time.*

> *It is not the quantity that is read, but the manner of reading, that yields us profit. Those who read fast, reap no more advantage, than a bee would by only skimming over the surface of the flower, instead of waiting to penetrate into it, and extract its sweets. Much reading is rather for scholastic subjects, than divine truths; to receive profit from spiritual books, we must read as I have described; and I am certain that if that*

method were pursued, we should become gradually habituated to prayer by our reading, and more fully disposed for its exercise.

(Madame Jeanee Guyon, *A Short and Very Easy Method of Prayer*, Ch. II. 3 Jan. 2002
<http://www.passtheword.org/DIALOGS-FROM-THE-PAST/methodofprayer.htm>)

Contents

Day: *8/20/08* Date: *Wednesday* Time: *10:32 am* Location: *patio table*

Fulfillment

Have you assumed that your ultimate fulfillment would be found in marriage? Have you privately entertained the notion that the only satisfied women are married women? Have you been expecting your career to satisfy you until you are married? If you have answered "yes" to any of these questions, then you have a prospect of disillusionment looming in the future. "…A woman becomes a woman when she becomes what God wants her to be."* This priceless truth can help keep your perspective clear in relation to true fulfillment in life. Too many Christian women think that the inner longings of their heart relate only to love, marriage, and motherhood. Look a little closer and see if that longing isn't ultimately for Jesus. Gary Chapman once remarked, "I feel very strongly that marriage is not a higher calling than the single state. Happy indeed are those people, married or single, who have discovered that happiness is not found in marriage but in a right relationship with God." Fulfillment for a Christian woman begins with the Lordship of Christ in every area of her life.

*Kenneth G. Smith, *Learning to Be a Woman* (Downers Grove, Illinois: InterVarsity Press, 1972), backcover, as cited in *Lady in Waiting*.)

The only way a woman of God can find true satisfaction is by letting go of her desire to control her life, dreams, desires and plans to get where she wants to be and what she wants to get, and confidently leaving them in the care and under the complete control and authority of Jesus. Easier said than done. Some of the things that

Keep me from surrendering my entire self are my doubts and fears (which are really irrational when I think about it) and in my natural human desire for control. When I am refusing to give up an area of my life (which I truly have no control over in the first place) I am forfeiting God's perfect plans for that area of my life. I am my own worst enemy. Countless times in the past, God has proven himself faithful time and time again to His people. Just like the Israelites, I too easily forget all the times God has blessed the lives of the people who had the faith to surrender everything to God, and how he has blessed my life and taken care of me.

Verses:

Ecclesiastes 12:13

Joshua 24:15

Matthew 6:33

Matthew 8:26

Jeremiah 29:11

Fulfillment for a Christian woman begins with the Lordship of Christ in every area of her life.

Day: _____ Date: _____ Time: _____ Location: _____

Journey Away From Rituals

Ruth moved from a false religion into the only true and eternal relationship. Too many women have been involved in a form of religious worship, but have never had a vital, growing relationship with Jesus...Has your faith been a lifeless ritual rather than a vital love relationship with Jesus? Why not spend some of your free hours as a single woman beginning a journey away from rituals into a deep relationship with Jesus Christ?

One single woman expressed this vital relationship with Jesus in the following way: "I desired that my relationship with the Lord be an adventure. One where I would find out what pleased Him and then do it, devoting as much energy to Jesus as I would in a relationship with a boyfriend. I am falling more in love with Jesus every day." Do you know more about pleasing a boyfriend than you do about pleasing the Lord Jesus?

_____

_____

_____

_____

_____

_____

_____

_____

_____

_____

_____

_____

_____

_____

_____

_____

_____

_____

_____

_____

_____

_____

_____

_____

_____

_____

_____

_____

_____

*Has your faith been a lifeless ritual rather than
a vital love relationship with Jesus?*

Day: _____ Date: _____ Time: _____ Location: _____

His Blueprints

Another costly aspect of Ruth's choice was the time frame in Israel's history. It was the age of the judges, a period of time described as "do your own thing"; "Everyone did what was right in his own eyes" (Judg. 21:25b). Ruth chose not only to break her family cycle, but also to challenge the lifestyle that many in Israel embraced. She wanted God's will, not hers; His blueprints, not her elementary scribbling; God's assignment, not her foolish plans.

Whenever a single woman decides to abandon herself completely to Jesus, as Ruth did, she will find herself out of step with society and, sometimes, even with her friends. A single woman today needs the boldness to challenge and break the cycle of the "American way" that exalts a relationship with a man as an answer to life. This "American way" blurs the reality of the ultimate answer to life found in a deep relationship with Jesus Christ. A modern-day Ruth wrote: " My deep satisfaction from my commitment to Jesus is constantly challenged by other believers. They treat me like some kind of Neanderthal, definitely out of step with the today's woman."

_____

_____

_____

_____

_____

_____

_____

_____

_____

_____

_____

_____

_____

_____

_____

_____

_____

_____

_____

*...His blueprints, not her elementary scribbling; God's
assignment, not her foolish plans...*

Day: _____ Date: _____ Time: _____ Location: _____

Tightly Bound

Ruth came to the God of Israel after years of living in darkness, but He gladly received her service even though she was a Moabite foreigner. She bound herself to the service of the Lord, interweaving her service with Him like the braiding of a heavy rope. Isaiah 56:6-7 (NIV) refers to a foreigner binding himself (or herself) to the Lord and His willingly receiving their "diligent" service: "And foreigners who bind themselves to the Lord to serve Him...these I will bring to My holy mountain...".

Are you tightly bound to the Lord, serving Him diligently, or has your relationship and service been unraveling over the years as you continue to be single and not married? Has resentment and self-pity unraveled what used to be a tightly woven labor for the Lord? You must be sensitive to the things and situations that distract you from redeeming your free time. "Whatever might blur the vision God had given [Elisabeth Elliot] of His work, whatever could distract or deceive or tempt others to seek anything but the Lord Jesus Himself she tried to eliminate."*

*Elisabeth Elliot, *A Chance to Die* (Old Tappan, New Jersey: Fleming H. Revell Company, 1987), p. 117, as cited in *Lady In Waiting*.

_____

_____

_____

_____

_____

_____

_____

_____

_____

_____

_____

_____

_____

_____

_____

_____

_____

_____

_____

_____

_____

_____

_____

_____

_____

Are you tightly bound to the Lord,
serving Him diligently...?

Day: _____ Date: _____ Time: _____ Location: _____

Mother Teresa

She was born Agnes Gonxha Bojaxhiu in 1910 in Skopje, Yugoslavia (now Macedonia). In 1928 she decided to become a nun and went to Dublin, Ireland, to join the Sisters of Loreto. From there she went to the Loreto convent in Darjeeling, India.

In 1929 she began to teach geography at St. Mary's High School for Girls in Calcutta. In those days the streets of Calcutta were crowded with beggars, lepers, and the homeless. Unwanted infants were regularly abandoned on the streets or in garbage bins. In 1946, Mother Teresa felt the need to abandon her teaching position to care for the needy in the slums of Calcutta.

Initially focusing her efforts on poor children in the streets, Mother Teresa taught them how to read and how to care for themselves. Many former students of St. Mary's eventually joined her order. Each girl who joined was required to devote her life to serving the poor without accepting any material reward in return.

(Mother Teresa. January 22, 1997. October 8, 1999. <http://www.nalejandria.com/utopia/english/ Mother Teresa-eng.htm/> as cited in Don Milam, *The Lost Passions of Jesus* [Shippensburg, Pennsylvania: MercyPlace, 1999], p. 131.)

My True Community

Keep giving Jesus to your people not by words, but by your example, by your being in love with Jesus, by radiating his holiness and spreading his fragrance of love everywhere you go. Just keep the joy of Jesus as your strength. Be happy and at peace. Accept whatever He gives—and give whatever He takes with a big smile. You belong to Him.

...

Meditations for the Heart

My true community is the poor—their security is my security, their health is my health. My home is among the poor, and not only the poor, but the poorest of them: the people no one will go near because they are filthy and suffering from contagious diseases, full of germs and vermin—infested; the people who can't go to church because they can't go out naked; the people who can no longer eat because they haven't the strength; the people who lie down in the street, knowing they are going to die, while others look away and pass them by; the people who no longer cry because their tears have run dry!

The Lord wants me exactly where I am—He will provide the answers.

(Eileen Egan and Kathleen Egan, *Suffering Into Joy* [Ann Arbor, Michigan: Servan Publications, 1994], pp. 22, 89.)

_____

_____

_____

_____

_____

_____

_____

_____

_____

_____

Accept whatever He gives—and give whatever He takes with a big smile. You belong to Him.

Day: _____ Date: _____ Time: _____ Location: _____

Life on Hold

Some singles see the lack of a mate as God denying them something for a more "noble purpose"—*a cross to bear*! Our selfish nature tends to focus on what we do not have rather than on what we do have—free time—that can be used for others and ourselves. Is your life on hold until you have someone to hold?

…Have you experienced…a crushing emotional blow?… Psalm 34:18 says, "The Lord is near to the brokenhearted, and saves those who are crushed in spirit." [A] brokenhearted woman had put her life on hold after her husband divorced her. Such a response is understandable, but…this now single woman decided to take her broken heart, her empty arms, and her loneliness and give them to Jesus. In exchange, Jesus taught her how to resist feeling sorry for herself and how to stop living in the arena of bitterness. After she made the choice of recklessly abandoning herself to Jesus as Lord, she was free to serve Him. This once brokenhearted single woman has been transformed into a fearless servant of the Lord.…

Have you also put your life on hold? Do you have an excuse for not serving Jesus?

_____

_____

_____

_____

_____

_____

_____

_____

_____

_____

_____

_____

_____

_____

_____

_____

_____

_____

_____

_____

_____

_____

_____

_____

Is your life on hold until you have someone to hold?

Day: _____ Date: _____ Time: _____ Location: _____

Adjust Your Vision

It is doubtful that there could ever be a better time to serve Jesus than this "moment" of singleness. Rather than wasting precious moments fantasizing about an earthly lover, take advantage of your free hours each day to serve the Lord of Heaven. If you are frustrated and distracted, rather than fruitfully serving Jesus, then ask Him right now to adjust your vision.

...Don't worry about that certain guy you have had your eye on for a while. If he is God's best for you, he will be there when you return....

Is there an opportunity of service that you have avoided because you can't give up your "post on the castle wall" looking for your knight in shining armor?...As you get older, you assume more obligations and responsibilities that demand your time and attention. Such distractions will make serving Jesus even more difficult. Have you given Jesus full reign over your time?

Limitless ministry opportunities exist for the Lady of Diligence. These ministries are available right this moment. They do not demand a Bible college education. The only requirement is a single woman who desires to use her time wisely in ministry.

_____

_____

_____

_____

_____

_____

Is there an opportunity of service that you have avoided
because you can't give up your "post on the castle wall"
looking for your knight in shining armor?

Day: _____ Date: _____ Time: _____ Location: _____

His Script

God providentially directed Ruth to the field of Boaz. You find this divine encounter in the second chapter of Ruth, verse 3: "...and she happened to come to the portion of the field belonging to Boaz...." The verb *happened* in Hebrew means "chanced upon." This leaves no room for manipulation. She had a chance and her chance transported her into the center of God's will and right to Boaz's field....

If Jesus wants you married, He will orchestrate the encounter. You have nothing to fear except getting in His way and trying to "write the script" rather than following His. Jesus does have your best interest at heart. He desires to bless you by giving you the best. Sometimes what you perceive as the best is nothing more than a generic version. Consider His wisdom and love in comparison to your own wisdom and self-love. In whom are you going to trust—all Wisdom and Everlasting Love or little ol' finite you? Ever since the Garden of Eden, women have often felt they could and should know as much as God. Much pain in our world has resulted from dependence on our wisdom rather than on our Father's.

_____

_____

_____

_____

_____

_____

_____

_____

_____

_____

_____

_____

_____

_____

_____

_____

_____

_____

_____

_____

_____

_____

_____

_____

_____

*You have nothing to fear except getting in His way and trying
to "write the script" rather than following His.*

Day: _____ Date: _____ Time: _____ Location: _____

Susanna Wesley

Susanna (Annesley) Wesley was born on January 20, 1669, in London, England and is most known for being the mother of the famous Wesley boys, John and Charles. Susanna was the youngest of 25 children. Her father was a minister and often let Susanna take part in theological discussions with his minister friends.

At the age of 19, Susanna married 26-year-old Samuel Wesley. He was a newly ordained Anglican priest who was named rector of the Epworth parish. During the absence of her husband, Susanna began a Bible study within her home. Neighbors, family, and friends soon heard of the Bible studies and the crowd soon grew to over 200 hungry souls.

Susanna regularly spent an hour in prayer and Bible reading every day. This practice was built into the lives of her children and bore fruit in their powerful preaching and passionate prayers.

Susanna passed away on July 25, 1742.

A Life Worthy of Eternity

This life is nothing in comparison of eternity;
so very inconsiderable, and withal so wretched,
that it is not worthwhile to be, if we were to die as the beasts.
What mortal would sustain the pains, the wants, the disappointments,
the cares, and thousands of calamities we must often suffer here? But
when we consider this as a probationary state...and that if we wisely
behave ourselves here, if we purify our souls from all corrupt
and inordinate affections, if we can, by the divine assistance, recover

the image of God (moral goodness), which we lost in Adam, and attain to a heavenly temper and disposition of mind, full of the love of God, etc., then we justly think that this life is an effect of the inconceivable goodness of God towards us...

I have such a vast inexpressible desire of your salvation, and such dreadful apprehensions of your failing in a work of so great importance; and do moreover know by experience how hard a thing it is to be a Christian, that I cannot for fear, I cannot but most earnestly press you and conjure you, over and over again, to give the most earnest heed to what you have already learned, lest at any time you let slip the remembrance of your final happiness, or forget what you have to do in order to attain it.

(George J. Stevenson, *Memorials of the Wesley Family*, Partridge, 1876, p. 185, as cited in Arnold Dallimore, *Susanna Wesley* [Grand Rapids, Michigan: Baker Books, 1993], pp. 91-92.)

_____

_____

_____

_____

_____

_____

_____

_____

_____

_____

"...if we can, by the divine assistance, recover the image of God... then we justly think that this life is an effect of the inconceivable goodness of God towards us..."

183

Day: _____ Date: _____ Time: _____ Location: _____

Become a Princess

When you picture the perfect man for you, what is your prince like? Do you see a man devoted to God? A man of character—teachable, loyal, faithful, gentle, and kind? What kind of woman do you think this godly man desires to marry—a shallow woman or a woman full of charm who knows how to dress and capture other men's attention? Is this the one he imagines he will one day want to spend the rest of his life with—the mother of his heirs? No way!!

To marry a prince, you must first become a princess. To marry into royalty, you must be appropriately prepared. Even Diana, the Princess of Wales, had to go through a period of "waiting and preparing" before marrying Prince Charles. She had to learn how to properly act, dress, and speak so she would honor the royal family. Is it any wonder that a heavenly princess must prepare inwardly for the calling to which she will give her life? As you set your attention on developing godly character, Christ will change you into the beautiful princess He created you to be.

_____

_____

_____

_____

_____

_____

_____

_____

_____

_____

_____

_____

_____

_____

_____

_____

_____

_____

_____

_____

_____

_____

_____

_____

_____

_____

_____

To marry a prince, you must first become a princess.

Lady *in* Waiting

Day: _____ Date: _____ Time: _____ Location: _____

Your Destiny

Do you think your ideals and standards are too high? Do you feel the pressure to compromise and settle for the generic version of life? Ruth lived in an era that was exactly like modern America. Judges 21:25 describes the era in which she lived: "In those days there was no king in Israel; everyone did what was right in his own eyes." We too live in a culture where it seems that no one fears God and people just "do their own thing."

You, like Ruth, will be greatly affected by your choices. Ruth's wise choices allowed her to break a godless family cycle and begin a new cycle that the Word of God triumphantly records. God has not changed—and neither have men. The high standards in God's Word are not irrelevant, but completely applicable to finding God's best for your life. Choices, guided by your convictions rather than by chance, determine your destiny....

You cannot make good choices without proper, biblical convictions. Don't carelessly leave your dating/relating standards to chance. Too much depends on your decisions in this area.

_____

_____

_____

_____

_____

_____

_____

_____

_____

_____

_____

_____

_____

_____

_____

_____

_____

_____

_____

_____

_____

_____

_____

_____

_____

_____

_____

_____

_____

Choices, guided by your convictions rather than
by chance, determine your destiny…

Day: _____ Date: _____ Time: _____ Location: _____

Back to the Basics

May we go back to the basics for just a moment? What is a conviction and how does one develop biblical convictions? A conviction is a standard that serves as a springboard for your choices. Consider where your standards, in the area of relating and dating, originated. Are your standards based more on Hollywood's terms of love and romance, or have you allowed God's Holy Word to shape your perspective?

The Lady of Conviction gives the Lord permission to renew her mind on a daily basis. She spends time searching the Word of God for standards that will guide her safely to God's best…She has surrendered her mind to a new persuasion: God's perspective on love and romance. The convictions that she establishes, based on the Word, allow her to resist being squeezed into the mold of this world. She is a non-conformist in a biblical sense, as in Romans 12:2 (NIV) which says, "Do not conform any longer to the pattern of this world, but be transformed by the renewing of your mind. Then you will be able to test and approve what God's will is—His good, pleasing and perfect will."

_____

_____

_____

_____

_____

_____

_____

_____

_____

_____

_____

_____

_____

_____

_____

_____

_____

_____

_____

_____

_____

_____

_____

_____

_____

*The Lady of Conviction gives the Lord permission
to renew her mind on a daily basis.*

Day: _____ Date: _____ Time: _____ Location: _____

A Need, A Right, A Completion

Every single woman must at some point come to grips with the fact that not all women will marry. Marriage is not a need, though God chooses to let marriage meet some needs a woman may have. Marriage is not a right, though God chooses to plan marriage for the majority of women. Marriage does not complete a person, though women who properly marry find that marriage rounds out some of their weaknesses. If marriage were a need, right, or completion for women, then all godly women would marry. There are many examples of true, God-honoring women who had no earthly mate but were still Ladies of Patience.

...

Don't let your impatient longings rob you of the life God wants to bless you with as a single. Realize you do not need marriage for happiness or a full life. If you are holding onto marriage as a right, relinquish this right so it will not keep you from God's fullest blessings. God knows what is best for you. His timing is perfect and He will take care of His Lady of Patience.

_____

_____

_____

_____

_____

_____

_____

_____

_____

_____

_____

_____

_____

_____

_____

_____

_____

_____

_____

_____

_____

_____

_____

_____

_____

_____

If marriage were a need, right, or completion for women,
then all godly women would marry.

Day: _____ Date: _____ Time: _____ Location: _____

Basilea Schlink

Basilea (Dr. Klara) Schlink was born in 1904. Her education included social welfare training and a doctorate in psychology. She was a leader of the Women's German Student Christian Movement and bravely stood against Nazi policy during the Hitler regime. She risked her life during World War II, publicly speaking out on the unique destiny of Israel as God's people. Mother Basilea appeared two different times before the German Gestapo for boldly proclaiming Jesus Christ as Lord; she was released despite her unwavering stance. As Mother Basilea and another leader, Mother Martyria, led Bible studies (even teaching the Old Testament that was forbidden by the Nazis) for young people, they began to see revival. The young girls encountered God in a fresh way; His holiness, His justice, His Lordship were experienced anew. Those who were lukewarm in their Christianity repented; hidden sins were confessed and forgiveness flowed.

(Adapted from "Who is M. Basilea Schlink? Who is M. Martyria Madauss?" 04 April 2001.
21 Jan. 2002 <http://www.Kanaan.org/Mother.htm>)

First Love, Divided Love

Jesus, who so often says "Whoever loves Me . . ." and asks "Do you love Me?" is concerned about our LOVE! He is concerned about a special kind of love. It is the love which is shadowed in the relationship between a bride and her bridegroom; that is, it is an exclusive love, a love which places the beloved, the bridegroom, above all other loves, in the first place. As a Bridegroom, Jesus has a claim to "first love". He who has loved us so much wants to possess us completely, with everything we are and have. Jesus gave Himself wholly and completely for us. Now His love is yearning for us to surrender ourselves and everything that we are to Him, so that He can really be our "first love." So long as our love for Him is a divided love, so long as our heart is bound to family, possessions, or the like, He will not count our love to be genuine. Divided love is of so little value to Him that He will not enter into a bond of love with such a soul, for this bond presupposes a full mutual love. Because our love is so precious to Jesus, because He yearns for our love, He waits for our uncompromising commitment.

(Basilea Schlink, "Bridal Love" ©2001 The Watchword. 3 Jan. 2002
<http://www.watchword.org/schlink/ww29d.html>)

_____

_____

_____

_____

_____

_____

_____

_____

_____

_____

_____

_____

As a Bridegroom, Jesus has a claim to "first love."

Day: _____ Date: _____ Time: _____ Location: _____

True Love

Seeking God is very similar to developing a friendship. You talk a lot, you listen, you write each other letters, you think about each other, you find out what the other likes and does not like, and you try to do things that please that person. The more you spend time together, the more intimately you know your friend. And the more intimately you know your friend, the greater your love will be. It works the same way with your relationship with God.

Jeremiah 29:12-13 promises that a woman who diligently seeks God with all her heart will find Him. Your heart is the key to devotion to God. A halfhearted search is not sufficient. This means you cannot seek God while you do your own thing.

Is God demanding too much to require that you seek Him with all your heart? No way!...

...giving Christ your heart means you are not free to give it away to other things or people that come into your life (in idolatry).... Devotion to the Lord Jesus Christ is giving everything or nothing at all. Your devotion to Christ must be a serious commitment....

_____

_____

_____

_____

_____

_____

Devotion to the Lord Jesus Christ is
giving everything or nothing at all.

Day: _____ Date: _____ Time: _____ Location: _____

Choose: Him or What He Can Give

Many seek God, but only for His hand. They don't want God as much as they want something from God, such as a man, happiness, or a family. This impure search for God is limited to what you can get. It is more of a self-love than a God-love. This seeking will end in misery, not in the union of love you desire. God...knows your motives. To grow in your knowledge of God, you must seek God correctly, which means you must also seek God with a pure heart.

A woman with a pure heart for God does not focus on what He gives, but delights in who He is. She seeks God's *face*, not just His *hand*. Would you want someone to say he loves you just so you would do something for him? To find God, you must seek Him with pure motives. Seek Him for who He is, not just for what He can do for you....

...

Singleness does not have to be a curse....Singleness puts you in an advantageous position because, more than likely, you have much more time to seek the Lord now than you will ever have if you marry.

_____

_____

_____

_____

_____

_____

_____

_____

_____

_____

_____

_____

_____

_____

_____

_____

_____

_____

_____

_____

_____

_____

_____

_____

*. . . you must seek God correctly, which means you
must also seek God with a pure heart.*

Day: _____ Date: _____ Time: _____ Location: _____

Your Gift

Since sex is desirable, why not have sex?...

God wants you to be a Lady of Purity because He wants to protect you from the consequences that sex before marriage brings. These consequences can be physical, emotional, relational, and spiritual....

Have you secretly opened a Christmas gift before Christmas Day and rewrapped it, putting it back under the tree? How thrilling and exciting it was when you saw the surprise. But what about the "big day" when the gifts were supposed to be opened for the first time? Where was the excitement when you opened your gift? The gift did not seem quite as special because it had already been opened for the first time. Each woman receives one "first time." God desires for your precious gift to be given to a committed lover who will cherish, keep, and protect you in marriage. God wants you and your gift to this man to be treasured and cherished, not trampled and conquered. Song of Solomon 8:4 (NIV) says, ... "Do not arouse or awaken love until it so desires." God wants to protect you from losing your virginity.

_____

_____

_____

_____

_____

_____

_____

_____

_____

_____

_____

_____

_____

_____

_____

_____

_____

_____

_____

_____

_____

_____

_____

_____

*God desires for your precious gift to be given to a committed
lover who will cherish, keep, and protect you in marriage.*

Day: _____ Date: _____ Time: _____ Location: _____

Hannah More

Born in 1745 in Bristol, England, Hannah More was to become a champion of the disenfranchised of the world. Instead of quiet domesticity, in obscurity, Hannah blazed a trail for women. As a powerful writer she earned a fortune which she used to set up a cottage industry that printed millions of moral tracts that were distributed around the world. She became friends with John Newton, the ex-slave trader, who became her mentor. She joined in with William Wilberforce in the battle against the slave trade.

She has the honor of making English ladies the foremost agent in the education of the poor. The intensity of her love for the Lord Jesus was reflected in a life given for His people.

What an example of balance: the hearts of Mary and Martha beating within the same bosom. Hannah More proves that you can be passionate about His presence and at the same time be a servant to fellow man.

(Tommy Tenney, *God's Favorite House Journal* [Shippensburg, Pennsylvania: Fresh Bread, 2000], p. 25.)

Do We Really Love God?

Our love to God arises out of our emptiness;
God's love to us out of His fulness. Our
impoverishment draws us to that power which can relieve and
to that goodness which can bless us. His overflowing love delights
to make us partakers of the bounties He graciously imparts. We can only
be said to love God when we endeavour to glorify Him, when we desire a
participation of His nature, when we study to imitate His perfections.

Meditations for the Heart

We are sometimes inclined to suspect the love
of God to us, while we too little suspect our own lack of love to Him....
When the heart is devoted to God, we do not need to be perpetually
reminded of our obligations to obey Him. They present themselves
spontaneously and we fulfill them readily. We think not so much of the
service as of the One served. [The motivation which suggests the work
inspires the pleasure.] The performance is the gratification, and the
omission is both a pain to the conscience and wound to the affections....

Though we cannot be always thinking of God, we may be always
employed in His service. There must be intervals of our communion with
Him, but there must be not intermission of our attachment to Him.

(Hannah More, *The Religion of the Heart* [Burlington, New Jersey: D. Allison & Co., 1811], updated by Donald L. Milam Jr., pp. 27, 33, 85-86, as cited in Tommy Tenney, *Mary's Prayers and Martha's Recipes* [Shippensburg, Pennsylvania: Fresh Bread, 2002], pp. 19-20.)

_____

_____

_____

_____

_____

_____

_____

_____

_____

Our love to God arises out of our emptiness;
God's love to us out of His fulness.

Day: _____ Date: _____ Time: _____ Location: _____

Don't Give Too Easily

Don't let your heart be given away too easily. If a man says he loves you, you don't have to echo the phrase. To men these three words can mean all kinds of things, like "I lust for you" or "I want you to kiss me." Or maybe he just can't think of anything else to say at the moment!... Gradually those "I love you's" can trap you emotionally and lead you on physically. To guard the key to your heart, make a commitment to say you love someone only if you love him with a committed love, not a casual love feeling. You will remain much more in control of your friendship. Real love will have time to blossom and grow without those three words. Guard and save them to be whispered when God reveals it is time. What a gift to tell your fiancé, "You are the first person I have ever said this to: 'I love you.' " Give meaning to those precious words, and you may use them and hear them with fondness through many happy years of marriage.

There's a second step you can take to guard your purity. It's a radical statement, but save all your kisses for your future husband....

A woman's kiss or embrace is not just another way of saying thank you! A kiss should say something more intimate.

_____

_____

_____

_____

_____

_____

_____

_____

_____

_____

_____

_____

_____

_____

_____

_____

_____

_____

_____

_____

_____

_____

_____

_____

_____

_____

. . . save all your kisses for your future husband.

Day: _____ Date: _____ Time: _____ Location: _____

Dating Standards

Don't set standards "as you go." Emotions can be tricky. You must make wise choices before the "flutters" and "heartthrobs" become so loud you cannot hear yourself think. Write them down and read them often! Commit them to God regularly in prayer.

…Here are some examples of "dating standards" that many godly women have made. They will help you resist the pressure too "open the gift" too early.…

I will date only growing Christian men. (You will most likely marry a man you date. This is important!!)

I will concentrate on the friendship—not romance. (Don't be tricked!)

I will not spend time with him at home when we are alone.

I will not give kisses and hugs freely.

I will not lie down beside a man.

…

Women are easily turned on by words.…Another way to protect your purity is to stand on guard when you hear "sweet talk."…

…words have trapped many ladies—beware! When you catch yourself rationalizing what you are doing and assuring yourself you are in control, make a second check. You'll be glad you did.

_____

_____

_____

_____

_____

_____

_____

_____

_____

_____

_____

_____

_____

_____

_____

_____

_____

_____

_____

_____

_____

Don't set standards "as you go."

Day: _____ Date: _____ Time: _____ Location: _____

It's Not Too Late

...If you are reading this "after the fact" and are dealing with the guilt of the lost gift, do not be discouraged. Although it is true that there is only one first time, God is the God of the first-time experience. Let Him heal your broken heart through forgiveness. Agree with God that you have sinned and leave the sin before Him. Then guard yourself from entering into that sin pattern again. Learn a valuable lesson, but do not continue to beat yourself with condemnation. Jesus paid for those sins at Calvary. Do not continue to allow yourself or the enemy to defeat you with remembering a sin once you have confessed it to God and those you have offended. There may be consequences of your sin, but you do not have to live with the guilt of it.

...

Even though you have been freed from the guilt by confession, do not use it as an opportunity to continue in sin or to leave yourself open to temptation. Continue to choose freedom over sin's mastery. Lay aside every encumbrance and the sin that so easily entangles you and run with endurance the race set before you (see Heb. 12:1).

_____

_____

_____

_____

_____

_____

_____

_____

_____

_____

_____

_____

_____

_____

_____

_____

_____

_____

_____

_____

_____

_____

Lay aside every encumbrance and the sin that so easily entangles you and run with endurance the race set before you.

Day: _____ Date: _____ Time: _____ Location: _____

Deficit of a Father's Love

Women tend to struggle with insecurity because of the unique way God created them. God made every little girl with the need to love and be loved by her earthly father. God designed His world with a picture of a family as the theme. The father protects, loves, and cares for his wife and their children. The ideal earthly father models the gentle, nurturing love of the heavenly Father. Many young women in our society did not have a father who followed God's design. This God-given need for a father's love caused a deficit in their lives.

...

As a little girl, you may remember feeling the desire to be cherished, loved, and accepted by your daddy. If he failed to show that love to you in God's way, perhaps you continued to search for a man who would. No man, not even a husband, can fill the need you have for secure love. Only Jesus, who "is the same yesterday and today yes and forever," will never disappoint or fail you (Heb. 13:8).

...the man you marry cannot meet your need for security. Only God's love brings security.

_____

_____

_____

_____

_____

_____

_____

_____

_____

_____

_____

_____

_____

_____

_____

_____

_____

_____

_____

_____

_____

_____

_____

_____

. . . the man you marry cannot meet your need for security.
Only God's love brings security.

Day: _____ Date: _____ Time: _____ Location: _____

Basilea Schlink

Waiting for Our Love

*Jesus is yearning to have fellowship with us and to hear words
of love drop from our lips. He is waiting for us. He wants us
to be close to Him. He wants to speak to us in our hearts, to
cultivate love's intimate relationship with us. Only in times of quiet
when no one else distracts us, and nothing else draws us away,
can Jesus visit us with His love. Let him who wishes to know the
presence of Jesus and who desires to enter into bridal love
for Jesus keep his times of quiet holy and faithfully for Him.*

*Jesus is waiting for our love. As important
as our sacrifices and our obedience to the
commandments are for God (the rich young ruler sacrificed, and kept the
commandments), they are not enough. Sacrifices and obedience do not
necessarily yield the "eternal, divine life." Love does not necessarily
pulsate through them. Jesus is pulsating life and love and He wants
to impart His nature to us. Therefore, only our love, which stems from
the divine, eternal life which He has granted to us, is the proper
response to His love for us. This love leads us to keep His
commandments, which are His wishes for us. It will lead us to bring
Him many gifts, and to offer Him sacrifices— but in a different spirit.*

*...Bridal love for Jesus is filled with delight. There is no greater,
happier, higher, richer love.*

(Basilea Schlink, "Bridal Love" © 2001 The Watchword. 3 Jan. 2002
<http://www.watchword.org/schlink/ww29d.html>)

_____

_____

_____

_____

_____

_____

_____

_____

_____

_____

_____

_____

_____

_____

_____

He is waiting for us. He wants us to be close to Him.
He wants to speak to us in our hearts, to cultivate love's
intimate relationship with us.

Day: _____ Date: _____ Time: _____ Location: _____

Manipulation

When you see a woman going after the guys, you probably don't immediately say, "Yes, I see that she really is insecure!" Insecurity dwells in the heart. What you see outwardly is a woman's age-old ability to manipulate and maneuver. When a woman manipulates a situation, she feels personal satisfaction because she believes she is in control.

...

Manipulation and maneuvering can also take the form of serving as a "surrogate (substitute) helpmeet." Many women want to marry as badly as they want to go to Heaven. They long to care for a man, so they run around trying to find at least a "generic" version of the real thing. These precious (but deceived) women constantly look for a man with a need and pounce on that need in hopes of eventually winning the affection of man. Any male in need irresistibly attracts them.

...Women may find more pleasure doing for a man than a woman because the potential "payoff" seems more valuable. She envisions surrendering her "surrogate" apron for an engagement ring....

...Allow God to use you to minister to brothers and sisters equally with no ulterior motives.

_____

_____

_____

_____

_____

_____

_____

_____

_____

_____

_____

_____

_____

_____

_____

_____

_____

_____

When a woman manipulates a situation, she feels personal satisfaction because she believes she is in control.

Day: _____ Date: _____ Time: _____ Location: _____

Pre-Romantic Stress Disorder

You have just returned home from a great singles retreat where you once again surrendered your frustration as a single in exchange for God's peace and contentment. As you listen to your answering machine, you hear a certain voice. The most sought-after bachelor you know asks you for a date next weekend. Do you remain calm and give your expectations to the Lord? Or do you jump back in your car and head to the mall to register your china and look at some wedding gowns? Would the prospect of a date with the most eligible bachelor in town cause you to experience the "Pre-romantic Stress Disorder"? Or would you surrender your expectations to Jesus?

For a single woman to experience genuine contentment while soloing in a "couple's world," she must avoid the ditches of discontentment. She needs to learn the mystery of contentment and its power over the restless torture of her desire.

...

Circumstantially, Ruth had the perfect excuse to be discontented. Widowed at a young age, her circumstances provided the perfect breeding ground for self-pity and bitterness....Yet Ruth chose to cling to the God of Israel, whom she found to be trustworthy even in difficult circumstances.

_____

_____

_____

_____

_____

_____

_____

_____

_____

_____

_____

_____

_____

_____

_____

_____

Would the prospect of a date with the most eligible
bachelor in town cause you to experience the
"Pre-romantic Stress Disorder"?

Day: _____ Date: _____ Time: _____ Location: _____

Julian of Norwich

Julian is the most popular of the English mystics. She lived as a Benedictine nun in Norwich, beside the St. Julian Church, from which she most likely took her name. Little is know about Julian's life, although she is mentioned by her contemporary, Margery Kempe.

Julian's book, *Revelations of Divine Love*, entitled her to become the first great female writer in the English language. Despite her disclaimers of being unskilled as an author, she wrote lively prose in a style all her own. She was well trained in the Bible as well as in the teachings of the Church.

Her theology is based upon her mystical experiences. She became ill at the age of 30 and, in the midst of suffering, prayed for a vision of Christ's sufferings. Once in a time of prayer Julian heard the words, "I am the foundation of your praying"—words that greatly influenced her spiritual life. She always pointed to the goodness and love of God, a light in time of darkness for Julian, who lived in an age of social unrest and the fear of the Black Plague.

(Tommy Tenney, *The God Chasers Daily Meditation & Personal Journal*
[Shippensburg, Pennsylvania: Destiny Image Publishers, 1999], pp. 80-81.)

Revelations of Divine Love

...Oftentimes our trust is not full. We are not sure that God hears us, as we think because of our unworthiness, and because we don't feel right (for we are as barren and dry oftentimes after our prayers as we were before)...For thus have I felt in myself.

Meditations for the Heart

*And all this brought our Lord suddenly to my mind, and He showed me
these words. He said, "I am the Ground of your asking: first it is my
will that you have it; and afterwards, I make you to will it; and then,
I make you to ask it and you do ask for it. How should
it then be that you do not have what you ask for?"*

. . .

*For it is most impossible that we should ask mercy and grace, and
not have it. For everything that our good Lord makes us to ask, Himself
has ordained it to us from without beginning. Here may we see that
our asking is not cause of God's goodness; and He showed that
in all these sweet words when He sad: I am [the] Ground. — And
our good Lord wills that this be known of His lovers in earth; and the
more that we know [it] the more should we ask, if it be wisely
taken; and so is our Lord's meaning.*

(Adapted from Julian of Norwich, *Revelations of Divine Love*, Grace Warrack, ed. [London:Methuen & Co. Ltd.,
1901]. Ch. XLI, 14th Revelation. 7 Jan. 2002 <http://www.ccel.org/j/julian/revelations/home.html>)

_____

_____

_____

_____

_____

_____

*I am the Ground of your asking: first it is My will that you
have it; and afterwards, I make you to will it; and then,
I make you to ask it and you do ask for it.*

217

Day: _____ Date: _____ Time: _____ Location: _____

Biblical Dating Standards

What is a Bozo? A Bozo is a guy whose outward appearance is a façade. It is hard to discern who he really is because of the "makeup and costume" he wears. What he appears to be physically, socially, and even spiritually is just a performance. A Bozo is a counterfeit of a Boaz.

It is possible to avoid such a clown. Your standards and convictions will help you recognize the difference....

...As a prerequisite to every date, you should examine your motive.... Some women even give up their biblical convictions in order to get a date with a certain guy.

Have you dated more Bozos than Boazs? If your answer is yes, you may need to develop higher ideals. A very attractive and popular high school girl was challenged to develop a list of biblical dating standards and to put them into practice. She carried a copy of those standards in her wallet for five years. Thus she dated more Boazs than Bozos because her convictions helped her clearly see the type of guys with whom she was relating and ultimately dating. Do you carry God's standards for dating in your heart as well as in your wallet?

_____

_____

_____

_____

_____

_____

_____

_____

_____

_____

_____

_____

_____

_____

_____

_____

_____

_____

_____

_____

_____

_____

_____

*Some women even give up their biblical convictions in order
to get a date with a certain guy.*

Day: _____ Date: _____ Time: _____ Location: _____

Date Fast

Clear standards for dating and relating will guard you against compromise and making wrong choices out of sudden emotion rather than a God-directed will. These guidelines for your dating friendships will keep God as your focus rather than allowing the guy to become the focus (idol). Clear standards coupled with accountability to a sister in Christ will help you walk in the convictions you establish. To guard you against haphazard meetings or just the "WFs" (weird feelings) in your heart, you need standards for which you will be accountable.

…The issue of standards is most relevant, but may seem simplistic. We acknowledge that some women find it difficult to raise their standards and change their patterns because they are still entangled in the past. Unresolved conflicts with a father, a brother, or an ex-boyfriend may overshadow and control the attraction to Bozos. In this case we suggest a possible date fast, a period of time during which you refrain from accepting another date until you can sort out some of the unresolved conflicts from the past.…During the "date fast," you can find time to search for new ways of relating and dating biblically.

_____

_____

_____

_____

_____

_____

_____

_____

_____

_____

_____

_____

_____

_____

_____

_____

_____

_____

_____

_____

_____

_____

_____

*During the "date fast," you can find time to search for
new ways of relating and dating biblically.*

Day: _____ Date: _____ Time: _____ Location: _____

Missionary Dating

"Here comes the bride all dressed in...chains!" Hey, wasn't that supposed to be "all dressed in white"? The last word in the chorus was changed to "chains," not because the bride is marrying a member of a motorcycle gang, but because she made the unwise choice of marrying an unbeliever. The chains symbolize what she has to look forward to as a believer married to an unbeliever. The Word of God speaks clearly about a partnership with an unbeliever....

...

When a single woman experiences a prolonged period of datelessness, loneliness tempts her to compromise her conviction concerning dating a growing Christian. Her dateless state may pressure her to surrender to the temptation of dating an unbeliever. She may justify such a date in the guise of being a witness for Jesus. Many single women have been trapped emotionally with an unbeliever when it all began with "missionary dating." Ponder this: Every unbelieving marriage partner arrived as an unbeliever on the first date. As trite as it may seem, every date is a potential mate. Avoid dating an unbeliever.

...You must set a higher standard and resist dating a guy who is not growing in his intimacy with Christ.

_____

_____

_____

_____

_____

Every unbelieving marriage partner arrived as
an unbeliever on the first date.

Day: _____ Date: _____ Time: _____ Location: _____

Marriage is Not a Dream

Realizing that marriage is not a dream but real life can also help you to wait patiently. Instead of merely being envious, get with a godly woman and see the extra load she carries. Look at all she cannot do, instead of the fact that she has a man in her house. Understand that in reality, married life is not constant communication, daily roses, hugs and kisses, breakfast in bed, and sheer bliss. Marriage is every bit as much work as it is wonderful, even in God's way and time. It is good, but don't be deceived into mistaking it for Heaven.

Since no spouse is perfect, learning to live "as one" is not without its tears. Marriage alone is not a cure-all or answer to every heartfelt need. If you think it is, you had better just keep waiting, for that kind of marriage doesn't exist. Although there is a romantic inside every one of us, you must be realistic regarding marriage or the shock could be devastating.

. . .

Developing patience is hard. Getting married ahead of God's timing is worse. God may not work according to your time schedule, but He does have your best interests in mind.

_____

_____

_____

_____

_____

_____

Although there is a romantic inside every one of us,
you must be realistic regarding marriage
or the shock could be devastating.

Day: _____ Date: _____ Time: _____ Location: _____

Breaking Your Alabaster Box

What is in your alabaster box? Is your box full of fantasies that began as a little girl while you listened to and watched fairy tales about an enchanting couple living happily ever after? Have you been holding on tightly to your alabaster box of dreams, frantically searching for a man worthy of breaking your box? Take your alabaster box to Jesus and break it in His presence, for He is worthy of such honor. Having responded to your heavenly Bridegroom in such a manner, you can wait with confident assurance that, if it be God's will, He will provide you with an earthly bridegroom.

How do you know if you have broken your alabaster box at the feet of Jesus? Such a decision will be reflected in reckless abandonment to the Lordship of Jesus Christ....Take your alabaster box, with your body, soul, and dreams, and entrust them to Jesus. When He is your Lord, you can joyfully walk in the path of life that He has for you.

...Have you broken the valuable alabaster box yet?

_____

_____

_____

_____

_____

_____

_____

_____

_____

_____

_____

_____

_____

_____

_____

_____

_____

_____

_____

_____

_____

_____

_____

_____

*How do you know if you have broken
your alabaster box at the feet of Jesus?*

Day: _____ Date: _____ Time: _____ Location: _____

Waiting Periods

...Wherever you are, whatever your circumstances may be...be assured that God has not lost your address or your file. He knows exactly where you are and what you need....

You make the most important decision in life, giving your life to Jesus Christ, "by faith." The second most important decision concerns your life-mate. This decision also demands the element of faith. Waiting for one's life-mate and then saying "I do" to him demands secure faith, like Ruth's faith in the God of Israel.

...Your faith during the "waiting period" pleases God.

Don't fear or resent the waiting periods in your life. These are the very gardens where the seeds of faith blossom....

This intruding anxiety about your lack of a life-mate is not reality, but rather a weakness that the Greater Reality is capable of handling. Just go to Jesus as soon as the intruder arrives. Such a practice will only enhance your life as a Lady of Faith. Many single women have not recognized that the trying, frustrating waiting period is the perfect classroom for the Lady of Faith. Don't skip class! Embrace those dateless nights and, by faith, rest in His faithfulness.

_____

_____

_____

_____

_____

_____

_____

_____

_____

_____

_____

_____

_____

_____

_____

_____

_____

_____

_____

_____

_____

_____

_____

_____

Your faith during the "waiting period" pleases God.

Day: _____ Date: _____ Time: _____ Location: _____

Cleanup Time

If you are to know God intimately, then you must seek Him, not only with a whole heart, but also with a clean heart. When you think of the word *bride*, you probably first imagine a beautiful, clean, pure woman in white. No grime or dirt mars the image of purity. As a Christian you are part of the Bride of Christ. Any grime or dirt of sin will mar your image before Him.

The Lord's fiancé must have a clean heart. You must clean up any blot of sin that may arise between you and your heavenly Sweetheart. Sin…is disgusting to Him; He will not abide with it. Picture a couple deeply in love. He loves to be near her—so near he can breathe the fresh aroma of her sweet breath!…What do you think she does before she sees him if she has eaten onions?…Not only does she brush, but she also "Scopes, Close-ups, and Gleems." She doesn't want to offend her love!… Sin is far more repulsive to God than even onion breath…. If you want your devotion to God to be complete, don't merely brush at sin lightly. Get in there and confess it, clean it up, and clear it out.

_____

_____

_____

_____

_____

_____

_____

_____

_____

_____

_____

_____

_____

_____

_____

_____

_____

_____

_____

_____

_____

_____

_____

_____

_____

If you want your devotion to God to be complete,
don't merely brush at sin lightly.

Day: _____ Date: _____ Time: _____ Location: _____

Madame Jeanne Guyon

Madame Jeanne Guyon was born at Montargis, France. When she was only 15, she married an invalid who was 38 years old. Unhappy in her marriage, she sought happiness in her devotional life. She lived in a convent under royal order for a year and then was imprisoned in Vincennes and the Bastille because of her religious beliefs. Almost 25 years of her life were spent in confinement. Many of her books were written during that period.

Writing that compels the reader to move into a living experience of Jesus Christ is Madame Guyon's great contribution to devotional literature. *Experiencing the Depths of Jesus Christ* (sometimes entitled *A Short and Very Easy Method of Prayer*) has had a wide influence: Watchman Nee saw that it was translated into Chinese and made available to every new convert in the Little Flock; Francois Fénelon, John Wesley, and Hudson Taylor all highly recommended it to the believers of their day.

(Tommy Tenney, *The God Chasers Daily Meditation & Personal Journal* [Shippensburg, Pennsylvania: Fresh Bread, 1999], pp. 114-115.)

The Effectual Touch in the Will

The Soul then receives an effectual Touch in the Will, which invites it to recollection, and instructs it that God is within, and must be sought there; that He is present in the Heart, and must be there enjoyed.

This discovery, in the beginning, is the source of very great joy to the Soul, as it is an intimation or pledge of happiness to come; in its very commencement, the road it is to pursue is opened and is shown to be that of the Inward Life. This knowledge is the more admirable, as it

Meditations for the Heart

is the spring of all the felicity of the Soul, and the solid foundation
of interior progress; for those Souls who tend toward God merely
by the intellect, even though they should enjoy a somewhat spiritual
contemplation, yet can never enter into Intimate Union, if they
do not quit that path and enter this of the Inward Touch,
where the whole working is in the Will.

(Madame Jeanne Guyon, *The Way to God*, parapraphs 2 and 3. 3 Jan. 2002 <http://www.passtheword.org/DIALOGS-FROM-THE PAST/waytogod.htm>)

_____

_____

_____

_____

_____

_____

_____

_____

_____

_____

_____

The Soul then receives an effectual Touch in the Will,
which invites it to recollection, and instructs it that God
is within, and must be sought there; that He is present
in the Heart and must be there enjoyed.

Day: _____ Date: _____ Time: _____ Location: _____

Don't Sin Against Yourself

Have you ever been dieting but treated yourself to a huge piece of rich chocolate cake with fudge icing to celebrate some special occasion? Cake is good. Cake is desirable. The more cake, the more pleasure. But cake, in the midst of a strict diet, can really make one sick! The pleasure of a big, luscious piece of cake depends on the right timing, just as the pleasures of sex do.

God also wants to protect you from the sexually transmitted diseases that could affect not only you, but also your future husband....

God also desires to shield you from an unwanted pregnancy. Although precautions exist, pregnancy always remains a possibility. A rushed marriage, adoption, or abortion only complicate the consequences.

God desires to shield you from the negative physical consequences of premarital sex. He wants to protect you from sinning against your body. First Corinthians 6:18 (NIV) says, "Flee from sexual immorality. All other sins a [woman] commits are outside [her] body, but [she] who sins sexually sins against [her] own body."

"He wants you to be free from an addiction to premarital sex. Passionate physical exchange is a short-lived high. As with drugs, you keep wanting more intense highs."*

*Tim Stanford, "The Best of Sex," *Campus Life Magazine*, February, 1992, pp. 25-26, as cited in *Lady In Waiting*.

_____

_____

_____

_____

_____

_____

_____

_____

_____

_____

_____

_____

_____

_____

_____

_____

_____

_____

_____

_____

_____

_____

_____

. . . cake, in the midst of a strict diet, can really make one sick!

Day: _____ Date: _____ Time: _____ Location: _____

Spiritual Pain

Passion makes it difficult to see that God also set physical limits to protect you spiritually. Hebrews 13:4 (NIV) very clearly says that "marriage should be honored by all, and the marriage bed kept pure, for God will judge the adulterer and all the sexually immoral." God judges the sin of immorality. It feels awful to be separated from your Lord by the guilt of sin.

Actions speak louder than words, and this is especially true regarding premarital sex. It is difficult to share Christ with one who knows your reputation. Your actions can also cause weaker brothers and sisters to stumble. One night of passion can totally destroy a reputation you have built over a lifetime. "The spiritual side of sex is often overlooked. Even many Christians are not aware of the profoundly spiritual nature of their sex lives. A person will feel acute spiritual pain and separation from God when engaging in sex outside of marriage, but may not even realize how spiritually beneficial and unifying sex is within marriage."*

God does not intend to deny you pleasure. He protects you so you might enjoy physical health, emotional stability, relational intimacy, and spiritual blessings.

*Tim Stanford, "The Best of Sex," *Campus Life Magazine*, February, 1992, pp. 25-26, as cited in *Lady In Waiting*.

_____

_____

_____

_____

_____

_____

_____

_____

_____

_____

_____

_____

_____

_____

_____

_____

_____

_____

_____

_____

_____

_____

_____

_____

_____

It feels awful to be separated from your Lord by the guilt of sin.

Lady *in* Waiting

Day: _____ Date: _____ Time: _____ Location: _____

Your Assignment: Wait

Naomi told [Ruth] that Boaz was a candidate for being their kinsman-redeemer.... This simply meant that the Mosaic Law allowed Boaz, as the closest kin, to redeem the childless widow and keep the family name alive....

Naomi instructs Ruth to approach Boaz and ask him if he would be their kinsman-redeemer...His willingness was directly related to the character he had noticed in her responses to life and God.

...

Naomi's response to Boaz's willingness may have put a damper on most single women's racing heartbeat. "Then Naomi said, 'Wait, my daughter, until you find out what happens. For the man will not rest until the matter is settled today'" (Ruth 3:18 NIV). Who has to *wait*? The woman must wait. Who is the one who will not rest? The man, Boaz, will not rest.

Wait. Such an assignment is not to cause suffering, but prevent it. Women experience so much needless pain when they run ahead of God's format. Naomi knew that there may exist an even closer kinsman who would qualify to redeem her and Ruth....Naomi did not want Ruth's heart to race ahead into disappointment in case the circumstances did not go as assumed.

_____

_____

_____

_____

_____

_____

_____

_____

_____

_____

_____

_____

_____

_____

_____

_____

_____

_____

_____

_____

*Wait. Such an assignment is not to
cause suffering, but prevent it.*

Day: _____ Date: _____ Time: _____ Location: _____

Hannah Smith

Hannah Smith is the author of the popular classic, *The Christian's Secret of a Happy Life*, which was published in 1875. Its spiritual secrets of walking with God have been a great source of spiritual strength to many generations....

The search for God finds its greatest hope as we look within, deep into our spirit, where Christ lives. Smith gives us a series of clues for developing our inner life for receiving the "Divine Seed" and preparing our spirit for ultimate union with Christ.

(Tommy Tenney, *Mary's Prayers and Martha's Recipes* [Shippensburg, Pennsylvania: Fresh Bread, 2002], p. 21.)

You Must Move In

A large part of the pain of life comes from the haunting "fear of evil" which so often besets us. Our lives are full of supposes. Suppose this should happen, or suppose that should happen; what could we do; how could we bear it? But, if we are living in the "high tower" of the dwelling place of God, all these supposes will drop out of our lives. We shall be "quiet from the fear of evil," for no threatenings of evil can penetrate into the "high tower" of God. Even when walking through the valley of the shadow of death, the psalmist could say, "I will fear no evil"; and, if we are dwelling in God, we can say so too.

But you may ask here how you are to get into this divine dwelling place. To this I answer that you must simply move in. If a house should be taken for us by a friend, and we were told it was ready, and that the lease and all the necessary papers were duly attested and signed, we should not ask how we could get into it—we should just pack up and move in. And we must do the same here. God says that He is our dwelling place, and the Bible contains all the necessary papers, duly attested and signed. And our Lord invites us, nay more, commands us to enter in and abide there. In effect He says, "God is your dwelling place, and you must see to it that you take up your abode there. You must move in."

(Hannah Smith, *The God of All Comfort*, Ch. 8 3 Jan. 2002
<http://www.ccel.org/s/smith_hw/comfort/htm/VIII.htm#VIII.)>

"God is your dwelling place, and you must see to it that you take up your abode there. You must move in."

Day: _____ Date: _____ Time: _____ Location: _____

The Umpire Has the Final Word

...Your lack of contentment is because of *pride*. Pride can be described as an excessively high opinion of what one deserves. When a single's life is not moving in the direction she wants (husband, career children, house, etc.), the arguing often begins. With whom is the single woman arguing? It is none other than the umpire, the arbitrator: Jesus. "And let the peace of Christ rule [arbitrate, umpire] in your hearts..." (Col. 3:15).

The struggle with the Umpire is not limited to the single women up to bat! Every woman who has descended from Eve must learn to trust the call of her heavenly Umpire. The trouble from the beginning was a woman not listening to the Umpire, but reaching for a life on "her terms." Why would a woman argue with such an all-wise Umpire? "Pride only breeds quarrels" (Prov. 13:10a NIV).

...Exchange your pride for Jesus' strength so you may accept whatever assignment the Umpire has for you from this moment forward. Dating is not a reward or a prize for living for Jesus. A Friday night without a date is often a night of "being spared" by an all-wise Umpire.

_____

_____

_____

_____

_____

_____

_____

_____

_____

_____

_____

_____

_____

_____

_____

_____

_____

_____

_____

_____

_____

_____

_____

_____

_____

_____

_____

Why would a woman argue with such an all-wise Umpire?

Day: _____ Date: _____ Time: _____ Location: _____

Take the Radical Route

Does it seem too unrealistic for today's woman to set her sights on a knight in shining armor?...A single friend (a modern Ruth) wrote a letter in which she admitted that her high ideals often made her feel like the "Long Ranger." She said, "So often I meet women who don't want to go to the deeper, more radical route of separation from our culture in seeking after God's standards." Do we lower our standards because we seem out of step with all our peers? Does the woman in Proverbs 31 seem obsolete? Maybe for the "cosmopolitan" woman she is obsolete, but not for the Lady of Conviction. God has the best in hand for those who seek Him.

Ruth's choice to wait for God's best resulted in her union with a Boaz rather than a Bozo. Ruth not only married a man who was a "pillar of strength" (Boaz), but she also was blessed by the privilege of bearing a son (Obed) who would be part of the lineage of Jesus Christ. Ruth's wise choices resulted in her experiencing God's overwhelming goodness.

_____

_____

_____

_____

_____

_____

_____

_____

_____

_____

_____

_____

_____

_____

_____

_____

_____

_____

_____

_____

_____

_____

_____

_____

". . . women. . . don't want to go to the deeper,
more radical route of separation from our culture
in seeking after God's standards."

Day: _____ Date: _____ Time: _____ Location: _____

No End to the Wait

Take courage, single friend. You are not alone in your wait; neither are you alone in the feelings and struggles you encounter. Many godly women have waited and won. Many women have lost hope and compromised. Wait patiently and win triumphantly the future your Father has planned for you. It will always be designed with you in mind and is worth being patient to discover.

Ruth was a wonderful example of a Lady of Patience. Ruth did not allow her circumstances or lack of male companionship to cause her to be impatient. Instead she concentrated on developing companionship with her heavenly Father and chose to let Him bring a husband to her if He saw fit. Concern over the ticking of her "biological clock" did not make her fearful of the future. Instead she concentrated on being a lady of character, not on getting a man. She took one day at a time, knowing that God was not bound by circumstances nor her age. She used the wait to become the woman God wanted her to be. At the end of this personal preparation God chose to provide her with a husband.

_____

_____

_____

_____

_____

_____

_____

_____

_____

_____

_____

_____

_____

_____

_____

_____

_____

_____

_____

_____

_____

_____

_____

_____

_____

Many godly women have waited and won.
Many women have lost hope and compromised.

Day: _____ Date: _____ Time: _____ Location: _____

Compromise

Marriage to a non-Christian brings pain to the believing wife. As women, we long to be known and loved for all we are. A man who is spiritually dead can never know the very intimate spiritual part of you that is your heart. He would be blind to much of what you would try to share with him. He could never know and understand you fully.

Be careful when you begin to think that you are "in love" and you "just can't live without him." Think again. Think of the loneliness you will feel when your husband will not attend church with you. Think of the angry bickering that may take place between the two of you because he can never understand the depths of your spiritual awareness and, consequently, your convictions. If you do not think about this now, you may one day think, "Before I couldn't live without him; now I can hardly live with him."...

Please consider a greater consequence than being unhappily married to a man who does not know your Lord....Will it be worth the compromise when your children look up at you and ask why daddy doesn't love Jesus?

_____

_____

_____

_____

_____

_____

_____

_____

_____

_____

_____

_____

_____

_____

_____

_____

_____

_____

_____

_____

_____

_____

_____

_____

_____

_____

. . . you may one day think, "Before I couldn't live without him; now I can hardly live with him."

Day: _____ Date: _____ Time: _____ Location: _____

Hannah Smith

A Lesson in the Interior Life

By rejoicing in Him, however, I do not mean rejoicing in ourselves, although I fear most people think this is really what is meant. It is their feelings or their revelations or their experiences that constitute the groundwork of their joy, and if none of these are satisfactory, they see no possibility of joy at all.

But the lesson the Lord is trying to teach us all the time is the lesson of self-effacement. He commands us to look away from self and all self's experiences, to crucify self and count it dead, to cease to be interested in self, and to know nothing and be interested in nothing but God.

The reason for this is that God has destined us for a higher life than the self-life. That just as He has destined the caterpillar to become the butterfly, and therefore has appointed the caterpillar life to die, in order that the butterfly life may take its place, so He has appointed our self-life to die in order that the divine life may become ours instead. The caterpillar effaces itself in its grub form, that it may evolve or develop into its butterfly form. It dies that it may live. And just so must we.

(Hannah Smith, *The Christian's Secret of a Happy Life* [Christian Witness Co.], Ch. 18. 3 Jan. 2002
<http://www.ccel.org/s/smith_hw/secret/secret21.htm>)

_____

_____

_____

_____

_____

_____

_____

_____

_____

_____

_____

_____

_____

_____

_____

_____

_____

_____

_____

_____

_____

God has destined us for a higher life than the self-life.

Day: _____ Date: _____ Time: _____ Location: _____

Cause and Effect

When you marry, you do not choose blessings or curses for you alone; you choose for the generations after you. If you choose to wait patiently for your knight in shining armor, you will be blessed by the heritage that a prince brings. If you choose to run eagerly ahead of God's plan and marry a man with no conscience toward God, you will reap the life's course he follows, but not alone. Your children's and grandchildren's lives will be directly affected by the man you marry.

…

God warned His people in Deuteronomy of the long-term effect of their choices.…

Deuteronomy 28:2, 15, and 32 show that God has always desired to bless His people, but He will not force them to do what is best. In His Word He has often warned us to wait, to be careful, and to trust Him. He will not make us wait. His heart of love begs us to listen and obey so He may bless us and the dear ones who will one day look to and follow us.…

You must choose to wait patiently for God's best.

_____

_____

_____

_____

_____

_____

_____

_____

_____

_____

_____

_____

_____

_____

_____

_____

_____

_____

_____

_____

_____

_____

_____

_____

_____

_____

_____

_____

You must choose to wait patiently for God's best.

Day: _____ Date: _____ Time: _____ Location: _____

Single Hours

The perfect time to make the most of every opportunity is while you are single. Every believer should use time wisely as Ephesians 5:15-17 (NIV) says....

Rather than staying home worrying about another "dateless" Saturday night, realize how much valuable time has been entrusted to you at this point in your life. Rather than resent your many single hours, embrace them as a gift from God—a package that contains opportunities to serve Him that are limited only by your own self-pity and lack of obedience.

...Countless single women stay home rather than travel alone into the unknown. They not only miss out on being encouraged by others, but also are not exposed to new relationships when they remain at home tied up by cords of fear and feeling sorry for themselves.

If a single woman allows the fearful prospect of meeting new people and new challenges to keep her at home, she may find herself bored and lonely while all the time missing many satisfying and fulfilling experiences....

Are you busy serving Jesus during your free time, or do you waste hours trying to pursue and snag an available guy?

_____

_____

_____

_____

_____

_____

_____

_____

_____

_____

_____

_____

_____

_____

_____

_____

_____

_____

_____

_____

_____

Rather than resent your many single hours,
embrace them as a gift from God. . .

Lady *in* Waiting

Day: _____ Date: _____ Time: _____ Location: _____

Madame Guyon

The Prayer of the Heart

Let all pray: you should live by prayer, as you should live by love. "I counsel you to buy of me gold tried in the fire, that ye may be rich." (Rev. iii. 18.) This is very easily obtained, much more easily than you can conceive.

Come all ye that are athirst to the living waters, nor lose your precious moments in hewing out cisterns that will hold no water. (John vii. 37; Jer. ii. 13.) Come ye famishing souls, who find nought to satisfy you; come, and ye shall be filled! Come, ye poor afflicted ones, bending beneath your load of wretchedness and pain, and ye shall be consoled! Come, ye sick, to your physician, and be not fearful of approaching him because ye are filled with diseases; show them, and they shall be healed!

Children, draw near to your Father, and he will embrace you in the arms of love! Come ye poor, stray, wandering sheep, return to your Shepherd! Come, sinners, to your Saviour! Come ye dull, ignorant, and illiterate, ye who think yourselves the most incapable of prayer! ye are more peculiarly called and adapted thereto. Let all without exception come, for Jesus Christ hath called ALL.

(Madame Jeanne Guyon, *A Short & Very Easy Method of Prayer*, Ch. I. 3 Jan. 2002
<http://www.passtheword.org/DIALOGS-FROM-THE-PAST/methodofprayer.htm>)

256

---

*Children, draw near to your Father, and He will embrace
you in the arms of love! Come ye poor, stray,
wandering sheep, return to your Shepherd!*

Day: _____ Date: _____ Time: _____ Location: _____

Prayer Partner

Do you have a prayer partner? Or do you only have someone with whom you have regular pity parties? If you do not have a prayer partner, ask the Lord right now for such a gift. A prayer partner can help you pray for others....

...Praying regularly with someone (or a small group) is such a vital part of your service to God. To intercede on behalf of someone else's need is a privilege. When you intercede with a partner, the "duet" of harmony before God can change your world. Matthew 18:19 (NIV) describes this harmonious duet: "Again, I tell you that if two of you on earth agree about anything you ask for; it will be done for you by My Father in heaven." That little verb *agree* refers to harmony. Do you have someone with whom you can prayerfully approach God in harmony? Rather than searching for a life-partner, look for a prayer partner. Together you can participate in God-given prayer projects. Together you can discover how you can take your concerns for others and turn them into prayer projects.

_____

_____

_____

_____

_____

_____

_____

_____

_____

_____

_____

_____

_____

_____

_____

_____

_____

_____

_____

_____

_____

_____

_____

_____

_____

When you intercede with a partner, the "duet" of harmony
before God can change your world.

Day: _____ Date: _____ Time: _____ Location: _____

Madame Guyon

Meditative Reading

*There are two ways of introducing a soul into prayer, which
should be pursued for some time; the one is meditation,
the other is reading accompanied by meditation.*

*Meditative reading is the choosing some important practical or
speculative truth, always preferring the practical, and proceeding
thus: whatever truth you have chosen, read only a small portion of it,
endeavoring to taste and digest it, to extract the essence and substance
of it, and proceed no farther while any savor or relish remains in the
passage: then take up your book again, and proceed as before,
seldom reading more than half a page at a time.*

*It is not the quantity that is read, but the manner of reading,
that yields us profit. Those who read fast, reap no more advantage,
than a bee would by only skimming over the surface of the flower,
instead of waiting to penetrate into it, and extract its sweets.
Much reading is rather for scholastic subjects, than divine truths;
to receive profit from spiritual books, we must read as I
have described; and I am certain that if that method were
pursued, we should become gradually habituated to prayer
by our reading, and more fully disposed for its exercise.*

(Madame Jeanne Guyon, *A Short & Very Easy Method of Prayer*, Ch. II. 3 Jan. 2002
<http://www.passtheword.org/DIALOGS-FROM-THE-PAST/methodofprayer.htm>)

_____

_____

_____

_____

_____

_____

_____

_____

_____

_____

_____

_____

_____

_____

_____

It is not the quantity that is read,
but the manner of reading, that yields us profit.

Day: _____ Date: _____ Time: _____ Location: _____

Spiritual Eye Wash

In order to have "eyes of faith," you may have to use a spiritual eye wash to remove the debris that the enemy has dropped into your eyes. The Lady of Faith will have times when her secure eyes of faith begin to blink into an anxious twitch of insecure, sensual sight. She can admit her insecurity to her heavenly Fiancé and He can calm the twitching eyes. Spending some quality time in the Word is the best "eye wash" for "eyes of faith."

…A Lady of Faith…can only be content in this trying situation if she has her "eyes of faith" properly focused on the ultimate relationship—with her heavenly Bridegroom. Datelessness is a common type of debris that irritates the "eyes of faith," but the eye wash treatment—quality time with Jesus and reading His Word—is always effective.

…

One young lady faithfully attended her church for years. Often she needed reminding that "he's just not here yet." God brought her Boaz from across the country to where she was in Florida.…Many tears of faith had washed away the debris that often caused her to doubt if she would ever get married.

_____

_____

_____

_____

_____

_____

_____

_____

_____

_____

_____

_____

_____

_____

_____

_____

_____

_____

_____

_____

_____

_____

_____

_____

*Spending some quality time in the Word is the best
"eye wash" for "eyes of faith."*

Day: _____ Date: _____ Time: _____ Location: _____

Devotion

...It is hard enough for a single woman to keep her focus where it should be without friends making insensitive comments [about not being married]. How much better it would be for the Lady in Waiting if she were encouraged to pursue her undistracted devotion to the Lord Jesus Christ, instead of being made to feel like she does not quite measure up....

Much too often people view a single woman as though she should be pitied rather than envied. Nothing could be further from the truth. A Lady in Waiting has the advantage of being able to develop her love relationship with Christ without the distraction that a husband or family inherently bring to one's heart.

This has been God's plan from the beginning. He tenderly created woman to love Him and to experience the blessedness of fellowship with Him. In those first days, Eve communed with God in indescribable fellowship and oneness. When God came to walk in the cool of the day, there was no fear; only love. Eve had only positive feelings about God. She loved Him and knew He loved her. She enjoyed Him and devoted herself totally to His pleasure.

_____

_____

_____

_____

_____

_____

_____

_____

_____

_____

_____

_____

_____

_____

_____

_____

_____

_____

_____

_____

_____

_____

_____

_____

A Lady in Waiting has the advantage of being able to develop her love relationship with Christ without the distraction...

Day: _____ Date: _____ Time: _____ Location: _____

Amy Carmichael

Amy Carmichael was born December 16, 1867, in Millisle, Northern Ireland, the oldest of three sisters and four brothers. She was raised in the Presbyterian church.

During her adolescence Amy showed signs of a great poetic gift. In 1885 she had a mystical experience that set the course of her spiritual pursuit.

Amy's passion for missions was ignited in 1887 when she heard China Inland Mission founder Hudson Taylor speak. Five years later, God's words "Go ye" were all the confirmation she needed to set her course for foreign lands. She was rejected by C.I.M. because of her frail health, but in 1893 she served the Japanese mission as a "Keswick missionary," and in 1895 she departed for India. Miss Carmichael soon formed the evangelizing "Woman's Band" and took in her first "refugee."

In 1900 she moved to the infamous Dohnavur where she eventually founded the "Dohnavur Fellowship." In 1903 Amy's *Things as They Are* was published, launching her career as a prolific writer. In 1916 she founded "Sisters of Common Life," a spiritual support group.

Miss Carmichael was crippled by a fall in 1931; four years later, she became bedridden. She remained thus until her death on January 18, 1951, and was buried at her beloved Dohnavur.

(<www.heroesofhistory.com/page49.html> as cited in Tommy Tenney, *Mary's Prayers and Martha's Recipes* [Shippensburg, Pennsylvania: Fresh Bread, 2002], pp. 13-14.)

Distractions in Prayer

Sometimes nothing helps so much as to turn from trying to pray, and instead, to read on the knees of the spirit some familiar passage from the

Meditations for the Heart

Bible, for those words have a power in them to effect that of which they speak. Another sure way into peace is found in a literal obedience to Colossians 3:16. Turn a psalm or a hymn into prayer, read or repeat it aloud, for to speak to oneself deep down in one's heart, using words that one knows and loves, is often a wonderfully quickening thing to do, and nothing more quickly and gently leads one into the place of peace, where prayer is born....

Sometimes we cannot find words... do not be afraid of silence in your prayer time. It may be that you are meant to listen, not to speak. So wait before the Lord. Wait in stillness... And in that stillness, assurance will come to you.... You will know that you are heard; you will know that your Lord ponders the voice of your humble desires; you will hear quiet words spoken to you yourself, perhaps to your grateful surprise and refreshment.

(Amy Carmichael, *Thou Givest...They Gather* [Fort Washington, Pennsylvania: Christian Literature Crusade, 1958), pp. 45-48, as cited in Tommy Tenney, *Mary's Prayers and Martha's Recipes* [Shippensburg, Pennsylvania: Fresh Bread, 2002], pp. 14-15.)

_____

_____

_____

_____

_____

_____

_____

Do not be afraid of silence in your prayer time. It may be that you are meant to listen, not to speak.

Day: _____ Date: _____ Time: _____ Location: _____

What's Your View?

…"I [Naomi] went out full, but the Lord has brought me back empty. …the Lord has witnessed against me and the Almighty has afflicted me?' " (Ruth 1:21).

Would you be devoted to a God like Naomi's? In Naomi's bitterness, she no longer referred to God as "the Lord" as she had in verses 8 and 9, but with a title that can cause one to feel alienated and insignificant—"the Almighty." Though Ruth clung to Naomi as a mother, she did not accept her mother-in-law's view of God for herself. ["If we think of Him (God) as cold and exacting, we shall find it impossible to love Him, and our lives will be ridden with servile fear."]*

Your past experiences, present circumstances, or your parents' devotion or lack thereof may cause you to have an incorrect view of God. But nothing and no one can give you a clearer picture of the true God than slipping under His wings and discovering for yourself Who God really is, the refuge for which you long. He desires for you to come again "into the garden" and walk with Him in complete fellowship. This is the fullness of devotion.

*A.W. Tozer, *The Root of the Righteous* (Camp Hill, Pennsylvania: Christian Publishing, Inc. 1985), p. 5, as cited in *Lady In Waiting*.

_____

_____

_____

_____

_____

_____

_____

_____

_____

_____

_____

_____

_____

_____

_____

_____

_____

_____

_____

_____

_____

_____

_____

...nothing and no one can give you a clearer picture of the true God than slipping under His wings and discovering for yourself Who God really is...

Day: _____ Date: _____ Time: _____ Location: _____

Maximizing Fellowship With God

As a single, you have a wonderful opportunity to use your time to maximize your fellowship with God. When you love someone, you give them your heart, the center of your being. God asks for no less. He desires a totally devoted heart. Deuteronomy 6:5 says that you are to love Him with all your heart (deepest devotion), your soul (what you think and what you feel), and your might (your strength and energy).

Many women today are devoted, all right! They have devoted themselves to developing a love relationship, but not with the Lord. They erroneously seek for love in sensations and promises. The world's version of love is something they want to "fall into." Meanwhile, "true love" escapes them. True loves can only be found in undistracted devotion to Jesus Christ.

To love Him like this, you must know Him intimately....It is a personal, intimate knowledge. Do you have a devotion to God that causes people to marvel at how intimately you know Him? Do you know God in a way that causes Him to be an intimate, personal part of your being as you may desire a husband to one day be?

_____

_____

_____

_____

_____

_____

_____

_____

_____

_____

_____

_____

_____

_____

_____

_____

_____

_____

_____

_____

_____

_____

_____

*As a single, you have a wonderful opportunity to use your
time to maximize your fellowship with God.*

Day: _____ Date: _____ Time: _____ Location: _____

Contentment

Whether married or single,…the key to your enjoying this moment deals with your inner contentment….

…

Whether married or single, one must learn that it is Jesus who strengthens you to walk in the most dismal or delightful of circumstances. True contentment is learned. You are not born with it and you cannot buy it at one of Kmart's blue-light specials. Your classroom for learning is your daily life. Every shattered dream or unfulfilled expectation serves as a perfect opportunity to learn contentment. These circumstances are your classroom assignments for learning the mystery of contentment. Learning contentment will require complete dependence upon Jesus, for difficult circumstances without the strength of Jesus can rob you of potential contentment. Do not be deceived into thinking you do not need Jesus' strength to face the good circumstances as well as the bad. When the sun is shining with no clouds in sight, you may assume that you can securely bask in the sunshine without any prospect of rain; however, this full feeling can easily breed a tendency to ignore Jesus. "Otherwise, I may have too much and disown you and say, 'Who is the Lord?' " (Prov. 30:9a NIV)

_____

_____

_____

_____

_____

_____

_____

_____

_____

_____

_____

_____

_____

_____

_____

_____

_____

_____

_____

_____

_____

_____

_____

_____

*Every shattered dream or unfulfilled expectation serves as a
perfect opportunity to learn contentment.*

Day: _____ Date: _____ Time: _____ Location: _____

The Place of Rest

You don't know what tomorrow holds, but you do know who holds tomorrow. Say this with the psalmist:

O Lord, my heart is not proud, nor my eyes haughty; nor do I involved myself in great matters, or in things too difficult for me. Surely I have composed and quieted my soul; like a weaned child rests against his mother, my soul is like a weaned child within me. O [substitute your name], hope in the Lord from this time forth and forever (Psalm 131).

The place of rest that the psalmist found was a result of the choice he made. This quietness of soul did not come naturally to him. He actively chose to take himself out of involvement and quiet his soul (his mind, will, and emotions). He chose to put his hope in God. Are you trying to involve yourself in matters that are too great for you? Can you see into a man's heart? Can you know the future? You know Someone who does know men's hearts and the future. Patiently rest against His chest. He will bring you the peace you need....By an act of your will you must choose to trust God regardless of what happens.

_____

_____

_____

_____

_____

_____

_____

_____

_____

_____

_____

_____

_____

_____

_____

_____

_____

_____

_____

_____

_____

_____

_____

By an act of your will you must choose to trust God
regardless of what happens.

Day: _____ Date: _____ Time: _____ Location: _____

Madame Guyon

Prayer Divinely Explained

Prayer is the effusion of the heart in the
presence of God: "I have poured out my soul before
the Lord," said the mother of Samuel.
(1 Sam. i. 15.) The prayer of the wise men at the feet of Christ in
the stable of Bethlehem, was signified by the incense they offered.

Prayer is a certain warmth of love, melting,
dissolving, and sublimating the soul, and causing it to ascend unto God,
and, as the soul is melted, odors rise from it; and these sweet exhalations
proceed from the consuming fire of love within.

This is illustrated in the Canticles, [Song of Solomon] i. 12, where
the spouse says, "While the king sitteth at his table, my spikenard
sendeth forth the smell thereof." The table is the
centre of the soul; and when God is there, and we know how to dwell
near, and abide with Him, the sacred presence gradually dissolves
the hardness of the soul, and, as it melts, fragrance issues forth;
hence it is, that the Beloved says of his spouse, in seeing her soul
melt when he spoke, "Who is this that cometh out of the wilderness,
like pillars of smoke perfumed with myrrh and frankincense?"
(Cant. [Song of Solomon] v. 6; iii. 6.)

(Madame Jeanne Guyon, *A Short & Very Easy Method of Prayer*, Ch. XX. 3 Jan. 2002
<http://www.passtheword.org/DIALOGS-FROM-THE-PAST/methodofprayer.htm>)

_____

_____

_____

_____

_____

_____

_____

_____

_____

_____

_____

_____

_____

_____

_____

_____

_____

_____

_____

Prayer is the effusion of the heart in the presence of God.

Day: _____ Date: _____ Time: _____ Location: _____

Consider…Your Friends

When Ruth told Naomi, "your people shall be my people," she under-stood that she would not be able to grow closer to the God of Israel if she remained among the Moabites (her own people). Ironically, God called Moab His washbasin (see Ps. 60:8; 108:9). One rinses dirt off in a wash-basin. Ruth chose to leave the washbasin and head for Bethlehem which means the "house of bread."*

Even today there exist "Moabites" who will undermine your growth if you spend too much time with them.…Realizing that one's friends drive you either toward or away from God, you may need to find a "new people" who will encourage your growth and not hinder it.…

…When a woman stops growing spiritually, the lack of progress can often be traced back to a friendship that undermined her commitment to Jesus.

Take a moment to think about the spiritual depth of the girlfriend who influences you the most. Is she daily becoming all that Jesus desires? If so, her growth will challenge you to grow. On the other hand, her apathy may ultimately be contagious.

*Scofield Bible (New York: Oxford University Press, 1967), p. 51, as cited in *Lady In Waiting*.

_____

_____

_____

_____

_____

_____

_____

_____

_____

_____

_____

_____

_____

_____

_____

_____

_____

_____

_____

_____

...one's friends drive you either toward or away from God...

Day: _____ Date: _____ Time: _____ Location: _____

Behavior Patterns

Part of reckless abandonment is realizing how much our culture has affected our behavior patterns. You want to be Christlike, but your *lifestyle* is a reflection of *Vogue* magazine or *Cosmopolitan* rather a new creation in Christ. A.W. Tozer said, "A whole new generation of Christians has come up believing that it is possible to 'accept' Christ without forsaking the world."* Ruth had to forsake the familiar and comfortable in order to receive God's best for her life.

. . .

One single was persecuted, not by non-Christians but by Christians, because she chose to spend her summer studying at a Bible Institute rather than playing in the sunshine with her friends. They actually accused her of thinking she was better than them because she planned to study the Bible intensively for eight weeks. Unfortunately, our self-centered culture in America has penetrated the Church so much that a young woman not only has to choose against the American culture, but sometimes against the more subtle, worldly Christian subculture tainting the Body of Christ.

*A.W. Tozer, *The Pursuit of God*. (Camp Hill, Pennsylvania: Christian Publishing, Inc., 1982), p. 16, as cited in *Lady In Waiting*.

_____

_____

_____

_____

_____

_____

_____

_____

_____

_____

_____

_____

_____

_____

_____

_____

_____

_____

_____

_____

_____

_____

_____

_____

*Part of reckless abandonment is realizing
how much our culture has affected our behavior patterns.*

Day: _____ Date: _____ Time: _____ Location: _____

Imitations

There are many imitations of a true pearl, but with years, the shiny pearl paint cracks and wears off and all that is left is an unattractive bead hanging on a string. God's Spirit, however, produces true inner beauty, as you confess your sin, avoid displeasing God's Spirit, obey even the slightest of His promptings, and give the Holy Spirit full control of your life. Pearls of godly character take time to develop, but how blessed is the woman adorned by them.

You can settle for an imitation necklace of fake pearls by trying to simply cover over ungodly character, or you can allow the Holy Spirit to use the sands of singleness to create the real thing. If you want a cheap imitation, a modeling or charm school will be sufficient for what you seek. But if you want genuine pearls, you must allow the Holy Spirit to perform a special work in your life. Determine to string lovely pearl "necklace of virtue" as a treasure for your Lord.

"Providing lasting pleasure
potential beyond measure,
the rarest of treasure,
a reputation of virtuous character."
JMK

_____

_____

_____

_____

_____

_____

_____

_____

_____

_____

_____

_____

_____

_____

_____

_____

_____

_____

_____

_____

_____

_____

_____

*. . . if you want genuine pearls, you must allow the Holy
Spirit to perform a special work in your life.*

Day: _____ Date: _____ Time: _____ Location: _____

The Mom Maneuver

Another form of maneuvering is to become the guy's "mom." Insecure females all too often deceive themselves into thinking that because they do so much for a particular young man, they will surely win his love. *Wrong!* It is easy for a man, whether he is young or old, to let a woman sacrifice for him. Why? Most men are used to the sacrifices of a woman. Good ol' mom has been sacrificing for him since the womb. Sure, the young man will say, "Thanks," but young men do not marry their mothers! When a woman does something nice for a certain guy, he usually does not spend the rest of the day thinking about her unselfish service (he may be accustomed to receiving). The woman may begin to feel used.

Some women prepare meals, sew on buttons, and wash the guy's clothes—all the things a mom would do—assuming all this is practice for their future together. Inevitably, the man she has served so unselfishly may fall for a girl who can't bake or sew and thinks you take all the clothes to the dry cleaners that "fluff and fold."

_____

_____

_____

_____

_____

_____

_____

_____

_____

_____

_____

_____

_____

_____

_____

_____

_____

_____

Most men are used to the sacrifices of a woman.

Day: _____ Date: _____ Time: _____ Location: _____

Man Hunt

To quit the hunt and stop "going after the guys," you must first avoid maneuvering and manipulating. Ruth did, and God can give you the grace to do it too. Believe that God will take care of you regardless of your circumstances. Don't put your own devices to work. You can only see the outward man from today's perspective. God sees men's hearts from the perspective of eternity. With His perspective, He can see much better what you need. Trust Him and let Him show you His dependable love for you.

Second, you must put your security in Christ. He longs for you to be secure in His love. He wants to protect, lead, and love you. To develop security, give your heart and emotions to the Lord....

...To build security into your life, spend time in God's Word....

By spending time in God's Word, you will also learn what God thinks of you....

You are very special to God—so special that He has plans for you....

Do not allow insecurity to motivate you to maneuver or manipulate your relationships. Instead of hunting for a husband or boyfriend, concentrate on becoming a woman of excellence....

_____

_____

_____

_____

_____

_____

_____

_____

_____

_____

_____

_____

_____

_____

_____

_____

_____

_____

_____

_____

_____

_____

Instead of hunting for a husband or boyfriend,
concentrate on becoming a woman of excellence....

Day: _____ Date: _____ Time: _____ Location: _____

Julian of Norwich

Loved of God

*For as the body is clad in the cloth, and the
flesh in the skin, and the bones in the flesh, and the heart in the
whole, so are we, soul and body, clad in the Goodness
of God, and enclosed. Yea,
and more homely: for all these may waste and wear away,
but the Goodness of God is ever whole; and more near to us,
without any likeness; for truly our Lover desireth that our soul
cleave to Him with all its might, and that we be evermore
cleaving to His Goodness. For of all things that heart may think,
this pleaseth most God, and soonest speedeth the soul.*

*For our soul is so specially loved of Him that is highest, that it
overpasseth the knowing of all creatures: that is to say, there is
no creature that is made that may fully know how much and how
sweetly and how tenderly our Maker loveth us. And therefore
we may with grace and His help stand in spiritual beholding, with
everlasting marvel of this high, overpassing, inestimable Love
that Almighty God hath to us of His Goodness. And therefore
we may ask of our Lover with reverence all that we will.*

*For our natural Will is to have God, and the Good Will of God is
to have us; and we may never cease from willing nor from longing till
we have Him in fullness of joy: and then may we no more desire.*

Meditations for the Heart

*For He willeth that we be occupied in knowing and loving till the time
that we shall be fulfilled in Heaven; and therefore was this lesson of
Love shewed, with all that followeth, as ye shall see. For the strength and
the Ground of all was shewed in the First Sight. For of all things the
beholding and the loving of the Maker maketh the soul to seem less
in his own sight, and most filleth him with reverent dread and true
meekness; with plenty of charity to his even-Christians.*

(Julian of Norwich, *Revelations of Divine Love*. Grace Warrack, ed. [London: Methuen & Co. Ltd., 1901] Ch. VI
7 Jan. 2002 <http://www.ccel.org/j/julian/revelations/revelations.html>)

_____

_____

_____

_____

_____

_____

_____

_____

_____

_____

_____

_____

*"For as the body is clad in the cloth, and the flesh in the skin,
and the bones in the flesh, and the heart in the whole, so are
we, soul and body, clad in the Goodness of God."*

Day: _____ Date: _____ Time: _____ Location: _____

Sabotage!

...realize that a single woman can sabotage her own contentment by defrauding herself. A single woman can defraud herself as effectively as her male counterpart. Protect your contentment by adopting this "Eleventh Commandment": Thou shalt not defraud thyself.

Women defraud themselves by confusing ministry with matrimony. A guy tries to help a girl grow spiritually, and she sees his care and interest as leading inevitably to marriage. Another guy and girl work on a ministry team together and their spiritual intimacy is confused in her mind with romantic intentions.

Misread intentions between males and females put them on a collision course. The crash can be avoided if the Lady of Contentment would keep in mind that her emotions must be submitted to the facts: ministering together is a privilege as a believer, not an automatic marriage opportunity. Daily, throughout the world, women's hearts are broken because they allow their emotions to run ahead of commitments. Women, young and old, seem to resist controlling their emotions. As a result, they end up emotional cripples, angry at the men who failed to live up to their emotional fantasies.

_____

_____

_____

_____

_____

_____

_____

_____

_____

_____

_____

_____

_____

_____

_____

_____

_____

_____

_____

_____

_____

*. . .a single woman can sabotage her own contentment
by defrauding herself.*

Day: _____ Date: _____ Time: _____ Location: _____

Reality vs. Fantasy

An important method of limiting your own self-defrauding is through daily discipline over "prenuptial fantasies." Such fantasies may provide you an escape from monotonous reality, but these moments are dangerous. They will aggravate your struggle for contentment because they are not innocent daydreams, but an attack on your godly contentment. You may be so used to daily fantasies that you might not even realize when you begin daydreaming again about your prince.

Often a single woman's struggle with contentment can be traced back to her fantasies more than to her frustrating circumstances. Just think for a moment about three words from Second Corinthians 10:5 (KJV): "Casting down imaginations." Fantasizing about a future with guy you have been watching in Sunday school or at work is nothing more than your very active imagination. What should you do when you start daydreaming about a guy you've never dated or even formally met? You must take your thoughts to Jesus and leave them in His capable hands. This daily discipline of taking your fantasies to Jesus is the foundation for your future as a contented woman, whether you are married or single.

_____

_____

_____

_____

_____

_____

_____

_____

_____

_____

_____

_____

_____

_____

_____

_____

_____

_____

_____

_____

_____

_____

_____

_____

You may be so used to daily fantasies that you might not even realize when you begin daydreaming again about your prince.

Day: _____ Date: _____ Time: _____ Location: _____

Jessie Penn-Lewis

The Presence of God

"Oh God when Thou wentest forth before Thy people, when Thou didst march through the wilderness, the earth shook, the heavens also dropped at the Presence of God: even Sinai itself was moved at the Presence of God." (Psalm lxviii. 7-8)

What a glorious ringing shout of triumph there is in these words! They seem to vividly picture the victorious march of an all-conquering King with everything going down before Him. Habakkuk gives us the same conception of the all-victorious Presence of Jehovah. "Thou didst march through the land....for victory with Thine Anointed."
(Hab. iii. 13 R.V.)

The manifested Presence of God will alone move the "Sinais." How foolish we are to attempt to "push" them. The walls of Jericho fell down without one single push, yet we seem to think we must do our little best and then God will do the rest. Nay, it is "stand still and see the salvation of God." It is the manifested Presence of Jehovah we need; He must march forth before us and the biggest "Sinai" will be moved before Him. Oh the "Sinais"! How we groan over them! That Sinai of self, will it never go? That idol we have surrendered so often and yet there it stands still the same! That Sinai in our Christian work, and many others known best to God and ourselves. How we take our little spades, do our little best, push and push, dig and dig, failing utterly to make the least impression.

Meditations for the Heart

"Oh God…when Thou wentest forth…even Sinai itself…!"

It is the Presence of God we need. How can we obtain His Presence, thus moving so gloriously before us?

We must first be willing for His manifested Presence in us.

(Jessie Penn-Lewis, "The Presence of God," *The Overcomer* [January, 1929], p.1.)

_____

_____

_____

_____

_____

_____

_____

_____

_____

_____

_____

_____

_____

"It is the manifested Presence of Jehovah we need;
He must march forth before us and the biggest
'Sinai' will be moved before Him."

Day: _____ Date: _____ Time: _____ Location: _____

Wisdom and Grace

How many times a week do you find yourself in a position where some-one has shared a need with you and you want so much to respond with wisdom and grace? Isaiah 50:4 (NIV) says, "The Sovereign Lord has given me an instructed tongue, to know the word that sustains the weary. He wakens me morning by morning, wakens my ear to listen like one being taught." Do you have a hard time responding to such an early wake-up call? Rising early to develop the tongue of a disciple will open a door of ministry to those who are weary, whether they are at work, at church, or even at the grocery store. Your very words will be a ministry of healing and encouragement. "The tongue that brings healing is a tree of life, but a deceitful tongue crushes the spirit" (Prov. 15:4 NIV). Such predawn training will give you the privilege of becoming God's garden hose in a land of many thirsty people.

. . .

...purchase some pre-stamped postcards and try to send them regularly to different people who need a refreshing word. The Lord wants you to be involved in the lives of those around you....

_____

_____

_____

_____

_____

_____

_____

_____

_____

_____

_____

_____

_____

_____

_____

_____

_____

_____

_____

_____

_____

_____

_____

. . . predawn training will give you the privilege of becoming
God's garden hose in a land of many thirsty people.

Day: _____ Date: _____ Time: _____ Location: _____

Check Your Heart

If the Lord wants to give you a man, He does not need your clever "chance rendezvous." This is not advocating that you avoid men completely and expect the Lord to "UPS" His choice to your front door. You need to participate in activities that involve men and women, but be sensitive to your motives whenever you find yourself in the presence of "available men." Consider this Scripture whenever checking your motives and your pulse! Proverbs 16:2 (NIV) says, "All a man's ways seem innocent to him, but motives are weighed by the Lord."

You can prevent disappointing moments if you check your heart whenever you go to a singles' activity. Much preparation (like taking a shower, putting on makeup, styling your hair, doing your nails, and choosing the perfect outfit) precedes one's attending such an activity, yet so little heart preparation does. The gal with sensual sight can become so obsessed with finding her guy that she neglects her inner self. Orpah's style (logical sight) tends to become the norm, but Ruth offers an alternative to this vain search for Mr. Right. She demonstrates what it means to be a Lady of Faith.

_____

_____

_____

_____

_____

_____

_____
_____
_____
_____
_____
_____
_____
_____
_____
_____
_____
_____
_____
_____
_____
_____
_____
_____

You can prevent disappointing moments if you check your heart whenever you go to a singles' activity.

Day: _____ Date: _____ Time: _____ Location: _____

Eyes of Faith

...Ruth certainly must have considered the probability of remaining single if she went with Naomi. Even though it promised no prospects of a husband, she chose to follow Naomi and her God back to Bethlehem. Ruth chose to trust God with her future. She looked not with sensual sight, but through "eyes of faith." Even though Ruth was young in her faith in the God of Israel, she chose to trust with her heart for the future her eyes could not yet see.

...Your hope cannot be put in some dreamed-up future. It must be in the God who knows your past, present, and future, and loves you enough to give you the best.

...

Do you long to please Him? Then reconsider your circumstances and realize that what seems to be a hopeless situation (no prospects on the horizon) is just the flip side of the view through "eyes of faith."

Sometimes in an attempt to be a Lady of Faith, one can get sidetracked trying to hurry the "male order delivery" process.

...God knows when your heart aches for these precious things. But He also knows that these earthly things will not make you secure.

_____

_____

_____

_____

_____

_____

_____

_____

_____

_____

_____

_____

_____

_____

_____

_____

_____

_____

_____

_____

_____

_____

_____

Your hope cannot be put in some dreamed-up future.

Day: _____ Date: _____ Time: _____ Location: _____

Pearl of Great Price

One of life's most costly and beautiful objects is born out of pain and irritation—the pearl. A tiny piece of sand slips into an oyster's shell and begins to rub against the soft tissue, causing irritation. In response to the irritation, the oyster produces a hard substance. This substance eventually develops into one of the world's most beautiful jewels—a lovely luminous pearl. In fact, the greater the irritation, the more valuable the pearl!

...

Many single women view themselves as ugly oyster shells lying on the beaches of life, beset with the trials and problems that come with not being married. To make matters worse, they compare their crusty exterior to all the beautiful seashells around them and wonder how any man could ever give his attention to them.

If you are one of these women, be encouraged. Don't view the trials of singleness as irritating grains of sand to be discarded as quickly as possible. Realize that God has them there to create something beautiful in you....

God is using the sands of singleness to make you perfect and complete. He's developing pearls of character in your life.

_____

_____

_____

_____

_____

_____

Meditations for the Heart

_____

_____

_____

_____

_____

_____

_____

_____

_____

_____

_____

_____

_____

_____

_____

_____

The greater the irritation, the more valuable the pearl!

Day: _____ Date: _____ Time: _____ Location: _____

Virtue Is Irresistible

...If you attract a guy with only your looks, then you are headed for trouble, since looks don't last. As time goes on, we all end up looking like oysters. Therefore, what you look like on the inside is far more important than what you look like on the outside.

...What enabled Ruth to catch Boaz's attention? Was it her gorgeous hair or beautiful eyes? No! The answer is found in Boaz's response to her question in Ruth chapter 2.

> *Then she fell on her face, bowing to the ground and said to him,*
> *'Why have I found favor in your sight that you should take notice of*
> *me, since I am a foreigner?' And Boaz answered and said to her,*
> *'All that you have done for your mother-in-law after the death of*
> *your husband has been fully reported to me, and how you left your*
> *father and mother and the land of your birth, and came to a people*
> *that you did not previously know (Ruth 2:10-11).*

Boaz was attracted to the virtue or character displayed in Ruth's life. A woman of virtue is irresistible to a godly man.

_____

_____

_____

_____

_____

_____

_____

_____

_____

_____

_____

_____

_____

_____

_____

_____

_____

_____

_____

_____

_____

_____

_____

_____

_____

_____

_____

_____

A woman of virtue is irresistible to a godly man.

Day: _____ Date: _____ Time: _____ Location: _____

Hannah More

Religion of the Heart

*God is the fountain from which all streams of goodness flow.
He is the center from which all rays of blessedness shine. All
our actions are, therefore, only good insofar as they have a
reference to Him: the streams must revert to their Fountain,
the rays must converge again to their Center.*

*If love for God is the governing principle, this powerful spring will
actuate all the movements of the reasonable creature. The essence of
religious faith does not so much consist in actions as in affections.
Though right actions may be performed where there are not right
affections, they are a mere carcass, utterly devoid of soul, and
therefore, of virtue. On the other hand, genuine affections
cannot substantially and truly exist without producing right actions.
Let it never be forgotten that a devout inclination which does not
have life and vigor enough to ripen into action when the occasion
presents itself has no place in the account of real goodness.*

*What a model for our humble imitation is that divine Person who was
clothed with our humanity! He dwelt among us so that the pattern might
be rendered more engaging and conformity to it made more practicable.
His life was one of unbroken, universal charity. He never forgot that we
are compounded both of soul and body, and after teaching the multitude,
He fed them. He repulsed none for being ignorant, was impatient with
none for being dull, despised none for being loathed by the world, and*

Meditations for the Heart

He rejected none for being sinners. Our Lord encouraged those whose
forgiveness others criticized; in healing sicknesses He
converted souls; He gave bread and forgave injuries. Christians must
seek to express their morning devotions in their actions through the day.

(Hannah More, *The Religion of the Heart*, [Burlington, New Jersey: D. Allinson & Co., 1811], updated by
Donald L. Milam, Jr., pp. 27, 33, 85-86, as cited in Tommy Tenney, *Mary's Prayers and Martha's Recipes*
[Shippensburg, Pennsylvania: Fresh Bread, 2002], pp. 18-19.)

_____

_____

_____

_____

_____

_____

_____

_____

_____

_____

_____

_____

_____

_____

God is the fountain from which all streams of goodness flow.
He is the center from which all rays of blessedness shine.

Day: _____ Date: _____ Time: _____ Location: _____

Inward Beauty

The key to beauty is found in First Peter 3:4 (NIV): "Instead, it should be that of your inner self, the unfading beauty of a gentle and quiet spirit, which is of great worth in God's sight." This kind of beauty can only get better the older it gets....

When you look at the virtuous woman of Proverbs 31:10-31, you will see God's picture of a beautiful woman. There are 20 verses describing her. Only one verse mentions her outward appearance. If you were to spend 1/20 of your time on outward physical beauty and the other 19/20 on developing the other qualities God describes as beautiful, such as wisdom, kindness, and godliness, you would become the excellent woman Proverbs 31:10 says a man should try to find.

...King Solomon said in Proverbs 31:30 (NIV)..."Charm is deceptive, and beauty is fleeting; but a woman who fears the Lord is to be praised." There are many women who fear pimples, wrinkles, flabby thighs, and crow's feet, but very few women who really fear the Lord. With which are you attractive to men: the snares of Proverbs 5, 6, and 7, or the beauty of First Peter 3:4?

_____

_____

_____

_____

_____

_____

_____

_____

_____

_____

_____

_____

_____

_____

_____

_____

_____

_____

_____

_____

_____

_____

_____

_____

When you look at the virtuous woman of Proverbs 31:10-31,
you will see God's picture of a beautiful woman.

Day: _____ Date: _____ Time: _____ Location: _____

Two-Way Conversation

Have you ever tried to develop an intimate relationship with Jana Jabberbox? She's the gal who has lots to say and loves to hear herself say it. You try to say something when she takes a breath—which isn't often—but she keeps right on talking. She never listens. It's a one-way conversation, and you are left out. Even when someone is very special to you, you do not get too excited with a steady monologue. Listening is an important part of developing a closeness with someone else. If you want to get to know the Lord, you must seek Him not only with a whole, clean, and pure heart, but also with a listening heart.

As you spend time with God during your daily devotional time, learn to listen to Him as you read of His love and thoughts about you in the Bible. Think about what He is saying to you personally. Sit silently and write what impressions come to your listening heart. As you read and study His love letters, the Bible, you begin to see what He really thinks of you and what wonderful plans He has for you. As a result, your devotion grows and grows.

_____

_____

_____

_____

_____

_____

_____

_____

_____

_____

_____

_____

_____

_____

_____

_____

_____

_____

_____

_____

_____

_____

_____

If you want to get to know the Lord, you must seek Him
not only with a whole, clean, and pure heart, but
also with a listening heart.

Day: _____ Date: _____ Time: _____ Location: _____

Hannah Smith

The Lord Our Dwelling Place

"Lord, thou hast been our dwelling place in all generations."

The comfort or discomfort of our outward lives depends more largely upon the dwelling place of our bodies than upon almost any other material thing; and the comfort or discomfort of our inward life depends similarly upon the dwelling place of our souls.

Our dwelling place is the place where we live, and not the place we merely visit. It is our home. All the interests of our earthly lives are bound up in our home; and we do all we can to make them attractive and comfortable. But our souls need a comfortable dwelling place even more than our bodies; inward comfort, as we all know, is of far greater importance than outward; and, where the soul is full of peace and joy, outward surroundings are of comparatively little account.

It is of vital importance, then, that we should find out definitely where our souls are living. The Lord declares that He has been our dwelling place in all generations, but the question is, Are we living in our dwelling place? The psalmist says of the children of Israel that "they wandered in the wilderness, in a solitary way; they found no city to dwell in. Hungry and thirsty, their soul fainted in them." And I am afraid there are many wandering souls in the church of Christ, whom this description of the wandering Israelites would exactly fit. All their Christian lives they have been wandering in a spiritual wilderness, and have found no city to dwell in, and, hungry and thirsty, their souls have fainted in them. And yet all the while the dwelling place of God has been standing wide open, inviting them to come in and take up their abode there forever. Our Lord Himself urges this invitation upon us. "Abide in me," He says, "and I in you"; and He goes on to tell us what are the blessed results of this abiding, and what are the sad consequences of not abiding.

The truth is, our souls are made for God. He is our natural home, and we can never be at rest anywhere else. "My soul longeth, yea, even fainteth for the courts of the Lord; my heart and my flesh crieth out for the living God." We always shall hunger and faint for the courts of the Lord, as long as we fail to take up our abode there.

(Hannah Smith, *The God of All Comfort*, Ch. 8. 3 Jan. 2002
<http://www.ccel.org/s/smith_hev/comfort/htm/VIII.htm#VIII>)

_____

_____

_____

_____

_____

_____

_____

_____

_____

The truth is, our souls are made for God. He is our natural home, and we can never be at rest anywhere else.

Day: _____ Date: _____ Time: _____ Location: _____

The Answer to Life

Whenever a single woman decides to abandon herself completely to Jesus, as Ruth did, she will find herself out of step with society and, sometimes even with her friends. A single woman today needs the boldness to challenge and break the cycle of the "American way" that exalts a relationship with a man as the answer to life. This "American way" blurs the reality of the ultimate answer to life found in a deep relationship with Jesus Christ...

Often a woman will attempt to find delight in a career if Mr. Right has not arrived. In time, even her "great career" will prove to be less than satisfying. A career, marriage, or even motherhood is not enough to totally satisfy you by itself. God knows that you will never be complete until you really understand that you are complete in Jesus. Colossians 2: 9-10 says, "For in Him all the fullness of Deity dwells in bodily form, ...and in Him you have been made complete, and He is the head over all rule and authority."

When a single woman enters a career or even marriage without understanding that she is complete in Christ, she will be disillusioned and dissatisfied.

_____

_____

_____

_____

_____

_____

_____

_____

_____

_____

_____

_____

_____

_____

_____

_____

_____

_____

_____

_____

_____

_____

_____

_____

*. . . the "American way" . . . exalts a relationship with a man
as the answer to life.*

Day: _____ Date: _____ Time: _____ Location: _____

Do You Believe the Lie?

Why do women feel they have to go after the men? Many women have believed a lie. They think, "I must get the best for myself because God may not give it to me." What do you think would have been the outcome of Ruth's life if she had chosen to believe this lie? Would she have returned home with Orpah and married one of the local guys? Would she have followed Naomi to a new land, but taken control of her own destiny in choosing a mate to care for herself and her mother-in-law?...

Ladies, God gives you the choice between His plans and yours. In the midst of her circumstances, Ruth could not have possibly seen that a man like Boaz would one day be her prince. Neither can you with your limited perspective see who or where your prince will be. Only God has all things in view....Don't look back one day and regret that you made your "life mate" choice from a limited perspective because you longed for the security of a relationship. God can and will give you His best if you wait for it.

_____

_____

_____

_____

_____

_____

_____

_____

_____

_____
_____
_____
_____
_____
_____
_____
_____
_____
_____
_____
_____
_____
_____
_____
_____
_____
_____
_____
_____

Only God has all things in view.

Day: _____ Date: _____ Time: _____ Location: _____

The Motive Check

...Before you go to another activity to spend time with the available guys, as you check your hair and makeup and teeth, give yourself a thorough "heart flossing."...A woman with selfish motivation mentally plots the next maneuver to capture the attention of the man of her dreams. Ask the Lord to reveal any impure motive that resides in your heart...This is not to say that you cannot do nice things for a man; it is simply a warning to check your motives...Before you bake one more thing for a brother or purchase one more book or meaningful card, be very careful to check your motive and honestly respond to whatever the Lord shows you. You can save yourself many tears and much frustration if you are just willing to do a regular "motive check" on your heart.

Manipulation and maneuvering can be deadly. If you maneuver to get a man, you will have to maneuver to keep him! This is not implying that there is no work involved in a good relationship, but there is a huge difference between working and maneuvering. You recognize the difference between the two by discerning your motive.

_____

_____

_____

_____

_____

_____

_____

_____

_____

_____

_____

_____

_____

_____

_____

_____

_____

_____

_____

_____

_____

_____

_____

_____

_____

You can save yourself many tears and much frustration if you are just willing to do a regular "motive check" on your heart.

Lady *in* Waiting
Study Guide

DEVELOPING YOUR LOVE RELATIONSHIPS

Contents

Dearest Lady,

It is our prayer that the Meditation Journal and Study Guide will help you apply the thoughts and principles in *Lady in Waiting* to your personal life; thus helping you to succeed in your search for life's best.

You can use this Study Guide as an individual or in a group of any size. We recommend that after you read *Lady in Waiting* through once, then go through it again, chapter by chapter, with this Study Guide.

The final pages in this Study Guide are intended for your use in journaling—for writing your thoughts and prayers. You may want to use these pages after completing the Study Guide, or as you work through it.

The questions in this Study Guide are very personal. Thus, when you answer them, this book actually becomes another sort of journal. If you are using this Study Guide in a group setting, then you may or may not want to share your answers, but honest interaction in a group setting is of great benefit to everyone involved.

May the true King draw you ever closer to His heart.

—Jackie Kendall and Debby Jones

Lady in Waiting

is not about finding the right man,
but becoming the right woman.

The Lady in Waiting
recklessly abandons herself
to the Lordship of Christ,
diligently uses her single days,
trusts God with unwavering faith,
demonstrates virtue in daily life,
loves God with undistracted devotion,
stands for physical and emotional purity,
lives in security,
responds to life in contentment,
makes choices based on her convictions,
and waits patiently for God to meet her needs.

Ruth's Reckless Abandonment

In the Book of Ruth, a young widow made a critical decision to turn her back on her people, her country, and her gods because her thirsty soul had tasted of the God of Israel. With just a "taste," she recklessly abandoned herself to the only true God. She willingly broke her alabaster box and followed the Lord wherever He would lead her.

But Ruth said, "Do not urge me to leave you or turn back from following you; for where you go, I will go, and where you lodge, I will lodge. Your people shall be my people, and your God, my God" (Ruth 1:16).

Ruth had a determined heart, and the Lord honored her faith in moving away from all that was familiar and taking a journey toward the completely unknown. Ruth did not allow her friends, her old surroundings, or her culture's dead faith to keep her from running hard after God. She did not use the excuse of a dark past to keep her from a bright future that began with her first critical choice: reckless abandonment to the Lord God.

Lady of Reckless Abandonment

I. Read Ruth chapter 1.

1. What is happening in these two women's lives? _____

_____

_____

_____

2. How do the women feel? _____

_____

_____

_____

3. How do they respond to this time of crisis in their lives? _____

_____

_____

_____

4. What are their choices? _____

_____

_____

_____

their plans? _____

_____

_____

their hopes? _____

_____

_____

5. What are their dreams for the future? _____

_____

_____

_____

6. How do they respond to each other? _____

_____

_____

_____

7. What do you identify with? _____

_____

_____

_____

8. How can Ruth remain strong during such hardship? _____

_____

_____

_____

II. "Ruth moved from a false religion into the only true and eternal relationship. Too many women have been involved in a form of religious worship, but have never had a vital, growing relationship with Jesus."

1. What is the difference between religion and a relationship?_____

_____

_____

2. Read Isaiah 29:13 (NIV). Does this verse describe your religious experience? Why or why not? _____

_____

_____

3. Read John 3:16. How can one enter into a personal relationship with God? _____

_____

_____

_____

4. Describe how you entered into a personal relationship with the Lord. (If you are unsure that you have already done so or wish to make that choice, turn to page 9 for the good news of how you can trade religion for a vital relationship with God.) _____

_____

_____

_____

5. Which would make hard circumstances easier to live with: a religion of works or a relationship with a God who cares and helps? Why? _____

_____

_____

_____

6. How do you know from Chapter 1 of the Book of Ruth that Ruth's response to God was personal? What verses support your answer? _____

_____

_____

_____

"No one, not even the man you will marry one day,
can make you happy—only Jesus can."

III. "Too many Christian women think that the inner longings of their hearts relate only to love, marriage, and motherhood or career."

1. What do you think about this statement? _____

_____

_____

2. Do women long for something constant, something that will satisfy deep heart longings? _____

_____

_____

_____

Why? _____

_____

_____

What are some examples? _____

_____

_____

3. Discuss how each of the following can or cannot satisfy a woman's deepest needs. _____

_____

_____

_____

Possessions: _____

_____

_____

Positions: _____

_____

_____

People: _____

_____

_____

4. Have you assumed that your ultimate fulfillment would be found in things? a position? a relationship? marriage? children? Explain. _____

_____

_____

_____

5. Why can these never completely satisfy you? _____

_____

_____

_____

"You were not created to complete another,

but to complement. Completion is Jesus' responsibility and

complementing is a woman's privilege. A woman not complete

in Jesus will be a drain on her husband. Such a woman will

expect her husband to fill the gap that only Jesus can fill."

IV. Read Luke 7:36-50.

As explained in *Lady in Waiting*, the family of a young woman of marriageable age would give her an alabaster box filled with precious ointment as part of her dowry. The size of the box and the value of the ointment related to the family's wealth. When a young man came to ask for her in marriage, she would take the box and break it at his feet to show him honor.

1. Describe the past of the woman who broke the alabaster box in Luke 7.

_____

_____

_____

2. What was her situation in the present? _____

_____

_____

_____

3. Explain her hope for the future. _____

_____

_____

_____

Study Guide

4. What was she sacrificing? _____

_____

_____

_____

5. What was her reward? _____

_____

_____

_____

6. Is there something your heart clings to that is too valuable to give to Jesus? What? _____

_____

_____

7. Are you afraid to be without something or someone? What or who is it, and why? _____

_____

_____

_____

"Think about this: Could this 'holding on' to something possibly be keeping you from having open hands to receive something better from the Lord?"

The woman in Luke 7 wisely broke her alabaster box in the presence of the only One who can make a woman's dreams come true. What is in your alabaster box? Take your box, with your body, soul, and dreams, and entrust them to Jesus. Write here your prayer of release to His Lordship.

_____

_____

_____

_____

_____

Mary, the mother of Jesus, said, "I belong to the Lord, body and soul...let it happen as you say..." (Luke 1:38, Phillips).

V. Right now, choose to put mediocrity behind you. Determine to pursue Jesus with everything in you—heart, mind, will, and emotions. Whether you are single or married, now is the perfect time to establish a radical relationship with Jesus and to remove any "tokenism" from your Christian walk.

1. Is there anything holding you back from taking this step? _____

_____

_____

_____

2. What mediocrity is in your life that you can get rid of? _____

_____

_____

_____

3. Is what you are hanging on to taking your life where you want it to go? Explain. _____

_____

_____

_____

4. What can you do to make God more real in your life right now? _____

_____

_____

_____

5. How will you do this? List at least three practical steps you can take.

_____

_____

_____

Study Guide

"It will require a determined heart and more than a little courage to wrench ourselves loose from the grip of our times and return to Biblical ways."—A.W. Tozer

(A.W. Tozer, *The Pursuit of God*, Camp Hill, Pennsylvania: Christian Publishing, Inc., 1982, p. 29.)

Write your prayer of commitment. _____

_____

_____

_____

_____

"Incompleteness is not the result of being single, but of not being full of Jesus."

Prayer

Dear Jesus,

Thank you for always being there for me. Lord, I want to enter into a deeper relationship with you. I know that You are the One who paid the price for this relationship, who guaranteed it by dying on the cross for me. Yet, I have continued to sin. Now, I repent of all my wrongdoing. Forgive me. Make me a clean vessel, ready to receive all that You have for me. Fill my cup and run it overflowing. You are my Lord, My Savior—and my best friend. I can depend on You totally to meet all my needs. I belong to You. Today, I come to You in totality.

In Your name, Lord Jesus.
Amen.

Lady *in* Waiting

Day: _____ Date: _____ Scripture: _____

What does this Scripture say about me: _____

_____

_____

_____

_____

_____

What does it say about God: _____

_____

_____

_____

_____

_____

How will this change my attitude and action: _____

_____

_____

_____

_____

_____

Prayer: _____

_____

_____

_____

_____

_____

Study Guide

Day: _____ Date: _____ Scripture: _____

What does this Scripture say about me: _____

_____

_____

_____

_____

_____

What does it say about God: _____

_____

_____

_____

_____

_____

How will this change my attitude and action: _____

_____

_____

_____

_____

_____

Prayer: _____

_____

_____

_____

_____

_____

Lady *in* Waiting

Day: _____ Date: _____ Scripture: _____

What does this Scripture say about me: _____

_____

_____

_____

_____

_____

What does it say about God: _____

_____

_____

_____

_____

_____

How will this change my attitude and action: _____

_____

_____

_____

_____

_____

Prayer: _____

_____

_____

_____

_____

_____

Ruth's Diligence

Understanding God's promised provision for widows, Naomi sent Ruth to gather grain in the field of a kinsman. Ruth was willing to use her life to work diligently at whatever her Lord called her to do. She would not be paralyzed by her lack of a husband.

And Ruth the Moabitess said to Naomi, "Please let me go to the field and glean among the ears of grain after one in whose sight I may find favor." And she said to her, "Go, my daughter" (Ruth 2:2).

When she and Naomi moved back to Bethlehem, Ruth did not waste a moment in feeling sorry for herself. She went right to work. Instead of being drained by her discouraging circumstances, she took advantage of them and diligently embraced each day.

What more humbling work could Ruth have done than to gather grain for the survival of her mother-in-law and herself?

Chapter 2

Lady of Diligence

I. Read Ruth chapter 2.

1. Describe what is happening in Ruth's and Naomi's lives. _____

_____

_____

_____

2. What are they choosing to do with their time? _____

_____

_____

_____

3. What is Ruth's strength? _____

_____

_____

_____

4. Did God provide for them? How? _____

_____

_____

_____

5. What was Ruth's attitude? _____

_____

_____

_____

II. "Rather than staying home worrying about another 'dateless' Saturday night, realize how much valuable time has been entrusted to you at this point in your life. Rather than resent your many single hours, embrace them as a gift from God—a package that contains opportunities to serve Him that are limited only by your own self-pity and lack of obedience."

1. What do you think about this quote? Explain. _____

_____

_____

_____

2. In what ways is it true or not true about your life now? _____

_____

_____

_____

3. What would happen with your singles group or church if each person was constantly serving instead of waiting to be served? _____

_____

_____

_____

"Serving the Lord brings such inexpressible joy."

III. One single woman learned that she did not have to wait for a husband to enjoy beauty in her private life. She could unpack her china and crystal that were tucked away in a hope chest and use them for herself. Through this "full place setting" lesson, the Lord taught her to find satisfaction in serving Him.

1. What do you think about this "full place setting" philosophy? _____

_____

_____

_____

2. How have you seen the "hope chest" principle keep others from living life to its fullest? _____

_____

_____

_____

3. Name one way you can begin to be all the woman God desires you to be now. _____

_____

_____

_____

"For those of you who are diligently going after Jesus and the privilege of serving Him, here is a very special reminder: Sometimes you will be called to do some monotonous work that will not make the headlines."

IV. Some view their lack of a mate as God's way of setting them apart for a more "noble" task, or for a cross to bear. We tend to selfishly focus on what we don't have rather than on what we do have—like free time—that can be used to help others as well as ourselves.

1. Is there any area in your life that you have put on hold for something you want but haven't seen yet? What? _____

_____

_____

_____

2. What are some reasons you have given to not spend time serving? ___

_____

_____

_____

3. In what capacity do you presently serve the Lord? _____

_____

_____

_____

"Is your life on hold until you have someone to hold?"
"Do you have an excuse for not serving Jesus?"

V. Read Matthew 6:21,33.

1. How does the use of our time show where our heart is? _____

_____

_____

_____

2. List some ministry opportunities that exist where you live. _____

_____

_____

_____

3. Star (*) the opportunities you listed above that you will spend time doing.

"If all of our serving is before others,
we will be shallow people indeed." —*Richard Foster*

(Richard J. Foster, *Celebration of Discipline*, San Francisco, California: Harper & Row Publishers, 1978, p. 117.)

Write a love letter responding to what God has shown you about being a Lady of Diligence. Remember, He doesn't want you to be perfect, just to have a perfect heart toward Him and all that He asks you to do.

_____

_____

Lady *in* Waiting

Study Guide

Day: _____ Date: _____ Scripture: _____

What does this Scripture say about me: _____

_____

_____

_____

_____

_____

What does it say about God: _____

_____

_____

_____

_____

_____

How will this change my attitude and action: _____

_____

_____

_____

_____

_____

Prayer: _____

_____

_____

_____

_____

_____

Lady *in* Waiting

Day: _____ Date: _____ Scripture: _____

What does this Scripture say about me: _____
_____
_____
_____
_____
_____

What does it say about God: _____
_____
_____
_____
_____
_____

How will this change my attitude and action: _____
_____
_____
_____
_____
_____

Prayer: _____
_____
_____
_____
_____
_____

Study Guide

Day: _____ Date: _____ Scripture: _____

What does this Scripture say about me: _____

_____

_____

_____

_____

_____

What does it say about God: _____

_____

_____

_____

_____

_____

How will this change my attitude and action: _____

_____

_____

_____

_____

_____

Prayer: _____

_____

_____

_____

_____

_____

Lady *in* Waiting

Day: _____ Date: _____ Scripture: _____

What does this Scripture say about me: _____
_____
_____
_____
_____
_____

What does it say about God: _____
_____
_____
_____
_____
_____

How will this change my attitude and action: _____
_____
_____
_____
_____
_____

Prayer: _____
_____
_____
_____
_____
_____

Ruth's Faith

Ruth certainly must have considered the probability of remaining single if she went with Naomi. Even though it promised no prospects of a husband, she chose to follow Naomi and Naomi's God back to Bethlehem. Ruth chose to trust God with her future. She looked not with sensual sight, but through "eyes of faith."

She chose to trust with her heart for the future what her eyes could not yet see.

God providentially directed Ruth to the field of Boaz. You'll find this divine encounter in Chapter 2 of the Book of Ruth: "...and she happened to come to the portion of the field belonging to Boaz..." (verse 3).

This leaves no room for manipulation. Ruth's "eyes of faith" led her to the exact spot where she would meet Mr. Right, Boaz, whose name means "pillar of strength." God rewarded Ruth's faith with a husband who was a pillar of strength.

Chapter 3

Lady of Faith

I. Read Psalm 34:8-11.

1. What do these verses say? _____

_____

_____

_____

2. What do they mean to you? _____

_____

_____

_____

3. Are they true? _____

_____

_____

_____

4. Can God provide for those who seek Him? Why or why not? _____

_____

_____

_____

5. What is the good thing that you desire most? _____

_____

_____

_____

6. If it is good for you, will it come? How? _____

_____

_____

_____

7. What do you need to do while it is coming? _____

_____

_____

_____

"Faith does not eliminate questions.
But faith knows where to take them." —Elisabeth Elliot

(Elisabeth Elliot, *A Chance to Die*, Old Tapan, New Jersey: Fleming H. Revell Company, 1987, p. 117.)

II. "How can I be a Lady of Faith when I feel so insecure deep in my heart that God will deliver the goods? What if I have faith in God and end up being 98 and unmarried?" God knows what your heart aches for. But He also knows that earthly things will not make you secure.

1. Are you in what seems to be a "no-hope situation"? _____

_____

_____

_____

2. What were the situations Ruth and Naomi faced in Ruth chapter 1? __

_____

_____

_____

_____

_____

3. How would you react if you have faith in God and still end up being 48/58 and unmarried? _____

_____

_____

_____

4. Is it sometimes hard to trust God for a future that you cannot see? Why? _____

_____

_____

_____

5. Will worry and fret help or hinder your future? How? _____

_____

_____

_____

6. How would you feel when, after making plans for God with your limited sight, you find out that you have delayed the perfect plan He had designed from His eternal perspective? _____

_____

_____

_____

"A Lady of Faith has not numbed her longing to be married;
instead, she has embraced her Lord so tightly that she faces
her prolonged singleness with peace, not bitterness."

III. Read Psalm 138:8, Psalm 139, and Romans 8:32.

1. Who created you with the longings of your heart? How do you know?

_____

_____

_____

2. Who knows the future? Include a Scripture reference that backs up your answer. _____

_____

_____

_____

3. Who wants you to have the very best? How do you know? _____

_____

_____

_____

4. What should you do to cooperate with His plan? Include a Scripture reference. _____

_____

_____

_____

5. Can you really trust God with all your hopes and dreams? Why or why not? List some practical steps you can take to show your trust in God. _____

_____

_____

_____

6. How will you ever meet Mr. Right if you have "eyes of faith" and don't work at finding him? _____

_____

_____

_____

IV. Don't fear or resent the waiting periods that appear in your life. Rather, think of them as gardens where the seeds of faith blossom. Whenever circumstances stimulate you to deepen your faith, embrace them willingly (Heb. 11:6).

Lady *in* Waiting

"I do know that waiting on God requires the willingness
to bear uncertainty, to carry within oneself the unanswered
question, lifting the heart to God about it whenever it
intrudes upon one's thoughts." —Elisabeth Elliot

(Elisabeth Elliot, *Passion and Purity*, Old Tappan, New Jersey: Fleming H. Revell Company, 1984, pp. 59-60.)

1. How do you feel about waiting on God? _____

_____

_____

_____

2. What do you think about why God is making you wait? _____

_____

_____

_____

3. What is true about the reasons He may have for you to wait? _____

_____

_____

_____

4. Do unanswered questions capture your mind? How and when? _____

_____

_____

_____

5. Are you overtaken by the restlessness of singleness? When? _____

_____

_____

_____

6. What do you do when you feel restless? _____

_____

_____

_____

Study Guide

If I work...God will wait. If I wait...God will work.

For from of old they have not heard nor perceived by ear, neither has the eye seen a God besides Thee, who acts on behalf of the one who waits for Him (Isaiah 64:4).

7. What does this verse say to you? _____

_____

_____

_____

V. "You make the most important decision in life, giving your life to Jesus Christ, 'by faith.' The second most important decision concerns your life-mate. This decision also demands the element of faith. Waiting for one's life-mate and then saying 'I do' to him demands secure faith, like Ruth's faith in the God of Israel."

Only fear ("I'm afraid I missed, will miss, will never...") will block faith. Romans 10:17 shows one how to develop faith. If you have been full of fears, doubts, and anxiety about your future, take a few moments to confess these things to God and ask Him to develop faith in your life. ("I will, I can, I must wait and trust a God who sees, knows, and cares about my future.")

_____

_____

_____

_____

_____

_____

_____

"Your faith during the 'waiting period' pleases God.
Don't fear or resent the waiting periods in your life."

Lady *in* Waiting

Day: _____ Date: _____ Scripture: _____

What does this Scripture say about me: _____
_____
_____
_____
_____
_____

What does it say about God: _____
_____
_____
_____
_____
_____

How will this change my attitude and action: _____
_____
_____
_____
_____
_____

Prayer: _____
_____
_____
_____
_____
_____

Study Guide

Day: _____ Date: _____ Scripture: _____

What does this Scripture say about me: _____
_____
_____
_____
_____
_____

What does it say about God: _____
_____
_____
_____
_____
_____

How will this change my attitude and action: _____
_____
_____
_____
_____
_____

Prayer: _____
_____
_____
_____
_____
_____

Lady *in* Waiting

Day: _____ Date: _____ Scripture: _____

What does this Scripture say about me: _____

_____

_____

_____

_____

_____

What does it say about God: _____

_____

_____

_____

_____

_____

How will this change my attitude and action: _____

_____

_____

_____

_____

_____

Prayer: _____

_____

_____

_____

_____

_____

Ruth's Virtue

One of life's most costly and beautiful objects is born out of pain and irritation—the pearl. Like the oyster, Ruth experienced many irritations and trials in her young life. She grieved the deaths of her father-in-law, brother-in-law, and husband. She bravely faced the turmoil of change in the direction of her life as well as a move to a foreign land with a bitter mother-in-law. When she arrived in that strange land, the trials did not end. She was immediately thrown into a new working situation among total strangers with new customs. Through all this stress, her new faith began to wrap itself around the painful situations. The by-product was a pearl...

What enabled Ruth to catch Boaz's attention? Was it her gorgeous hair or beautiful eyes? No! The answer is found in Boaz's response to her question in Ruth chapter 2.

Then she fell on her face, bowing to the ground and said to him, "Why have I found favor in your sight that you should take notice of me, since I am a foreigner?" And Boaz answered and said to her, "All that you have done for your mother-in-law after the death of your husband has been fully reported to me, and how you left your father and your mother and the land of your birth, and came to a people that you did not previously know" (Ruth 2:10-11).

Boaz was attracted to the virtue and character displayed in Ruth's life. A woman of virtue is irresistible to a godly man.

Chapter 4

Lady of Virtue

I. Read Ruth chapter 3.

1. Write out every description of Ruth's outward appearance. Include the Scripture references that support your description. _____

_____

_____

_____

_____

2. Write out every description of Ruth from other people's perspectives. Include the Scripture references that support your description. _____

_____

_____

_____

_____

_____

3. What two things about Ruth attracted Boaz? _____

_____

_____

_____

"A woman of virtue is irresistible to a godly man."

For the lips of an adulteress drip honey, and smoother than oil is her speech (Proverbs 5:3).

To keep you from the evil woman, from the smooth tongue of the adulteress. Do not desire her beauty in your heart. Nor let her catch you with her eyelids (Proverbs 6:24-25).

With her many persuasions she entices him; with her flattering lips she seduces him (Proverbs 7:21).

4. What do these verses describe? _____

_____

_____

_____

5. Do you see these techniques in your magazines and ads? Explain. ___

_____

_____

_____

"Most dateless women think their condition is the result of the 'reflection in the mirror.' Consequently, women spend millions of dollars every year believing the myth that physical beauty is mandatory for marriage."

6. What do you think about this statement? _____

_____

_____

_____

"My wife's character is what caught my attention. Her inner beauty was irresistible. Now, thirty years of marriage and half a dozen children later, I am more attracted to and in love with her than when I first met her."—P. Lord

But let it be the hidden person of the heart, with the imperishable quality of a gentle and quiet spirit, which is precious in the sight of God (1 Peter 3:4).

II. Read Proverbs 31:10-31.

1. List every reference to outward beauty. _____

_____

_____

_____

2. List every reference to inward beauty. _____

_____

_____

_____

3. Which of these listed are most valuable? _____

_____

_____

_____

4. Of those listed, which ones get better with age? _____

_____

_____

_____

As Jackie once said, "If a man chose me for external beauty, his destiny would be hugging a prune. But, if a man chooses me for my internal beauty, his destiny will be unfading beauty even in the twilight years of marriage, because of Jesus."

Study Guide

*A pastor once said,
"Ladies, how you catch 'em is how you keep 'em."*

III. Take the virtue test on pages 58-59 of *Lady in Waiting*.

1. How did you do? In which of the columns did you score the highest?
Why? _____
_____
_____
_____

2. Are you using your single days to be the woman God created you to
be? Explain how. _____
_____
_____
_____

3. Name one negative quality that you have discovered in yourself. How
can you change it? _____
_____
_____
_____

4. What can you do to develop virtue? _____
_____
_____
_____

IV. To marry a prince, you must first become a princess. A Lady of
Virtue attracts admiration for qualities within instead of attention for
actions without.

1. When you envision your perfect man, what are the qualities you see
in him? _____
_____
_____
_____

2. Do you have those same wonderful qualities? Explain. _____

_____

_____

_____

3. Do you think that your perfect man is hoping for a woman whose only beauty is outward and whose skill is in attracting the attention of men? What do you think he is looking for? Explain. _____

_____

_____

_____

4. Are you seeking admiration or attention from the men around you? __

_____

_____

_____

5. Describe the difference. _____

_____

_____

_____

6. Are you a woman worth waiting for? Explain. _____

_____

_____

_____

*A man who has given you his attention can be
easily distracted when a more attractive body passes by,
but a man's admiration is for a lifetime.*

V. Read Ephesians 5:18.

How does a woman tap into "pearl-producing power"? In order for something to be filled, it must first be empty. To be filled by the Spirit means that you must be empty of yourself. Instead, you're full of God. You give the Holy Spirit complete and total control of your life. "When you became a Christian, you received all of the Holy Spirit. To be a virtuous woman, you must let the Holy Spirit have all of you."

1. Do you have the Holy Spirit's filling in your life? Explain. _____

_____

_____

_____

2. Read Galatians 5:19-23. Which of these are displayed in your life? ___

_____

_____

_____

But I say, walk by the Spirit, and you will not carry out the desire of the flesh (Galatians 5:16).

"...If you want genuine pearls, you must allow the Holy Spirit to perform a special work in your life. Determine to string a lovely pearl 'necklace of virtue' as a treasure for your Lord."

Write a prayer of commitment right now to walk by the power of the Holy Spirit instead of by your own flesh. This includes a daily practice of confessing your sin and asking God to fill your life with His power. You can begin now and watch the beautiful work of God take place in your life.

_____

_____

_____

_____

_____

_____

_____

_____
_____
_____
_____
_____
_____
_____
_____
_____
_____
_____
_____
_____
_____
_____
_____
_____
_____
_____
_____
_____
_____
_____
_____
_____
_____
_____
_____

"Pearls of character" are listed in Galatians 5:22-23 as love, joy, peace, patience, kindness, goodness, faithfulness, gentleness, and self-control.

Study Guide

Day: _____ Date: _____ Scripture: _____

What does this Scripture say about me: _____

_____

_____

_____

_____

_____

What does it say about God: _____

_____

_____

_____

_____

_____

How will this change my attitude and action: _____

_____

_____

_____

_____

_____

Prayer: _____

_____

_____

_____

_____

_____

Lady *in* Waiting

Day: _____ Date: _____ Scripture: _____

What does this Scripture say about me: _____

_____

_____

_____

_____

_____

What does it say about God: _____

_____

_____

_____

_____

_____

How will this change my attitude and action: _____

_____

_____

_____

_____

_____

Prayer: _____

_____

_____

_____

_____

_____

Study Guide

Day: _____ Date: _____ Scripture: _____

What does this Scripture say about me: _____
_____
_____
_____
_____
_____

What does it say about God: _____
_____
_____
_____
_____
_____

How will this change my attitude and action: _____
_____
_____
_____
_____
_____

Prayer: _____
_____
_____
_____
_____
_____

Lady *in* Waiting

Day: _____ Date: _____ Scripture: _____

What does this Scripture say about me: _____
_____
_____
_____
_____
_____

What does it say about God: _____
_____
_____
_____
_____
_____

How will this change my attitude and action: _____
_____
_____
_____
_____
_____

Prayer: _____
_____
_____
_____
_____
_____

Ruth's Devotion

Boaz spoke of Ruth's devotion to God when he said, "May the Lord reward your work, and your wages be full from the Lord, the God of Israel, under whose wings you have come to seek refuge" (Ruth 2:12).

Ruth chose to cling to her mother-in-law's God as her own even though Naomi had drawn a negative, harsh picture of Him.

And she said to them, "Do not call me Naomi; call me Mara, for the Almighty has dealt very bitterly with me. I went out full, but the Lord as brought me back empty. Why do you call me Naomi, since the Lord has witnessed against me and the Almighty has afflicted me?" (Ruth 1:20-21)

Would you be devoted to a God like Naomi's? Though Ruth clung to her as a mother, she did not accept Naomi's view of God for herself.

"If we think of Him (God) as cold and exacting, we shall find it impossible to love Him, and our lives will be ridden with servile fear." —A.W. Tozer

(A.W. Tozer, *The Root of the Righteous*, Camp Hill, Pennsylvania: Christian Publishing, Inc., 1985, p. 5.)

Chapter 5

Lady of Devotion

I. Read First Corinthians 7:34-35.

1. Paraphrase these verses in your own words. _____

_____

_____

_____

2. What does this passage mean to you? _____

_____

_____

_____

3. Compare your life with someone you know who is married and has a job and small children. Who has the most time to call her own? _____

_____

_____

_____

4. What does "undistracted devotion to God" mean to you? _____

_____

_____

_____

Singles have a wonderful opportunity
to maximize their fellowship with God.

II. Too often people view a single woman through eyes of pity rather than envy. A Lady in Waiting actually has the advantage of being able to develop her love relationship with Christ without the distractions that a husband or family inherently bring to a woman's heart.

1. List some advantages of your life as a single. _____

_____

_____

_____

2. How often do you think of these advantages? Explain. _____

_____

_____

_____

3. List some advantages that a married woman has. _____

_____

_____

_____

4. Do you also have some of these as a single? Explain. _____

_____

_____

_____

5. A woman can spend her entire single life wishing to get married, and then her entire married life wishing to be single. How can you avoid this scenario? _____

_____

_____

_____

III. Read Jeremiah 29:12-13.

Seeking God is like developing a friendship. Friends talk a lot, listen to each other, write letters, and think about each other. Friends find out what the other does and does not like, and do things that please that person. The more time friends spend together getting to know each other, the greater their love and friendship will be. Your relationship with God works the same way.

1. What are the elements of a dating relationship that help you get to know the other person? _____

_____

_____

_____

2. Which of these can be used in your relationship with your heavenly Fiancé? _____

_____

_____

_____

IV. Read Jeremiah 29:11.

1. List what God wants for you as expressed in this verse. _____

_____

_____

_____

2. In that list, circle what you want. _____

_____

_____

_____

3. What does a woman need to do to have what both she and God want? (Look at Jeremiah 29:12.) _____

_____

_____

_____

Do you think God demands too much in requiring you to seek Him with all your heart? Suppose Mr. Right comes one day and begins to speak of his devotion to you. His words are what you've always waited to hear: "I love you. I give you my heart completely. For 364 days of every year, I will devote myself to you and you only." Then he adds, "However, one day of each year I want to date others and see what I have missed. Don't worry, you can have all the rest. Will you marry me?"

4. What would your response be? _____

_____

_____

_____

5. Would you want this kind of devotion? Explain. _____

_____

_____

_____

6. Is it selfish of you to deny him his heart just one day a year to give to others? _____

_____

_____

_____

7. If you would not accept a proposal like this, is it wrong for God to want whole-hearted love? _____

_____

_____

_____

V. Read Psalm 16:11.

1. Where does this verse say joy and pleasures are found? _____

_____

_____

_____

2. Where have you been looking for pleasures and joy? _____

_____

_____

_____

3. How can you be at His right hand? _____

_____

_____

_____

VI. Your days of singleness are a precious, privileged time. Don't waste a single one! You will never have them again. Let them be treasure-finding days in your Father's Kingdom.

1. How can you fall in love with God? _____

_____

_____

_____

2. When will your first date with Him be? _____

_____

_____

_____

3. What will you do on your dates with Him? _____

_____

_____

_____

4. Read Hebrews 13:5-6,8. What does this say about God's love for you?

_____

_____

_____

It takes 21 days to develop a habit. Will you take the 21-day test? Spend 21 consistent days dating our First Love and you will fall so in love with Him that you'll want 21 weeks, then 21 months, then 21 years. What a love life you will enjoy with Someone who will never leave you, who will never change, who will always love you just the same.

Falling in Love With My Heavenly Fiancé

Each morning I will "date" my Lord. If I hit the snooze one too many times, I will set a lunch or afternoon "date." Before I go to bed at night I will make sure that I have spent at least 5 minutes falling in love with Him.

Beginning with 5 minutes for 21 days in a row:

MINUTE 1
(30 sec.) I will praise Him and tell Him that I am glad to have this time with Him.
(30 sec.) I will ask Him if there is anything wrong between us and apologize (or confess) any sin that He shows me.

MINUTE 2
I will read His love letters until they say something to my life. (Start with Psalms and read a few verses each day.)

MINUTE 3
I will write down in my love letter journal what I have found in His love letter:

A. Something it says about me.
B. Something it says about Him.
C. Something He likes me to do or not do.

MINUTE 4
I will "listen" or meditate on what I have read and written. (A date is no fun when only one person talks; each must listen to fall in love.)

MINUTE 5
I will tell Him my concerns and ask Him to help me please Him. We continue this conversation all day.

"Your Father will not force you...
but He longs to fellowship with you.
Come into His chambers
delight in His Presence.
May you be found in Him
—a Lady of Devotion."

Write a prayer of commitment to spend a least 5 minutes each day dating Him and reading His Word. _____

_____

_____

_____

_____

_____

_____

_____

_____

_____

_____

_____

_____

_____

_____

_____

_____

_____

_____

_____

_____

Study Guide

Day: _____ Date: _____ Scripture: _____

What does this Scripture say about me: _____

_____

_____

_____

_____

_____

What does it say about God: _____

_____

_____

_____

_____

_____

How will this change my attitude and action: _____

_____

_____

_____

_____

_____

Prayer: _____

_____

_____

_____

_____

_____

Lady *in* Waiting

Day: _____ Date: _____ Scripture: _____

What does this Scripture say about me: _____

_____
_____
_____
_____
_____

What does it say about God: _____

_____
_____
_____
_____
_____

How will this change my attitude and action: _____

_____
_____
_____
_____
_____

Prayer: _____

_____
_____
_____
_____
_____

Study Guide

Day: _____ Date: _____ Scripture: _____

What does this Scripture say about me: _____

_____

_____

_____

_____

_____

What does it say about God: _____

_____

_____

_____

_____

_____

How will this change my attitude and action: _____

_____

_____

_____

_____

_____

Prayer: _____

_____

_____

_____

_____

_____

Lady *in* Waiting

Day: _____ Date: _____ Scripture: _____

What does this Scripture say about me: _____

_____

_____

_____

_____

_____

What does it say about God: _____

_____

_____

_____

_____

_____

How will this change my attitude and action: _____

_____

_____

_____

_____

_____

Prayer: _____

_____

_____

_____

_____

_____

Ruth's Purity

When Boaz had eaten and drunk and his heart was merry, he went to lie down at the end of the heap of grain; and she came secretly, and uncovered his feet and lay down (Ruth 3:7).

You may read this at a glance and picture the beginnings of an X-rated scene in Ruth's story. But remember that Ruth was acting according to the customs of the time. She was not slinking into Boaz's bed to seduce him. In obedience to her mother-in-law's instructions, Ruth quietly lay at his feet for him to notice her, thus symbolizing her subjection to Boaz as her nearest of kin.

By doing this, Ruth gave him the opportunity, if he so chose, to take legal action for the well-being of herself and her mother-in-law. (A woman had no form of social security and very few rights in that culture without a man.)

So this was not a brazen act of seduction, but an act of obedience to God's plan for her provision in that day. One thing is certain. When she left to go home, she walked away as a Lady of Purity.

Chapter 6

Lady of Purity

I. Read Ruth chapter 3 again.

1. What did Naomi ask Ruth to do? Why? _____

_____

_____

_____

2. What was Ruth's response? _____

_____

_____

_____

3. Do you think Naomi's request may have caused Ruth to wonder? (Remember, she was a foreigner and had not been raised with these customs.) _____

_____

_____

_____

4. What does Ruth's obedience say about her character? _____

_____

_____

_____

5. Would you have obeyed your mother (or mother-in-law) even if her request seemed foreign to anything you had ever thought or heard about? Why or why not? _____

_____

_____

_____

6. What are the verses in Ruth chapters 1 and 2 that show Naomi had consistently tried to do what was best for her daughter-in-law? _____

_____

_____

_____

7. Do you think Ruth had to remind herself of this? _____

_____

_____

_____

8. Consider Boaz. What was happening in his life before he went to bed that night? _____

_____

_____

_____

9. What was his response to a woman in his bed? _____

_____

_____

10. What does his response tell you about his reputation as a single man?

_____

_____

_____

11. Consider the place where Ruth was lying. Was she seductive or pure in her behavior? (Include Scripture to support your answer.) _____

_____

_____

_____

12. Why did Boaz ask her to stay the night? _____

_____

_____

_____

13. Whose reputation was he most concerned with? _____

_____

_____

_____

14. Do the men whom you spend time with care more for their reputation and needs or for the women of excellence whom they date? _____

_____

_____

_____

15. Would the guys you date be surprised to find a woman in their beds after a party one night? _____

_____

_____

_____

16. What difference do these questions make to one's purity? _____

_____

_____

_____

II. Debby has said, "Early in my dating, I tired of giving a kiss at the door for a hamburger, coke, and fries. What would I have to give next for a steak dinner or a night on the town? After I was married I realized the decision not to give my kisses freely to my dates had an added bonus. For every kiss I denied dates at the door, the man I married received my kisses 'with interest' in our years of marriage. It was worth waiting for kisses before marriage—so they would be full of meaning—for years to come within marriage."

1. Do you think that women today should have to say yes to their dates in the sexual realm, just because he paid for the evening's activities? Explain. _____

_____

_____

_____

2. How about a simple smile and "Thank you"? Is this not enough? ____

_____

_____

_____

If a woman wants to say "Thank you for a wonderful evening," she can say it with her words rather than with a kiss.

III. "Lack of self-control before marriage is fornication. Lack of self-control after marriage is adultery. The seeds for adultery are planted in the 'hotbeds' of fornication. A woman subconsciously wonders, 'If he did not exhibit self-control with me before marriage, how can I be sure that he will not give in to temptation during marriage when an attractive younger woman comes along?' A young man who cannot control himself before marriage does not suddenly become a man of self-control because he wears a wedding band!"

1. Explain what this quote means to you. _____

_____

_____

_____

2. How does sexual impurity undermine not only one's dating relationship, but also one's future marriage intimacy? _____

_____

_____

_____

3. Are you encouraging romance (that changes with the tide of emotion) or a relationship (that stands the test of time)? _____

_____

_____

_____

4. How can you change from romance to relationship? _____

_____

_____

_____

IV. "Today's society seeks ultimate pleasure with no pain. But following society's example usually brings just the opposite. Look to your heavenly Father, your Creator, for the truth. God gives true sexual fulfillment to the lady who waits for this gift."

1. Read the following verses. What does each say about relating to the opposite sex and the area of sexual purity? _____

_____

_____

_____

Proverbs 4:23 _____

_____

_____

_____

Song of Solomon 8:4 _____

_____

_____

_____

Study Guide

1 Corinthians 6:18-20 _____

_____

_____

_____

1 Corinthians 15:33 _____

_____

_____

_____

1 Thessalonians 4:3-8 _____

_____

_____

_____

2. What do you lose when you wait for a physical display of affection in a friendship? _____

_____

_____

_____

3. What do you gain if you wait to begin physical affection in a friendship? _____

_____

_____

_____

4. Many women have said, "We were such good friends until we started dating." What did they do differently or add to their "friendship" when they began to "date"? _____

_____

_____

_____

"If you encourage your date to play with the bow on your package, he will want to untie the ribbon and unwrap the gift. Don't distract him with the bow. Allowing sex to enter into a relationship before marriage will almost always result in the loss of an intimate friendship with the one you desire to know you for you."

V. "Although it is true that there is only one first time, God is the God of the first-time experience."

1. What if it is too late? What if the gift of purity has already been given away? Read the following Scriptures and write their responses to these questions. _____

_____

_____

_____

Isaiah 43:25 _____

_____

_____

_____

Jeremiah 31:34 _____

_____

_____

_____

Philippians 3:13-14 _____

_____

_____

_____

1 John 1:9 _____

_____

_____

_____

2. Briefly, what do these verses say about God's response to your sin when it is confessed? _____

_____

_____

_____

3. Will you now confess that sin and commit to live a life of physical, emotional, and spiritual purity before God? Write your prayer of confession and commitment. _____

_____

_____

_____

One girl has been quoted as saying, "There is no condom which protects a woman's heart, mind, and self-esteem."

VI. "Each woman receives one 'first time.' God desires for your precious gift to be given to a committed lover who will cherish, keep, and protect you in marriage. God wants you and your gift to this man to be treasured and cherished, not trampled and conquered."

1. Why is it important for a Lady of Purity to have dating standards or boundaries established before dating rather than creating them as she goes?

_____

_____

_____

2. In the following space write out and pray over the dating standards you feel that God wants for you. (Try to be specific in your areas of known weakness.) _____

_____

_____

_____

God wants you to have the joy of saying to your knight on that special wedding night, "Here I am, clean and pure, emotionally and physically. No one has touched the treasure of my love. I kept myself for you."

Lady *in* Waiting

Day: _____ Date: _____ Scripture: _____

What does this Scripture say about me: _____

_____

_____

_____

_____

_____

What does it say about God: _____

_____

_____

_____

_____

_____

How will this change my attitude and action: _____

_____

_____

_____

_____

_____

Prayer: _____

_____

_____

_____

_____

_____

Study Guide

Day: _____ Date: _____ Scripture: _____

What does this Scripture say about me: _____
_____
_____
_____
_____
_____

What does it say about God: _____
_____
_____
_____
_____
_____

How will this change my attitude and action: _____
_____
_____
_____
_____
_____

Prayer: _____
_____
_____
_____
_____
_____

Lady *in* Waiting

Day: _____ Date: _____ Scripture: _____

What does this Scripture say about me: _____

_____
_____
_____
_____
_____

What does it say about God: _____

_____
_____
_____
_____
_____

How will this change my attitude and action: _____

_____
_____
_____
_____
_____

Prayer: _____

_____
_____
_____
_____
_____

Ruth's Security

Then he [Boaz] said, "May you be blessed of the Lord, my daughter. You have shown your last kindness to be better than the first by not going after young men, whether poor or rich. And now, my daughter, do not fear. I will do for you whatever you ask, for all my people in the city know that you are a woman of excellence" (Ruth 3:10-11).

Ruth, as a single, young, widowed woman, must have experienced the lonely longings for the warmth of a husband. But she lived in victory over the desire to "man hunt." Instead of "going after the boys," she sat still and let God bring her prince to her. She was a Lady of Security.

In the midst of her circumstances, Ruth could not possibly have seen that a man like Boaz would one day be her prince. Neither can you with your limited perspective see who or where your prince will be. Only God has all things in view.

Surrender to God the terrible burden of always needing life on your terms. God can and will give you His best if you wait for it.

Chapter 7

Lady of Security

I. Read Hebrews 13:4-8; Ruth 3:10-11; and Proverbs 1:33.

1. What does Hebrews say about marriage, money, and power—and their ability to provide security? _____

_____

_____

_____

2. What did Ruth refuse to look to in order to make her feel secure? ____

_____

_____

_____

3. According to Proverbs, how does a woman live securely? _____

_____

_____

_____

Security is building your life around something that cannot be lost, destroyed, or taken away.

4. Considering this definition for security, why can the following areas not make a person secure? _____

_____

_____

_____

Positions (who I am and what people think of me): _____

_____

_____

_____

Possessions (what I have): _____

_____

_____

_____

People (someone who will always be there for me, always understand, always love me without change): _____

_____

_____

_____

5. Read Rom. 8:38-39. What is the one position we can have that never changes, a Person whose love will never vary or change, and Someone who can never be lost, stolen, or taken away? _____

_____

_____

_____

6. Write your own thoughts and feelings about Romans 8:38-39. _____

_____

_____

_____

II. One reason that relationships have a hard time lasting is because they don't include true love.

1. Why would a single woman work so hard to have a relationship with a man? _____

_____

_____

_____

2. What is the need that "drives" a woman? _____

_____

_____

_____

3. How do women manipulate and maneuver to attract a partner? _____

_____

_____

_____

4. What tactics are successful? _____

_____

_____

_____

5. Compare some of the tactics listed above with love as described in First Corinthians 13. _____

_____

_____

_____

III. Did you know that manipulating is a propensity that originated with a curse on the first woman? (See Genesis 3:16. In the Hebrew, desire means to "stretch out after, to run over.") The temptation to maneuver and control is common for all Evettes.

Study Guide

1. Have you ever played the role of the "surrogate mom" when trying to manipulate a guy's attention? _____

_____

_____

_____

2. What should a single woman do to get the attention of a particular male? _____

_____

_____

_____

3. Re-read the advice given by Elisabeth Elliot on page 99 (pages 112-113 in first edition) of the book, *Lady in Waiting*. Do you agree with the quote? Where do you disagree? _____

_____

_____

_____

4. Who should you be serving when single? (See 1 Corinthians 7:34-35.)

_____

_____

_____

5. How can manipulation be a form of self-deception? _____

_____

_____

_____

6. Instead of her "knight in shining armor," who should the single woman be thirsting for? _____

_____

_____

_____

IV. Some single women are tempted to manipulate the opposite sex because of the "dry and weary desert of singleness." They may hope a relationship with a man will meet their heart's desires.

1. Read these verses and write what they say to your heart.

Psalm 39:7 _____

_____

_____

_____

Psalm 40:1-3 _____

_____

_____

_____

Psalm 62:5 _____

_____

_____

_____

Isaiah 64:3-5 _____

_____

_____

_____

James 1:17 _____

_____

_____

_____

2. Why is it harder to wait for God than to do things for ourselves? _____

_____

_____

_____

Oh God, you are my God; I earnestly search for you. My soul thirsts for you; my whole body longs for you in this parched and weary land where there is no water (Psalm 63:1, NLT).

V. Manipulation can be deadly. You can save yourself many tears if you will do a regular "heart check."

Study Guide

1. Take a moment now to do a thorough motive check of your heart. What are you finding? _____

_____

_____

_____

2. Write a prayer confessing any wrong motives for relationships, and asking God for motives that are founded on having security in Him first.

_____

_____

_____

"The man you marry cannot meet your need for security.
Only God's love brings security."

3. Can you give to the Lord the key to your love life? Can you allow Him to be your security and not the things that change in life? Write the desires of your heart here. Confess any attitudes of demanding life on your agenda.

_____

_____

_____

_____

_____

_____

_____

_____

_____

_____

_____

No good thing does He withhold from those who walk uprightly
(Psalm 84:11b).

Lady *in* Waiting

Day: _____ Date: _____ Scripture: _____

What does this Scripture say about me: _____
_____
_____
_____
_____
_____

What does it say about God: _____
_____
_____
_____
_____
_____

How will this change my attitude and action: _____
_____
_____
_____
_____
_____

Prayer: _____
_____
_____
_____
_____
_____

Study Guide

Day: _____ Date: _____ Scripture: _____

What does this Scripture say about me: _____
_____
_____
_____
_____
_____

What does it say about God: _____
_____
_____
_____
_____
_____

How will this change my attitude and action: _____
_____
_____
_____
_____
_____

Prayer: _____
_____
_____
_____
_____
_____

Lady *in* Waiting

Day: _____ Date: _____ Scripture: _____

What does this Scripture say about me: _____

_____

_____

_____

_____

_____

What does it say about God: _____

_____

_____

_____

_____

_____

How will this change my attitude and action: _____

_____

_____

_____

_____

_____

Prayer: _____

_____

_____

_____

_____

_____

Ruth's Contentment

If you consider the circumstances, Ruth had the perfect excuse to be discontented. Ruth's circumstances—widowhood at a young age—provided the perfect breeding ground for self-pity and bitterness.

Yet Ruth chose to cling to the God of Israel, whom she found to be trustworthy even in difficult circumstances.

Contentedly facing each day's task, Ruth received the attention of the most eligible bachelor in town.

Then Naomi said, "Wait, my daughter, until you find out what happens. For the man will not rest until the matter is settled today" (Ruth 3:18, NIV).

Wait. Such an assignment is not to cause suffering, but to prevent it. Women experience so much needless pain when they run ahead of God's format.

Naomi did not want Ruth's heart to race ahead into disappointment in case the circumstances did not go as they expected.

Chapter 8

Lady of Contentment

I. Psalm 16:11 says, "Thou wilt make known to me the path of life [married or not]; in Thy presence is fulness of joy [His presence, not marriage, brings joy]; in Thy right hand there are pleasures forever." What more could a girl ask for?

1. Read these verses and write out what they mean to you.

Psalm 84:11 _____

_____

_____

_____

Isaiah 30:18 _____

_____

_____

_____

Isaiah 64:4 _____

_____

_____

_____

2. Is God's Word true? _____

_____

_____

_____

3. Can God do what He says He will? _____

_____

_____

_____

4. Why would He make us wait if it is in His power to do a thing that we have asked for and waited for and we are tired of waiting? _____

_____

_____

_____

5. When He makes us wait, does it mean that He is angry with us or trying to hurt us or doesn't love us? _____

_____

_____

_____

6. How can we be sure? _____

_____

_____

_____

7. What verses do you know that back up what is true regardless of how our feelings receive the assignment to wait? _____

_____

_____

_____

II. "It has been said that suffering is having what you do not want (singleness), and wanting what you do not have (a husband)."

1. Do most single women think that the ache and empty feeling inside come from the lack of a man to love? _____

_____

_____

_____

"If I find in myself a desire which no experience in this world can satisfy, the most probable explanation is that I was made for another world."—C.S. Lewis

(As found in Dr. Larry Crabb, *Finding God*, Grand Rapids, Michigan: Zondervan, 1993, p. 55.)

2. Consider what C.S. Lewis said about that ache inside all people (not just singles). What are your thoughts? _____

_____

_____

_____

3. Can a single woman learn to be content? Consider the reply of a famous single: Read Philippians 4:11-12. _____

_____

_____

_____

4. Discuss the meaning of the words content and contentment (Gr., "sail away"). Can you trust the sails of your singleness to the wind of God (see Jn. 3:8)? _____

_____

_____

_____

Study Guide

III. The new "Eleventh Commandment" is, "Thou shalt not defraud thyself." Misread intentions between males and females put them on a collision course. An innocent gesture on the part of a male friend can produce the most elaborate fantasy in a woman's mind.

1. How can a discontent single woman be easily defrauded by single men? List again the ways women can be defrauded see pages 108-112 of *Lady in Waiting.*_____

_____

_____

_____

2. Do single women defraud themselves more frequently than they are defrauded by single guys? _____

_____

_____

_____

3. Read Second Corinthians 10:5. How can you discipline prenuptial fantasies (which intensify discontentment)? _____

_____

_____

_____

IV. Do you have an accountability partner? Naomi encouraged Ruth to be calm and wait (see Ruth 3:18).

1. Every single woman needs an accountability partner ("spiritual monitor") to help her control fantasy and self-defrauding. Who is your spiritual monitor? How specifically has she helped you? _____

_____

_____

_____

2. List some ways in which you can act as a spiritual monitor. _____

_____

_____

_____

*Too often it is our friends who
accelerate our prenuptial fantasies!*

V. Read Psalm 55.

1. What can you do when you are discontent? _____
_____
_____
_____

2. What can you do when you feel afraid? _____
_____
_____
_____

3. What can you do when you face hard situations? _____
_____
_____
_____

*A discontent single who gets married becomes
a discontent wife. Marital status does not remove
discontentment from a heart.*

4. Take your discontented feelings to Jesus and leave them in His capable hands. Write a prayer of commitment here to daily discipline yourself to take your fantasies to Jesus and to begin enjoying contentment in His arms.

_____
_____
_____

*And the peace of God, which surpasses all understanding, will
guard your hearts and minds through Christ Jesus* (Philippians 4:7
NKJV).

Study Guide

Day: _____ Date: _____ Scripture: _____

What does this Scripture say about me: _____
_____
_____
_____
_____
_____

What does it say about God: _____
_____
_____
_____
_____
_____

How will this change my attitude and action: _____
_____
_____
_____
_____
_____

Prayer: _____
_____
_____
_____
_____
_____

Lady *in* Waiting

Day: _____ Date: _____ Scripture: _____

What does this Scripture say about me: _____
_____
_____
_____
_____
_____

What does it say about God: _____
_____
_____
_____
_____
_____

How will this change my attitude and action: _____
_____
_____
_____
_____
_____

Prayer: _____
_____
_____
_____
_____
_____

Study Guide

Day: _____ Date: _____ Scripture: _____

What does this Scripture say about me: _____
_____
_____
_____
_____
_____

What does it say about God: _____
_____
_____
_____
_____
_____

How will this change my attitude and action: _____
_____
_____
_____
_____
_____

Prayer: _____
_____
_____
_____
_____
_____

Day: _____ Date: _____ Scripture: _____

What does this Scripture say about me: _____
_____
_____
_____
_____
_____

What does it say about God: _____
_____
_____
_____
_____
_____

How will this change my attitude and action: _____
_____
_____
_____
_____
_____

Prayer: _____
_____
_____
_____
_____
_____

Ruth's Convictions

The Book of Ruth gives not only the story of a Lady in Waiting, but also the profile of a Knight in Shining Armor.

Ruth's choice to wait for God's best resulted in her union with a Boaz rather than a Bozo. Not only did Ruth marry a man who was a "pillar of strength," but she also was blessed by the privilege of bearing a son who would be part of the lineage of Jesus Christ.

Ruth's wise choices resulted in her experiencing God's overwhelming goodness.

Ruth did not allow the past influences of a heathen culture to keep her from setting new standards and making wise choices that would honor God. She chose to break her family's sin cycle and establish a new godly cycle.

Have you dated more Bozos than Boazes? If your answer is yes, then you may need to develop higher ideals.

Chapter 9

Lady of Conviction

I. Read the following verses and compare a BOZO with a BOAZ (works of the flesh versus fruit of the Spirit). What convictions do you have on whom to date and marry?

1. Proverbs 16:32. A BOZO is controlled by his emotions (lust, anger, etc.); a BOAZ is able to control his emotions (patience). _____

_____

_____

_____

2. Romans 8:28,32. A BOZO is angered when he doesn't get his way; a BOAZ can rise above disappointment (faith, peace). _____

_____

_____

_____

3. First Corinthians 13:4. A BOZO doesn't notice the needs of others, and is often rude; a BOAZ is courteous toward others, not just trying to impress them (kindness). _____

_____

_____

_____

4. Colossians 3:12-14. A BOZO is very critical of others, and often intolerant; a BOAZ is tolerant of imperfection (he has a clear view of himself) (love). _____

_____

_____

_____

5. Philippians 2:3-4. A BOZO is self-centered, always wanting life on his terms. (Amnon is a classic example...he never heard Tamar's pleading); a BOAZ is other-centered, looking out for the interests of others (meekness).

_____

_____

_____

6. Second Timothy 2:24-25. A BOZO is rigid, and his viewpoint is the only right conclusion; a BOAZ is teachable (ultimate meekness) and has an open heart and mind (patience/meekness). _____

_____

_____

_____

7. Colossians 3:23. A BOZO always has excuses for not doing a task well; a BOAZ strives to do his work to the best of his ability and to the glory of Jesus (faithfulness). _____

_____

_____

_____

8. Ruth 3:13-14. A BOZO lacks integrity and good character traits; a BOAZ displays kindness and integrity (goodness). _____

_____

_____

_____

Because Ruth waited on God, she was showered with blessings through His vessel: Boaz.

II. "You want to marry someone for the qualities he possesses now, not for qualities you hope he will develop. The most common mistake made by marriage partners is marrying someone they intend to change."

1. Are the men you find yourself befriending Bozos or Boazes? Why or why not? _____

_____

_____

_____

2. List some characteristics you want to find in your Boaz. _____

_____

_____

_____

III. Before Ruth found her Mr. Right, she broke an ungodly family cycle (see Ruth 1:16).

1. What was her past? _____

_____

_____

_____

2. What did she choose to do in order to break it? _____

_____

_____

_____

3. Is there a family cycle you need to break? _____

_____

_____

_____

4. What can you do to break it? _____

_____

_____

_____

"Your destiny is not something that is left to chance or fate; it is the product of wise choices."

IV. When you concentrate on the real thing, the Bozos become more apparent.

1. Briefly describe the difference between a Boaz and a Bozo. _____

_____

_____

_____

2. How many dates would it take for you to discern if the guy was a Boaz or a Bozo? (See Matthew 12:34.) _____

_____

_____

_____

3. Are the qualities listed on page 128 of *Lady in Waiting* too high for a Mr. Right in this generation? _____

_____

_____

_____

It's not how much you know...but how much you live that makes the difference.

V. "Do you want to marry a knight in shining armor? Then set your standards high. To be married to a man who loves the Lord and wants to serve

Him is one of life's highest privileges. It is worth whatever wait, whatever cost."

Write a prayer to the Lord committing yourself to only spend time with men of convictions and standards like yours. Tell the Lord what changes you are willing to make in your life to be a Lady of Conviction. _____

_____

_____

_____

_____

_____

_____

_____

_____

_____

_____

_____

_____

_____

_____

_____

_____

_____

_____

_____

_____

_____

_____

"...the female child of a king is a princess. Act like the valuable princess you are, and expect to be treated as royalty."

Study Guide

Day: _____ Date: _____ Scripture: _____

What does this Scripture say about me: _____
_____
_____
_____
_____
_____

What does it say about God: _____
_____
_____
_____
_____
_____

How will this change my attitude and action: _____
_____
_____
_____
_____
_____

Prayer: _____
_____
_____
_____
_____
_____

Lady *in* Waiting

Day: _____ Date: _____ Scripture: _____

What does this Scripture say about me: _____
_____
_____
_____
_____
_____

What does it say about God: _____
_____
_____
_____
_____
_____

How will this change my attitude and action: _____
_____
_____
_____
_____
_____

Prayer: _____
_____
_____
_____
_____
_____

Study Guide

Day: _____ Date: _____ Scripture: _____

What does this Scripture say about me: _____

_____
_____
_____
_____
_____

What does it say about God: _____

_____
_____
_____
_____
_____

How will this change my attitude and action: _____

_____
_____
_____
_____
_____

Prayer: _____

_____
_____
_____
_____
_____

Lady *in* Waiting

Day: _____ Date: _____ Scripture: _____

What does this Scripture say about me: _____
_____
_____
_____
_____
_____

What does it say about God: _____
_____
_____
_____
_____
_____

How will this change my attitude and action: _____
_____
_____
_____
_____
_____

Prayer: _____
_____
_____
_____
_____
_____

Ruth's Patience

Ruth was a wonderful example of patience. Ruth did not allow her circumstances or lack of male companionship to cause her to be impatient. Instead she concentrated on developing companionship with her heavenly Father and chose to let Him bring a husband to her if He saw fit.

Concern over the ticking of her "biological clock" did not make her fearful of the future. Instead she concentrated on being a lady of character, not on getting a man.

She took one day at a time, knowing that God was not bound by circumstances nor her age.

She used the wait to become the woman God wanted her to be.

Chapter 10

Lady of Patience

I. Read Psalm 46:10 and Isaiah 40:31.

1. Do you think that single women struggle the most in the area of being patient? _____

_____

_____

_____

2. Does waiting renew your strength or drain it? _____

_____

_____

_____

3. If God is faithful, why is it so easy to lose patience, so hard to wait? Why is it easier to settle for less than God's best? Expound. _____

_____

_____

_____

II. Read Deuteronomy 30:19.

Study Guide

1. What is the blessing life longs to give, described in this chapter? _____

_____

_____

_____

2. What is the "curse" He longs to protect us from? _____

_____

_____

_____

3. Have you ever been tempted to date a non-believer because of a long season of datelessness? What do Second Corinthians 6:14 and Joshua 23:12-13 say concerning this? _____

_____

_____

_____

III. "Marriage teaches us that even the most intimate human companionship cannot satisfy the deepest places of the heart. Our hearts are lonely 'til they rest in Him." —Elisabeth Elliot

(Elisabeth Elliot, *Loneliness*, Nashville, Tennessee: Oliver Nelson, 1988, p. 16.)

1. Does loneliness hinder the development of your patience? _____

_____

_____

_____

2. What develops patience besides prolonged singleness? _____

_____

_____

_____

3. Consider this source of patience: "We can rejoice, too, when we run into problems and trials, for we know that they are good for us—they help us learn to endure. And endurance develops strength of character in us, and character strengthens our confident expectation of salvation" (Romans 5:3-4, NLT).

IV. Read Isaiah 30:18 and Proverbs 3:5-6 and write below what they mean to you.

1. Do you know how profoundly your patient waiting affects God? Explain. _____

_____

_____

_____

2. What are some specific ways you can "trust in the Lord"? _____

_____

_____

_____

"Take courage, single friend. You are not alone in your wait; neither are you alone in the feelings and struggles you encounter. Many godly women have waited and won. Many women have lost hope and compromised. Wait patiently and win triumphantly the future your Father has planned for you. It will always be designed with you in mind and is worth being patient to discover."

Developing patience is hard.
Getting married ahead of God's timing is worse.

3. Write here your response to God's tug at your heart to be a Lady of Patience. _____

_____

_____

_____

For your husband is your Maker, whose name is the Lord of hosts...
(Isaiah 54:5).

Rest in the Lord and wait patiently for Him...(Psalm 37:7).

Study Guide

Now, dear Lady in Waiting, take a moment to consider what your heart has been telling you during the study of this book and take a moment to pen those thoughts as a prayer, as a love letter to the King. _____

_____

_____

_____

_____

_____

_____

_____

_____

_____

_____

_____

_____

_____

_____

_____

_____

_____

_____

_____

_____

_____

_____

_____

_____

_____

_____

Lady *in* Waiting

Day: _____ Date: _____ Scripture: _____

What does this Scripture say about me: _____

_____

_____

_____

_____

_____

What does it say about God: _____

_____

_____

_____

_____

_____

How will this change my attitude and action: _____

_____

_____

_____

_____

_____

Prayer: _____

_____

_____

_____

_____

_____

Study Guide

Day: _____ Date: _____ Scripture: _____

What does this Scripture say about me: _____

_____

_____

_____

_____

_____

What does it say about God: _____

_____

_____

_____

_____

_____

How will this change my attitude and action: _____

_____

_____

_____

_____

_____

Prayer: _____

_____

_____

_____

_____

_____

Lady *in* Waiting

Day: _____ Date: _____ Scripture: _____

What does this Scripture say about me: _____
_____
_____
_____
_____
_____

What does it say about God: _____
_____
_____
_____
_____
_____

How will this change my attitude and action: _____
_____
_____
_____
_____
_____

Prayer: _____
_____
_____
_____
_____
_____

Study Guide

Lady *in* Waiting

Study Guide

Lady *in* Waiting

Study Guide

Lady *in* Waiting

Study Guide

_____
_____
_____
_____
_____
_____
_____
_____
_____
_____
_____
_____
_____
_____
_____
_____
_____
_____
_____
_____
_____
_____
_____
_____
_____
_____
_____
_____

Lady *in* Waiting

Suggested Reading

Eros Defiled by John White

Too Close, Too Soon by Talley/Reed

Passion and Purity by Elisabeth Elliot

Pursuit of God by A.W. Tozer

Finding God by Dr. Larry Crabb

Search for Significance by Robert McGee

Trusting God by Jerry Bridges

For More Information

Both authors are available for speaking engagements. For more information, call or write:

Debby Jones
Crossover Communications International
P.O. Box 211755
Columbia, SC 29221
1.803.691.0688

Jackie Kendall
Power To Grow Ministries
P.O. Box 114
Loxahatchee, FL 33470
1.407.795.4792

Help for Finding God's Best in a Mate

HOW TO AVOID A BOZO
Jackie Kendall

Why are so many Christians making such poor choices in life mates? Do you want to find God's best—Mr. Right? Learn from this video the differences between a man worth waiting for and a BOZO. Discover how to avoid the counterfeit and find the real thing!

0-7684-0070-8